THE EXPANDING CASE

for the

U F O

Books by M. K. Jessup

M. K. JESSUP

The Expanding Case for the

UFO

Library of Congress Catalog Card Number 57-6206. Manufactured
in the United States of America.

Copyright © 2014 by: New Saucerian Books
Point Pleasant, West Virginia
ISBN: 149910510X
ISBN-13: 978-1499105100

TABLE OF CONTENTS

III
ECHOES OF HISTORY

IV
SELENOLOGY SPEAKS

The Satellite

The Moon

V

ETHNOLOGY SPEAKS

ILLUSTRATIONS

Unless otherwise indicated, all illustrations from OUR MOON *were drawn by its author, Mr. H. P. Wilkins, and are used with the permission of Frederick Muller, Ltd., publisher.*

THE EXPANDING CASE
for the
UFO

A FABLE

There was a Mexican Indian named Juan, who tended a small milpa, or cornfield, every year, at the base of a mountain.

Its face was sculptured in the form of a human figure, crouching in a posture of deep thought. According to Indian tradition this was one of the giants of a past civilization, existent before floods and cataclysms. His intellect was in proportion to his size, and he was thinking out a problem that the gods had given him to solve. They had sentenced him to sit immobile, congealed into stone, throughout uncounted ages until the problem was solved.

Juan took a great deal of comfort from the uncomplaining presence of the thoughtful giant, before whom his own frustrations paled in comparison.

One summer day as Juan tended his corn, he heard a rumbling and groaning. Something like a great yawn reverberated over the valley, and the cornfield trembled as with a quake or tremor. Then Juan was startled to see the ponderous stone figure slowly rising to his full towering height.

But Juan was not frightened. He had lived with this giant too long. Tacitly, at least, they were friends. Juan had been pondering also.

Raising his little voice to a shout, he called upward to the giant: "What have you been thinking about?"

Gazing down until he located the human mite at his feet,

11

the giant said: "Many years ago, the great gods of my people gave me a problem. I was told to work out the mathematics of a solar system with three suns, moving around each other in accordance with the laws of nature, and having nine planets, three moving in a retrograde direction, each with moons. I have completed the problem."

"Then," said Juan, "you are a free man?"

"Yes," said the giant.

"And may I, a mere mortal, ask you a question, the answer to which is beyond my reach?"

"Surely. Why not?"

"Perhaps you can tell me," said Juan, "for I have been wondering these many dull years. To whom was God speaking when he said: 'Let there be light'?"

And the giant said, "Um-m-m-m," and slowly sat down.

To this day he has not yet moved again.

Juan told his story in the village tavern that night. Only one man believed him and this man was not credited in the village with having much intelligence. Why, only last week, he said he had seen a great, silvery, disc-like object darting across the sky! It looked, he said, just like a great big shining saucer.*

* I have been unable to trace the authorship of this little story.

WE BEGIN AGAIN

The publication of my book, *The Case for the UFO*, marked the first step in my efforts to bring some order out of chaos by correlating previously observed data and drawing conclusions therefrom. But "Let there be light" continues to nag at the mind, and, whereas certain order was achieved, further investigation was required. Not only did startling new fields of research suggest themselves, but the voice I raised has echoed in the cave of research and I must, perforce, begin by reporting some of those echoes.

Suppose you wanted to prove *The Case for Mankind*, but had to do so without actually seeing a human being. Suppose that human beings were invisible, yet all their works were manifest.

Now suppose that you were trying to prove to a man from Mars that there really is a human race. How would you go about it? What evidence would you present to the man from Mars? How would you present the evidence to the man from Mars who reiterates: "There is no such thing as a human being. Until you show me one, I must continue to regard you as the victim of an overactive imagination, or worse"?

The phenomena you would exhibit to your man from Mars are the kind I exhibit to you on behalf of the UFO and their innate intelligences. The evidence for the UFO *and* for Mankind, if

13

not identical, are parallel and complementary to an impressive degree.

Many of your contemporaries *are* pointing to UFO and saying: "There are UFO," and you, perhaps, answer: "I do not see them, therefore there are no UFO."

But if I point to the *works* of UFO, and you persist in doubting their existence, then I must ask you to explain them by another rational method. Can you?

In what follows, we will often have to weigh one incredibility against another. And, sometimes we shall be driven to consider different orders of impossibility.

Some of my old school teachers may tell me there are no degrees of impossibility; "impossible" is not a "comparative" term. A thing or event is possible or impossible, period! Yet, you find that some incredibilities are more incredible than others. Such as . . .

It is impossible to see a black cat in a dark room. Yet, with infra-red we can photograph the cat, and with one of those ultra-modern military gadgets we might see the cat, via "invisible light." So, the impossibility of seeing a black cat in a dark room depends on how you look at the cat. Consequently we have progressive impossibility—or is anything really impossible?

On the other hand, I agree that it is manifestly impossible to pick up an orange from the table if no orange is there. Call this a *first order* impossibility if you like, but isn't this more conceivable than picking up the Great Pyramid of Gizeh or the planet Mars from the table? So here is what we might call a *second order impossibility.*

Not so long ago the thought of picking up a flying saucer, fresh from space, off the dining table, would have been reckoned at least a *third order* impossibility. The mere suggestion would have indicated insanity. But now?

Well, thousands of God-fearing, respectable people tell us, tell the press, and even make affidavits that they have seen Unidentified Flying Objects which are *not* planes, balloons, planets or atmospheric-temperature inversions. There may possibly be smoke in their eyes, but, if you persist in telling them so, there is certainly going to be fire. When a man or woman of intelligence, able to make a living among his fellow men, and of good standing in his community, says he saw something, I would rather try to find out what it was that he saw, and why it was there, than try to persuade him that he never saw it.

Like Roy A. Marshall, Jr., of Mannboro, Virginia, who says, in *Fate* (October, 1952):

"I saw my first saucer in the fall of 1926, while working for W. L. Price. I was on top of a seventy-foot tower at Paces, Virginia, about ten miles from South Boston, about four in the afternoon when I saw an object approaching from the South. I know all types of aircraft, but this object didn't make sense. There was no prop turbulence or motor noises. It seemed to glide toward me. As it passed overhead at about five thousand feet, I could hear an almost inaudible, high-pitched whine. Its details were fairly plain. I have sketches of it, and an aluminum model, from these and others sightings."

I think almost any astronomer would have a tough time making this observant, out-of-doors fellow believe he had seen a mirage, a searchlight, a balloon, a cloud . . . or that old astronomer's standby, the planet Venus! And don't let your attention wander: note that date. It's *1926*, quite a spell before Arnold.

So, as you say to me: "Impossible," I say right back at you, "How impossible?"

We *are* venturing, here, into a field where we are going to have to stretch possibility farther than anyone but a metaphysicist has ever done. I am going to ask you to do more than face the reality of UFO, I am going to ask you to confront a whole new philosophy regarding the world around us. I will not ask you to accept this philosophy—just to inspect the new concepts with an open mind.

Through the following pages you will have to contemplate new *types* of life, as well as new ways of life.

Let me say that I do not have all the answers. I may not have all of the questions. You may have those that I have missed; but as for the answers—that is a joint problem, and we must attack it together. It is unimportant *what* the answer turns out to be. It *is* important that we get closer to truth. If I offer postulates and they look like conclusions, please be patient. These are working hypotheses—proposals, nothing more.

After writing *The Case for the UFO*, I was accused of being the world's prize conclusion-jumper. No; but I *may* be the world's greatest hypothesizer, and I would gladly accept the appellation. Of such stuff is born *qualitative knowledge*.

If you have followed my speculations through the ramifications of my previous books, you are now familiar with the concept that there is life in space around this planet. You may not have accepted it—that is neither here nor there. You may have other ideas, for your background is not identical to mine. If you can come up with an acceptable common-denominator of explanation for an equal number of the phenomena which our groping race still has to solve, I will gladly listen to the case *you* make.

Meanwhile, here we are! Confronted with an overwhelming mass of observational data which says that there are beings around us.

From where do they come? What do they desire? Are they friends or enemies? What is their physical makeup? Are their minds like ours? Are they godlike, or men and women of a higher development than ours?

Were they originally earthlings? Or have they come from faraway space? Have they recently arrived? Or have they been here since before the dawn of our emergent civilization?

The presence of UFO accounts for a multitude of phenomena erroneously called supernatural or occult, or just plain oddities. Space flight, and life in space, alone can explain them. This explanation is so simple . . . so straightforward . . . so obvious and so overwhelming that it is awesome. Some of these phenomena were sketched briefly in *The Case for the UFO*. Subsequent research has broadened the evidential base. The degree of the intermingling of UFO activities with our personal and racial life has reached an astounding level. I feel as if I had opened a cosmic Pandora's box!

There are those who do not accept the reality of the UFO. They find abhorrent the idea that there is life—intelligent, perhaps even real flesh-and-blood life—inhabiting the space between planets and satellites of the solar system. They reject the possibility of space being cluttered with debris or space junk of all sorts, some of which arrives on earth as meteoric material other than iron and stone. Yet we are confronted with evidence accumulated over centuries that there is a *vast amount* of matter in space, usable to space dwellers, which does fall to earth now and then—and we have actually seen manifestations of space life.

There has been endless dissension between those who have seen UFO and those who reject the idea of UFO. The die-hards will not accept visual evidence. It is partly to these recalcitrants that this book is addressed.

I intend to show that we are tapping a vast reservoir of circumstantial evidence that space-life exists. I will let other writers present the personal reports of hundreds of good people who *have seen* the UFO's. I have made it my task to supply supporting evidence from other, chiefly scientific sources.

Many have assumed that the UFO come from another planet. Other equally intelligent people conclude that they come from planets in other, far-distant galaxies of stars—simply because the regimented astronomers arbitrarily declare that no other planets in the solar system are habitable. Some, on the other hand, appalled at the distances involved, have found their way out by insisting that the UFO are "materialized from multi-dimensional, or ethereal space," about which we have only the vaguest inkling at present. I suggested, previously, that it is an improbability of lesser order to postulate that UFO and the entities associated with them live in the space immediately around the earth—denizens of the earth-moon binary-planet system.

The UFO constantly seen in such numbers and variety offer almost a priori proof that UFO originate on or close to the earth. The idea of life in space in constructed dwellings, then, is an improbability of lesser order than any assumption that space vehicles or intelligent entities, come in great numbers from planets circling around distant stars, or even from the nearest planets of our own system.

The distances involved are too great to permit of such traffic, unless we are to assume speeds and modes of travel completely beyond the scope of present-day physics. Such travel is not unthinkable; but, to me, space intelligence in the earth-moon binary system is a more acceptable improbability and involves nothing incompatible with today's sciences. It is a basic postulate of science that the simplest explanation is best.

An alternative? We have only the concept of materializations of "ethereals" from multi-dimensional continuii of a different order than our three-dimensional world or space. I do not deny the possibility of such materializations, in the face of such phenomena as *teleportation* and *apportation* and the voluminous work of such investigators as the Borderland Sciences Research Association, conducted by Dr. Meade Layne. Although the belief that UFO are ethereal, or that they materialize at will from inter-penetrating and circumambient "spaces" is to me a higher order of improbability, we must not close our minds to such hypotheses.

In this book, as in *The Case for the UFO*, I must limit myself to the field of accepted physical law, as I see it. I must leave the occult and ethereal to more experienced students of those subjects.

I am trying to explain as much as possible on the basis of already established, albeit incomplete sciences. As a working hypothesis, I believe that life, and/or intelligence, inhabiting space around us, is less improbable than materialization, tele-portation, or cummutation from other planets. Should I ultimately be proven wrong, I will gladly accept the correction. Meanwhile, let us be hospitable to other lines of study. Together we are expanding the confines of qualitative knowledge.

In short, I believe that intelligence, in space, inhabiting the earth-moon binary system may be just as "natural" as life and intelligence on the earth itself, that this hypothesis provides clues to phenomena which have been denied scientific cognizance, because they could not be explained by conventional assumptions.

There is profound significance in the fact that our investigations seem to be closing the gap between formalized science and the newer and less inhibited developments coming from such workers as the B.S.R.A. (Borderland Sciences Research Association). At no point in our analysis of recorded data do we come into any irresolvable conflict. True, we do not reach identical conclusions, but we have shown that the B.S.R.A. conclusions are not as unacceptable to scientific cognizance as they were previously thought to be. As long as all of us are seeking *truth*—there can hardly be any basic conflict between "science" and any other investigatory procedure. And it is encouraging to see evidence that analysis of UFO phenomena, from diverse viewpoints, is narrowing the gulf between these fields of research.

In this volume I will continue the drive toward reality and rationality. For our present purposes I must repeat what was postulated in *The Case for the UFO*: that UFO were either originated by an ancient civilization of pre-flood days, or are indigenous to open space from whence they come to earth. Perhaps they brought the earth's first *civilization* with them. I incline to the former: that UFO, now living naturally in open space, originated on earth aeons ago.

I have taken a hard look at the possibility that intelligence does not necessarily mean life—carnate life as we understand it. There is considerable data to substantiate the latter speculation. Of two types of spatial UFO, the solid, structure-like, and the nebulous, cloud-like, it may be that the former originated on earth and the latter in space. But such speculative and debatable possibilities are innumerable.

In *The Case for the UFO* I developed the thesis that three branches of learning meteorology, history, and astronomy—when collated and analyzed, support the existence of intelligence functioning in space. In meterology we scrutinized things, living and dead, organic and inorganic, that fall from the sky, and peculiar storms and clouds which seem to have intelligent direction. Under the general heading of history we correlated data on inexplicable disappearances of people and things; mysterious engravings and tracks left in stone and on artifacts; incomprehensible tracks left in snow; indications, in ancient megalithic structures, that a power of levitation unknown to us was used for lifting vast stones, etc.

In the astronomical field, having space for only a small fraction of the evidence, I concentrated on observations by astronomers who saw UFO in space, passing across or near the sun. I made only cursory comment on shadows and lights on the moon, and shadows thrown from space on our own clouds. I now find that much remains to be said in all of those fields, and that several others demand attention.

I

ECHOES OF METEOROLOGY

◆ Falling Ice ◆

Strangely enough, evanescent ice meteorites seem to have been observed more often at or near their time of impact than any other objects from space. Their appearance, of course, makes them stand out, but their lack of permanence requires that they be seen falling, or immediately afterwards. Yet records are plentiful.

There is an account in the English scientific magazine *Nature*, November 1, 1894, of two-pound hailstones, and the *Chambers' Encyclopedia* listed some three-pounders. In the *Reports* of the Smithsonian Institute, (1870, p. 479) two-pound hailstones were verified, and six-pounders were reported. About the year 1800 a hailstone fell at Seringapatam, India, said to be the size of an elephant.

When they come that big, obviously they are not hailstones.

In 1841, near Sheffield, England, there was a fall of fish and small frogs intermingled with pieces of melting ice. That was in July, and we are asked by scientists to believe this mixture was picked up by a whirlwind and carried hundreds of miles!

But to prove that ice is arriving from outer space we must

21

get away from material which can be dubbed hailstones. Many of us may have seen hailstones as large even as turkey eggs, but anything larger almost certainly comes from space. Space origin is probable if the ice had a *rectangular* or irregular shape and/or a homogenous texture, that is, of solid or uniform inner structure. Normal hailstones are made up of concentric layers of moisture, successively frozen.

The *Monthly Weather Review*, June, 1877, described chunks of ice too large to be grasped in one hand, which fell in a tornado in Colorado on June 24 of that year. The same official government magazine reported a twenty-one inch mass of ice falling in an Iowa hailstorm in June, 1881. And four-and-a-half-inch lumps of ice were reported falling at Richmond, England, on August 2, 1879, according to *Symons Meteorological Magazine*. All this within the "Incredible Decade"—1877-1886.

On June 16, 1882, perhaps the most remarkable year of the decade, lumps of ice fell at Dubuque, Iowa, containing living frogs. Some pieces were up to seventeen inches in circumference and the largest weighed about three-quarters of a pound. The remarkable thing is that some of these lumps of ice (which were not called hailstones) had *icicles* upon them at least a half inch in length, which could not have formed upon wind tossed hailstones. The questions arise: how were these lumps formed; what held them stationary while icicles formed upon them; from where did they come?

The *Monthly Weather Review*, June, 1889, reports ice falls at Oswego, New York, on June 11 which resembled broken icicles; and others, the size and shape of lead pencils cut into short sections, falling on Florence Island in the St. Lawrence River, August 8, 1901.

Fauth, an arduous lunar mapper, in his book *The Moon*, says:

"Many terrestrial phenomena, especially the dreaded heavy hailstones with blocks of ice four inches thick (or more) which still puzzle the meteorologist, point to an accession of ice from outer space . . ."

and:

". . . the moon, with its coat of ice is an eloquent witness to the existence of ice in the solar system."

We are forced by contemporary evidence, and that of centuries past, to agree that ice is continually arriving from space. Therefore, there is water in space for the UFO dweller if he cares to pick it up. Fauth, at least, is *one* scientist who accepts the evidence of sound observation at its face value and helps to establish that conditions in space may support life as well as intelligence.

The "Carolina Bays" were almost certainly made by a huge swarm of ice meteors or space-icebergs which may have been partially instrumental in causing "the Flood." If ice meteors continually strike the earth, why not the moon, also?

The "modernists" of any century are prone to dismiss their predecessors as ignoramuses, unable to observe accurately, or interpret properly what they did observe. In case you find yourself dismissing past observations on such grounds, consider some recent reports.

Inland from the Bristol Channel, in England, is a wild stretch of moorland, heath, and rolling down, called Exmoor, given up to sheep-grazing. On the morning of November 11, 1950, a farmer named Edward Latham went into his fields at dawn and found a ewe lying dead as if struck by lightning; there was a deep wound in her neck. A few yards away lay a fourteen-pound block of ice, obviously fallen from the sky. It had dug itself into the ground to a depth of several inches. Yet, the weather had been mild. Around the field and along the roadway were lumps of ice as large as dinner plates. Other farmers found ice among their cattle, and pieces were strewn on the roadway four miles away.

The same thing had happened on the *same moor* in 1910 under similar conditions, killing three sheep. No explanation had been given by the British Air Ministry. There were no large metallic airplanes from which ice formations could have dropped down. A British weather official stated: "The conditions do not suggest that this is any *normal* meteorological weather phenomenon."

On November 24, 1950, ice fell out of a clear blue sky onto the asbestos roof of a garage at Wandsworth, London. The chunk was a foot square and the concussion was so great that a night watchman thought a boiler had burst. The Air Ministry thought it might have dropped from a plane using de-icing equipment. *But no planes were known to have been over the area!*

On the 26th of November, 1950, Reginald Butcher of Stebbing, Essex, found on his garden path something fallen from the sky which appeared to be ice, but on examination was found to be of an unknown substance. It weighed about a pound and was a foot long, and *it did not melt!* It was not ice nor was it glass nor crystalline, although it was translucent. The police took the substance, and the whole affair remains a mystery.

On November 27, 1950, a block of ice a foot long and four inches thick, weighing five pounds, fell out of the sky. It landed unbroken at the feet of a startled member of the Royal Automobile Club, Mr. Tunmore, of Braughing, Hertfordshire.

That piece of ice was actually seen in the process of coming down from a clear sky. No one had to await its impact in order to *surmise* that it *did* come from the sky. The puzzled Air Ministry experts and meteorological experts called for help from professors at Durham and Cambridge universities.

Professor F. A. Pameth, at Durham University, and authority on meteorites thought this object might be an "ice meteorite," but admitted that he could not explain their origin. A meteorological expert of the Air Ministry was not so modest. He conjectured that the block was ice, fired into space from *one of the ice-coated inner satellites of the planet Saturn* which was bombarding the earth.

An Air Ministry inspector who examined the Wandsworth block of ice said it probably had been formed against a smooth flat surface, but lacking an airplane overhead nobody has suggested what that surface might be.

On December 3, 1950, again at Wandsworth, a block of ice weighing two pounds fell on a house. Four days later, at Wycomb, a schoolboy saw a block of ice about nine inches *square* fall from the sky onto the road and splinter to pieces. No plane was in the sky. These falls of ice were given official attention. The

Parliamentary Secretary of the British Ministry of Civil Aviation admitted, in the House of Commons, on December 13, that

"Four cases of falling ice have been reported in which there is no evidence that aircraft were involved. *It is not considered that meteorological phenomena were responsible, and investigations are being continued.*"

Ice-falls persisted. In Southwest London a twenty-inch cylinder (whether of ice or metal was not specified) fell into a garden. There was no airplane overhead at the time.

On December 26, 1950, a block of ice weighing over *one hundred and twelve pounds* crashed on a road at Dumbartonshire, Scotland. The police who collected the splinters said that some pieces bore marks of apparent *slots and rivets.*

On December 21, a block of ice weighing a pound fell from the sky and glanced off the scarf on the head of Miss Margaret Patterson, twenty-four of Lingwell Road, Tooting, London. No plane seen or heard at that time.

On January 10, 1951, a six-foot icicle fell near Düsseldorf, Germany, and killed a carpenter.

There must be some significance in these repeated falls over *localized areas.* It is important to note that UFO observations had been considerably stepped up during this interval. Was it a bombardment or accidental falls from hovering UFO?

On January 15, 1953, a chunk of ice thirteen inches long and six inches wide, followed by smaller pieces, narrowly missed a woman and her child at Whittier, California. An egg-shaped chunk weighing about fifty pounds fell, at approximately 10:20 A.M., on February 18, 1953, at Freeport, Long Island, and smashed a rose trellis. The Air Force said *it could not have been formed on a plane.*

About fifty large blocks of ice fell on cars in parking lots in Long Beach, California, damaging them severely, on June 4, 1953. Some chunks were up to four feet long. The fall continued for about two minutes. Even after shattering, some chunks weighed twenty-five pounds when picked up. The parent pieces were estimated at three hundred pounds.

A Russian named Shwedoff postulated cosmic or meteoric hailstones in the early 80's; but as of 1956 science has not seen fit to admit these to respectability.

In the summer of 1951, the city of Bennington, Vermont, was battered for ten minutes by large hailstones which caused much damage. In the center of each ice particle was found a bit of *black metal* which has completely baffled meteorologists.

While the fall of ice from space does not necessarily prove the existence of UFO, it does prove the existence of vast amounts of ice and water in space, along with other miscellaneous debris. Would you agree that such materials contribute support to the case for space life?

Our contention is that when an impact is noted or damage is done by something from the sky, and no object is found, there has been a fall of some volatile substance such as ice. A case in point is the report printed in *Doubt* that on August 16, 1954, something from a clear blue sky struck, or fell into the chimney of a house in Eltham, London. The chimney was smashed, fuses were blown and the living room was smothered with soot—but nothing was found.

There is also the report of a Mrs. Campbell, of Leeds, who was sitting on a cliff watching jet aircraft fly overhead. Something struck her head and she was taken to a hospital almost unconscious. However, no object was found in a later search. (London *Daily Mail*, September 8, 1954).

A particularly puzzling feature of such arrivals of miscellaneous matter from space is that material of the same kind often falls repeatedly in the same locality, such as the repeated falls of ice on and near London.

Throughout our research we have been looking for evidence of intelligence, and it is the association of intelligent action with falls such as this that makes us tie them in, no matter how remotely, with UFO. Selectivity of the materials implies intelligence, and the selection inherent in many of these falls is very rigid. Seldom do we have more than one kind of material falling at the same time, and in mixtures ice is often combined with certain living organisms. These manifestations of intelligence may be capricious, but if so, we merely point out that capriciousness is also an indication of mentality.

◆ Falling Stones and Shapes ◆

The earth is certainly a landing field for all manner of inanimate space debris, and some things which we wouldn't care to call inanimate. They may be friendly—or sinister.

In studying the arrivals from space, one soon notices at least two types of material. The better known is geological debris—the common iron and stone meteorites. The other material comprises heterogeneous items.

The volume and diversity of this influx from space leads me to believe ordinary meteorites are but a part of the total space debris. And it is so characteristic of planetary surfaces that I am inclined to view many of them as housekeeping items of a planetary vivisphere—including items sometimes swept under the cosmic rug.

Some of the non-geological items can be called organic, or artificial in character—that is, they bear evidence of intelligent shaping or manipulation. Such evidence includes shape, material, physical condition, orientation, function, selection, peculiar and delimited distribution, purposefulness, timing, etc.

On June 20, 1887, at the end of the "incredible decade," a small stone fell from the sky at Tarbes, France. It was thirteen millimeters in diameter and five millimeters thick—about one-fifth of an inch by half an inch—and weighed about two grams. It was delicate, as though shaped by tiny hands, and was definitely *artificial* in character. If there is no life in space, from where did it come?

Meteorites of iron and stone, once damned by the savants, have now been admitted to respectability. But falling ice and intelligently shaped artifacts are still of the damned. Nevertheless people continue to see falling paper, wool, resin, beef, blood and stones with strange inscriptions—and snails, toads, peri-winkles, etc.

There are numerous reports of falls of cinders and slag. It is perhaps significant that stones often fall during storms, or at least the falls are connected with storms. Many examples are listed in the *Reports of the British Association for Advancement of Science, The Annual Register,* the *Intellectual Observer, Gregg's Catalogue,* and others.

A violent storm in 1794 dumped many stones on Sienna. There were repeated falls of small black stones on Wolverhampton, England, about May, 1869, after severe storms. Similar stones had fallen in nearby Birmingham the year before.

On October 13, 1872, a peculiar stone fell near Lake Banja, in Serbia. Being of an unknown type, the stone was named Banjite, after the lake. Seventeen years later, on December 1, 1889, another rock of Banjite fell at the nearby town of Jelica. Why did these stones of a material not known on earth fall in the same locality, seventeen years apart? Selective repetition may be considered a characteristic of intelligence. Significantly, the falls of these two pieces of Banjite spanned the time of the "incredible decade."

Mr. Lee Gould, an Australian scientist, saw a tree which had been broken off close to the ground. Nearby was an object which resembled a ten-inch shot, obviously from the sky. With equal surety, the "shot" had been shaped by some kind of intelligence.

In *Nature* (Vol. III, page 512, and Vol. IV, page 169) are reports of fish that fell with, or at least were found among, the fragments of a meteor.

A hollow globular piece of quartz fell in Canada on December 1, 1889. Other pieces of quartz or quartz pebbles have been reported, showing that many types of stone, as well as other materials, are adrift "out there."

These items might be unimportant to us, if they had no bearing on UFO problems. The point is they show that space contains much miscellaneous material, a great deal of it the stuff we would expect from an exploding planet. Such stuff would be useful to UFO in space. Some of it may come *from UFO*.

A block of limestone fell in a field near Middleburg, Florida, on March 9, 1888. The experts said it could not have fallen for there is no limestone in the sky!

We also have numerous cases of falling sandstone—some of it worn smooth. One piece was found embedded in a full-grown peach tree. This might not be significant except that it appears to have been *red hot* for it charred the tree around the point of penetration.

The following are especially significant because of repetition within a local area.

In February, March and at later dates, rocks fell at Chico, California, according to the New York *Times* of March 12, 1922. Many were large and smooth and seemed to come straight down from the clouds. No satisfactory explanation was offered by investigators. They were said not to be of meteoric origin because two showed signs of cementation, either natural or artificial. Our thought is that these may have come from an exploded planet in space.

Some investigators brought back evidence which seems to show that these rocks falling on Chico were actually apports. They may have been, for they seemed to appear immediately over the buildings on which they fell, rather than to have come from great heights.

Chico, California, seems to be a concentration point for peculiar events. The New York *Times*, September 2, 1878, in the "incredible decade," reported a fall of small fish there on the 20th of August, covering several acres. They fell from a cloudless sky! On the night of March 5-6, 1885, a large, hard object weighing several tons fell near Chico. In 1893, an iron object, said to be meteoritic, was found at Oroville, near Chico, where in 1887 an occurrence, dismissed as an earthquake, was described by townsmen as detonations heard in the sky. Why all this near Chico?

Bush Creek, California, where miner Black saw a flying saucer and "little people," is not very far from Chico.

◆ Falling Organic Matter ◆

We have records of falls of hair, flesh (no bones—I wonder why?), snakes, frogs, fish, insects, iron, steel, slag, ashes, birds, blood, mud, algae, stones, vegetable matter, discs, snails, lizards, lichens, mussels, periwinkles, and *warm* water.

Any single instance of these might be ignored or laughed off as a mistaken observation, hoax, or freak. And, throughout history, until Charles Fort began to list them, they *were* ignored, probably because no one had taken the trouble to compile and group the reports to obtain the weight of concentrated evidence.

I suppose if a little green man suddenly materialized at a scientific assemblage, he could be ignored as the product of mass hallucination—or as an isolated example, unverified by "controlled experiments"! But ten little green men would be, to most people, more convincing.

As regards this list of items fallen from the sky or from space—one or two we could forget. But dozens . . . hundreds . . . thousands . . . though seemingly unrelated to each other, become hard to ignore—as, also, the intelligence that seems to direct their distribution.

Try, by easy stages, to get used to the idea that intelligence does not necessarily mean *human* intelligence. I realize that it can be the latest and most severe blow to our ego to accept that our racial intelligence is anything but the culminating point of a creative, good and infinite universe or God. But in that way, will we grasp the nature of the universe—or at least the portion in our vicinity—and our proper place in it?

The *Monthly Weather Review* (1917, 45-220) is a gold mine of information regarding falls of live and organic matter over a period of centuries. This is a coldly scientific review of the subject, presented in as readable a manner as the conventional scientists can muster. The reader who wishes to investigate the subject of falling animal matter and to make an unemotional evaluation of such phenomena can find no better source. The author, Mr. McAttee, a bona fide scientific worker, does not, of course, espouse our line of thinking, for he obviously had not thought of such possibilities. Yet he acknowledges that innumerable recorded falls of living and organic matter from the sky are authentic.

One instance among those of which Mr. McAttee admits the authenticity is the following (*Descript. de St. Dominque,* by Morea de St. Mary, t-2, p. 413): From November, 1785, to May 5, 1786, on the island of Haiti—Santo Domingo, there was a terrible drought. On May 5, 1786, during a strong east wind, there fell, in several parts of the city of Port au Prince, quantities of black eggs which hatched the following day. M. Mazard preserved about fifty of these small animals in a water flask, where they shed their skins several times. They *resembled* tadpoles.

That's as near as we come to tadpoles among falling space life. There is, for us, some significance in the statement that these animals *resembled* tadpoles. What, in fact, *were* they?

According to the Los Angeles *Daily News* of September 24, 1954, a Mrs. Hoffman of Los Angeles reported hearing a loud thump in her back yard. There she found a "hunk of yellowish waxy stuff about fifteen inches long, six inches wide and one inch and a half thick." No plane had been heard overhead.

The Fortean Society magazine, *Doubt* (Number 47) reported that on October 7, 1954, large quantities of birds and bats died under unexplained circumstances. The New York *Times* took an inventory of the casualties found on the roofs of the Empire State Building: 125 birds of about thirty species and four bats.

One explanation was offered: that they were blown against the building by a strong wind. Selectivity again? A selective wind? It would be difficult to believe that so great a number, regardless of species, could be blown against *one* building by an *uncontrolled* wind. Could such an explanation account for more than 200 dead birds found, the same morning, at Mitchell Field, strewn over the open parade ground and runways? *Some had cracked skulls* but others appeared to have died from something resembling *heart failure.* Associated Press reports revealed the same thing happening on the same night in Alabama, Georgia, South Carolina, Kansas, Tennessee, Pennsylvania, and North Carolina. A biologist at Salina, Kansas, is reported to have performed autopsies on fallen birds which indicated asphyxiation.

This is a companion piece to the report of hundreds of birds of different species which rained down on Baton Rouge, Louisiana, in the period of the great comets in the 19th century. We suggest that only intervention from space can account for this. Such intervention need not necessarily have come from controlled space-craft; but either this or the impingement of noxious clouds into our atmosphere must be assumed. If noxious clouds, how do we account for the peculiar distribution? If we assume a space-craft, it must have swept up birds for some purpose and subsequently dumped them. Alternatively the craft may have emitted poisonous gases, but how does "gas" crack bird's skulls?

If poisonous gas entered from space, how did it penetrate our dense atmosphere so close to the surface? Why were there no deleterious effects on human beings or other animals on the surface? What is *your* theory?

There is a postscript to those accounts of dead birds, and strangely enough it arrived while I was writing these paragraphs. Some readers of *The Case for the UFO* were thoughtful enough to send in the clippings. The South Carolina *State* published the following on September 28, 1955:

Charlotte, September 27, (AP)—Scores of dead birds fell from the skies today at Douglas Municipal Airport near here, and *elsewhere in the vicinity*. It happened less than twenty-four hours after hundreds of dead birds plummeted to the streets of Troy, 73 miles east of here.

That clipping was sent to me by James H. Palmer. A more elaborate account was sent in by Fred A. Taylor. Protesting bird lovers blamed an airport gadget called a "ceilometer," using a 25,000,000-candlepower light for attracting and dazzling night-migratory birds. But what happened to those at Troy, seventy-three miles away? And those said to have fallen by day? *And did they have a ceilometer in Baton Rouge in the decade of the great comets?*

My hypothesis of a marauding UFO may not match the ceilometer; but I have a memory of something walking across the English landscape, leaving those "devil's footprints" in a long unhindered single line. Something holding something up. A force thrusting down . . . penetrating snow . . . marking stones— and cracking bird's skulls when birds and forces meet high up somewhere?

According to the Worcester (England) *Daily Times*, May 30, 1881, and a publication called *Land and Water*, June 4, 1881, periwinkles fell along a road into Worcester. The dictionary describes periwinkles as small marine snails, and Worcester is about fifty miles inland. There were great quantities of periwinkles— a few hermit crabs and small crabs of a species which could not be identified. But the agency which had dropped these living creatures had been very selective; they fell free of sand, pebbles, other shells or seaweed.

Mostly the people of Worcester were incredulous. However, some went out to see and returned with periwinkles for supper.

A Mr. J. Lloyd Bozward, a writer on meteorological subjects, investigated the reports. His findings were published in the Worcester *Evening Post* on June 9th.

He stated that the value of the periwinkles was sixteen shillings a bushel, which was real money at that time. A wide area on both sides of the road was heaped with periwinkles and crabs. Any thought of a fishmonger trying to get rid of overstock must be discounted. There as no glutted market at the time.

Gardens were covered even though there were high walls around them. Mr. Bozward asserts that, to his knowledge, about ten sacks of periwinkles had been picked up, at a value of about twenty pounds, and sold in the markets at Worcester. Crowds had filled pots, pans and boxes before he got to the place. He concluded from all available evidence, that these things had fallen from the sky during a thunderstorm. This resembles the usual partial and unsatisfactory explanation that a "whirlwind" capable of selectively sifting and washing them had picked them up at one place and deposited them somewhere else.

The conventional explanation in the journals was that an

overstocked fishmonger had gotten rid of them along the road. But why would he want to get rid of periwinkles that fetched twenty pounds? And why did he mix them with hermit crabs, and *particularly with crabs of undetermined species?* And, on the day before, no periwinkles were on sale in Worcester.

There are many reports of low types of animal life falling from the sky. Selection, segregation, and *localization* are common characteristics of such falls. They invariably cover small areas, usually narrow, elongated strips of land. My assumption is that such falls were dumpings from tanks in which space-craft transport, and perhaps grow, food for their own consumption. The Worcester periwinkles were distributed along a road for at least a mile over a narrow space. Such a pattern suggests that they were dumped from some contrivance moving parallel to the road.

As in the case of the "devil's footprints" in Devonshire, high walls proved no hindrance. Periwinkles and crabs were found inside garden walls, as well as along the road and in the fields. Was there something, pretty large, moving overhead near Worcester that day in 1881—the year of one of the greatest comets?

For the skeptics who point out that the storm must have picked up the periwinkles and crabs at the seashore fifty miles away and transported them inland to Worcester, we can point out that one of the greatest hurricanes in Irish history only succeeded in blowing a few small fish some fifteen yards from the edge of a lake.

Many falls of fish are recorded and have been authenticated by the *Monthly Weather Review* and the *Zoologist.* There is a nice detail to report about a fall of fish on the property of a Mr. Nixon of Mountain Ash, Glamorganshire, Wales, on February 11, 1859. This report provoked much debate in scientific journals. People nowhere near the place denied, of course, that any such thing happened; but, according to the *Annual Register,* the fish had fallen by pailfuls. A bigger question was posed by those who insisted the fish were already on the ground before the storm.

The most important thing to us is that the way the fish

and periwinkles fell could not be attributed to the mechanics of a whirlwind or tornado. The fish were on a narrow strip of land about eighty yards long and twelve yards wide. Another fall of fish occurred upon the same narrow strip of land ten minutes later. Even arguing that a whirlwind or tornado could stand still, it would discharge materials around its periphery; and it could hardly have dropped some, to carry off the rest, and then return ten minutes later to drop them. Science attempted to laugh off the whole occurrence, remarking that someone had soused someone else with a pailful of water containing minnows. However, it is stated that the roofs of some houses were covered with fish, some of which were five inches long. Small ones were placed in both salt and fresh water. Those placed in salt water died almost instantly but not those placed in fresh water.

Again we have extreme selection and localization which are attributes of intelligence. I propose that the size of area covered bears some relation to the size of a door in a space structure, which could be used for dumping the material from tanks while cleaning, or preparing to refill. There are many such instances of limited falls of live specimens of lower forms of life, particularly toads, frogs, snakes and varied marine life.

Fish and frogs usually fall in deluges and torrents of rain. But it has often been reported that the rain was not actually rain but dropping masses of water, again suggesting the emptying of huge tanks in vast contraptions flying overhead.

In a fall of fish over Calcutta on September 20, 1839, the fish fell in a straight line about eighteen inches in width. This was reported in *Living Age* (volume 52, page 186). If they didn't come from a tank, then from where?

Attributes of intelligent placement: straight line; along a road; and only about eighteen inches in width. Direction, control, and selection—can these be without purposefulness? Clouds formed in a cloudless sky; torrents, deluges of water. Big torpedo shapes crossing the face of the sun. Great black things poised like a giant crow over the moon. Can you seriously believe that all of this is unrelated to UFO?

Worms—do they bother you? These bother me. Enormous

numbers of unidentifiable brown worms fell from the sky near Clifton, Indiana, on February 4, 1892.

On February 14, myriads of scarlet worms fell in Massachusetts, covering several acres after a snowstorm. Something seemed to be specializing in the transportation and distribution of immature and larval forms of life in the middle of February, 1892. There were four other falls, or mysterious appearances of worms, early in 1892; some of the specimens could not be identified. At Lancaster, Pennsylvania, in a snowstorm, worms landed on umbrellas.

I call to your attention that falls of live things from the sky have usually been confined to marine life and the lower forms of life in general, such as snails, worms, reptiles, insects, fish, crabs, snakes etc. Most of these have high reproductive rates, simple living habits, require little food and a minimum of attention to raise. They live in water, or in a very damp habitat, and some are scavengers. Again, tanks are suggested.

If all such falls are hoaxes, then we have some heroic and persistent hoaxers.

One does not find many frogs in a desert. Yet, in a very dry desert in Nevada called Newark Valley, Mr. Stoker drove through a thunderstorm and a shower of frogs fell on his wagon. Again we note the connection between falling life and accompanying storms. Falls usually take place in masses of water and we question: are all storms caused by ordinary meteorological conditions? Or are there local storms of other origin? The storm of Newark Valley was isolated in a region where it could not pick up frogs. Several people, including personal friend, George Mullins, reported similar experiences.

On August 18 and 19, 1922, innumerable little frogs fell on London streets during a thunderstorm. According to the London *Daily News*, September 5, 1922, little toads had been dropping from the sky in France for two days. Fish of an unknown species fell at Seymour, Indiana, August 8, 1891. On February 6, 1890, a shower of fish fell in Montgomery County California, also of an unknown species.

According to the New York *Sun*, May 20, 1892, (the year of falling worms) eels showered down at Coalburg, Alabama. There were piles of eels in the streets and farmers carted them away for fertilizer. They were said to be of a species known in the Pacific Ocean. Do *you* think those eels were brought by a whirlwind?

In August, 1886, snails showered down during a heavy thunderstorm near Redruth, Cornwall, England.

The *Scientific American* reported that on July 3, 1860, a resident of South Granville, New York, had a stunned snake fall at his feet during a heavy shower. It came to life and glided away. It was grey and about a foot long.

According to the *Monthly Weather Review,* January 15, 1877, a great quantity of snakes appeared at Memphis, Tennessee, immediately after a violent storm. They covered a space of two blocks, crawling on sidewalks and in yards. There were masses of them. None were seen to fall, but who would have been out in such a storm to see them? Again, why such a limited space— two city blocks? And if they were picked up by a storm why were there no stones, fence rails, limbs of trees, leaves and other debris? Again we say—the snakes were dumped.

There were falls of toads, ants and fish in 1889. Ants fell in England in the summer of 1874, and *some were wingless.* Ants of an unknown species, about the size of wasps, fell in Manitoba in June, 1895. Worms fell in Devonshire in 1837. In 1876, in midwinter, worms were found crawling on ground frozen too hard for them to have come up from it, much less have been grown there from larvae.

Some whitish-colored frogs fell at Birmingham, England. Would not frogs grown in tanks, away from sunlight, lose their pigment?

In the winter of 1876, in different parts of Norway, worms were found crawling upon icy ground. They could not have come up from the frozen ground, therefore they must have dropped from the sky. In 1827 vast numbers of black insects fell during a snowstorm at Pakrov, Russia, and again at Orenburg, on December 14, 1830 during a snowstorm (reported in the *American Journal of Science,* volume I, page 375). On November 18, 1850, worms were found on snow near Sangerfield, New York.

The *Scientific American* for February 21, 1891, reported a

puzzling phenomenon in Randolph County, Virginia. Worms whose origin could not be explained had appeared several times on snow. Later similar worms were reported upon the snow near Utica, New York, and in Oneida and Herkimer Counties.

The most reasonable explanations for such falls in extremely localized rainstorms or snowstorms, often with a linear distribution, is that these live things are brought by some contrivance which uses storms for concealment, or creates storms by its presence.

We will close with an eyewitness account given to the author by Peter Kamitchis, a writer and editor in New York. He recalls a date he had during his adolescence back in Oklahoma. He and the young lady were caught in a typical Oklahoma cloudburst. But, un-typically, a steady mass of tiny white toads or frogs rained down. They skittered on the road in white waves, and the car-wheels spun a track through their smashed bodies.

◆ Water and Clouds ◆

The echoes remind us that controlled and organically shaped clouds make an attractive field for research, and several responsible observers, notably an English scientist, have stated that we would do well to take note of them for future reference.

Clouds may have a purposeful air about them, as shown in cloud photos released by the U. S. Navy in 1955. Those photos recall the phenomenal formation once seen over the Madeira Islands by Piazzi Smythe, Astronomer Royal of Scotland.

The city of Funchal, Madeira, lies in tropical repose on the slopes of a mountain 3,000 feet high. The white buildings with their red-tiled roofs reach all the way up from the beach to the tourist hotel on the summit where clouds take over. There, back in the 1880's, the Astronomer Royal was vacationing.

One afternoon, he saw a strange isolated cloud forming at a

great altitude over the bay. A solitary mountain peak may form clouds by the up-draft it produces, but this cloud was not of that sort. It was awesomely stationary, as if it had a purpose. Not only did it stay in the same place, for hours, but under it, like an offspring, another similar but larger cloud formed, then a third, a fourth, a fifth, all stationary and on the same vertical axis. Smythe's account could almost be a description of the clouds the Navy photographed off the coast of France. The formation had all the appearance of being intelligently controlled, and each cloud maintained its position until sunset. After dark the clouds disappeared in the reverse order of their formation. The highest remained visible in striking colors long after sunset, because of its very great height, at which it reflected the sinking sun. It *remained luminous* until 10:00 P.M., long *after* there were sun's rays to reflect. The formation was verified by ships at sea, and the great height is confirmed by a sighting distance of almost 150 miles.

This may have been a natural formation, but it had mathematical features and elements of control which held a hardheaded, skeptical analyst, and made him pause and record the facts.

That is the sort of thing we have in mind when talking about "artificial," or "organic"-appearing clouds and storms. Here we have examples, unusually symmetrical, often severely so, of the spindle shape so familiar to students of UFO lore. There are the familiar features of localization and of hovering in one place despite steady winds. If the clouds were even in part above the level of wind action, then what materials formed them? The group of clouds were obviously held rigid in a deliberate geometrical relationship by forces outside the range of ordinary meteorological conditions. They were apparently formed one from another on a vertical axis, as though the upper ones were parents to the lower. Especially notable is their similar shape, and their ability to hold vast concentrations of water without rain falling, like a mass that moved over Ontario and then dropped to cause a local flood.

In brief, this cloud formation of 1881 had the appearance of being "something special." Have you seen anything with these "special" characteristics?

We can thank Thompson's *Introduction to Meteorology,* for some of the following records of clouds of almost, if not quite, paranormal nature:

In the district of Cheribon, Java, there occurred a remarkable cloud and electrical disturbance at midnight on the 11th of August, 1772. The mountain was seen enveloped in a cloud of unusual appearance, and at the same time loud reports like artillery fire were heard. The cloud rolled down the mountainside and overtook those who were unable to flee, enclosing them in darkness and concealing the land for miles around, and tossed the terrified victims like waves on a troubled ocean. It emitted globes of fire, so vivid and numerous that night was dispelled. For twenty miles everything was devastated and 2,140 people were killed, and thousands of animals.

In Malta, October 28, 1867, about three quarters of an hour after midnight there appeared, to the SW, a great black cloud which, as it approached, changed its color until at last it became like a flame of fire mixed with black smoke. It made a dreadful noise and passed over part of the port where it totally destroyed an English ship and broke up all small boats in its path. It did a lot more damage, including blowing away the lighthouse and steeples of churches.

These two "storms" have the unusual characteristics of coming at midnight, and the second especially resembles an old-fashioned American tornado. Tornadoes at midnight, however, are rare.

At Venice, January 8, 1815, about 6 P.M., the sky was overcast, the temperature at 2° above zero (certainly abnormal enough, it would seem, although we believe that winters were generally colder then). Suddenly and silently a flame was seen to rise from the earth above houses and spread over a big church. It lasted four minutes and was very vivid.

Near Quito, Ecuador, about 9 P.M. one night, a globe of fire seemed to rise from a neighboring peak, pass from west to east until intercepted by another mountain, and was so effulgent that it lit the city. It was said to be "a foot in diameter," but who knows how big it was or how far away?

A meteorite fell on August 7, 1823, at the American town of Nobleborough, about 5 P.M. The sky was perfectly clear except for a small, whitish cloud, apparently about forty feet *square,* near the zenith, and the air perfectly calm. A noise like musketry came from the cloud which then *spiraled downward,* and the stone fell from it.

Can we afford to overlook a square cloud which spirals downward and expectorates a meteoric stone? The following account is from the New Orleans *Picayune*, July 11, 1893:

Bright, clear day near Pittsburgh, Pennsylvania. From the sky swooped a wrath which incited a river. It was one bulk of water: two miles away, no rain fell. A raging river jeered against former confinements. Some of its jibes were freight cars. It scoffed with bridges. Having made a highwater mark of rebellion, it subsided into a petulance of jostling rowboats. Monistically, I have to accept that no line of demarcation can be drawn between emotions of minds and motions of rivers. (Charles Fort)

Notice that it was a clear day; that the deluge rose and subsided suddenly; that there was no rain to produce flood drainage from surrounding territory—just one bulk of water.

The year 1954 was another of those years of world-wide deluge, and was made the subject of an international meteorological inquiry. We want to know whether or not they are periodic. Are they related to any known cycle of physical events such as sunspots or meteoritic orbital motions? This flood year reminds us of similar ones, 1889 and 1913. In Southern Morocco three days' rainfall exceeded the precipitation for three years. England was deluged and so were Italy, Germany, Spain, Switzerland, Belgium, and France. In the Western Hemisphere, Mexico, Honduras and some parts of South America had floods. Australia reported deluges. Asia was hardest hit, and record rainfall afflicted Tibet, India, Pakistan and China.

We still contend that these world-wide deluges are caused by masses of water or moisture arriving from orbits in space. Evaporation from the surface of the earth is not sufficient to account for them. Open space must contain a tremendous amount of miscellaneous material, including water.

J. S. Holden of Glenarm, Ireland, reported on the 15th of September, 1870, that about 8:30 P.M. he saw a bright meteor in the northwest. It first appeared like a first magnitude star, then assumed a comet shape, moving in a westerly direction. Then it turned into a *white opaque ring of cloud*, well-defined and luminous! From its expanding rim, it ejected a tail which curved earth-wards. Finally it faded to a fleecy wraith of cloud, the entire phenomenon lasting for about five minutes. This may have been the atmospheric disturbance created by an ordinary meteor, but the geometrical shapes are puzzling.

An old French work, *Traité Physique et Historique de l'Aurore Boréale*, lists 1,441 auroral phenomena from the sixth century to 1754. A number of displays here called auroral are obviously of a UFO nature. One described an aerial show of November 14, 1574:

. . . were seen in the air strange impressions of fire and smoke to proceed forth from a black cloud in the north, towards the south. That the next night the heavens from all parts did seem to burn marvelous ragingly . . . as if in a clear furnace.

This is not what we think of as an aurora. History contains many descriptions of these strange black clouds from which come smoke and fire and sometimes debris. These and other of the reported events must have been of UFO origin.

Astronomer Herschel once saw a cloud bank "precipitate so fast" that it crossed the whole sky at a speed of at least 300 mph. Obviously a UFO storm, not an ordinary meteorological storm.

In 1955 the U.S. Navy released photos of "organic" clouds seen off the coast of France. There were two, both like flattened spheres, black and isolated in the sky. Obviously they were not cut from the same meteorological cloth as other clouds. They had a "live" appearance suggesting purposefulness. They were clearly of a UFO nature; why were the photos released?

II

ECHOES OF ASTRONOMY

◆ More Mysteries of Space ◆

The total solar eclipse of 1869 was visible in the American Middle West. At St. Paul's Junction, Iowa, a number of observers, including trained scientists, saw what must have been a UFO. The account appeared in the Des Moines *State Register* of October 8, 1869; and in many science journals.

The planet Mercury, then close to the sun, was available as a reference point. Mr. W. S. Gilman Jr. placed the object close to Mercury, and horizontally to its right. The "star" as he called it, was independently found by Mr. and Mrs. Farrell, a Mr. Phelps and a Mr. Lockland. Each saw it both with the naked eye and telescopes. Each was positive of the sighting, and located the "star" a little to the right of, and below, the moon's center.

The UFO appeared to be about 1/6th the size of Mercury and of star-like brightness. It appeared very nearly in line with the Sun-Moon eclipse, and so near that it must have been within the penumbra of the moon's shadow and would then have been red as were Watson and Swift's UFO in 1878.

This is clearly a sighting of one of the space UFO discussed in *The Case for the UFO*.

This sighting alone would have been conclusive demonstration of UFO in the earth-moon system, probably at the gravitational neutral—but there was more evidence.

During this same eclipse, August 7, 1869, many people, at Mattoon, Illinois, noticed faint, whitish objects moving past their glasses at the time of totality. These were not then deemed important. It came out in later discussion and comparison of notes, that these "little" objects moved in the same direction—in a stream so to speak—from northwest downwards to southeast. No acceptable explanation was advanced. Minds were too shackled to conceive of space flight in those days. To us, now, no other explanation could do. Wind-blown fluffy seeds have been suggested as explanation in similar cases in England. To skeptics not involved in the sightings, such "explanations" seem logical. But . . . that was at Mattoon . . . and the phenomenon was not local, far from it.

Alvin G. Clark, America's most famous grinder and polisher of telescopic lenses, observing from Shelbyville, Kentucky, on the same date (August 7, 1869) states: "I saw, through the finder* of the Shelbyville Equatorial,** about twenty small objects crossing the field [of view] of the finder." He called them to the attention of Professor Winlock, who confirmed them.

A Mrs. Murphy, observing from Falmouth, Kentucky, saw two "meteors" during the same totality.

There is still more.

General Albert J. Meyer, observing at, or near, Abingdon, Virginia, saw "a shower of bright specks," just prior to totality. On reading descriptions of the other sightings, he concluded that he had seen the same things.

This was one of the clearest of all reports of UFO in space. To be seen *against the moon-sun eclipse*, from such widely separated points, these "things" *had to be* far out in space, toward the moon, as far as the earth-moon gravitational neutral, otherwise they would have been displaced by parallax.†

---

* A small telescope attached to a large one for sighting and aiming purposes, on exactly the same principle as the telescopic sight on a rifle.
** Equatorial: a telescope mounted on an axis parallel to the earth's axis, so that it swings parallel to the equator.
† Parallax means the shift in apparent position of an object against a

In other parts of volume VII of the *Astronomical Register,* Arago announced that *two* luminous meteors were seen to cross the sky in a direction *towards the sun and moon* at the moment of total eclipse, July 8, 1842. The reference says nothing about their speed. Of this same eclipse, M. Wullerstoff, observing at Venice, said that the moon's disc was occasionally crossed by light streaks. M. Piola, from observations at the same date said that some shooting stars and a bollide were visible at totality and that the bollide seemed to detach itself from the moon. These must have been UFO, possibly arriving at and departing from the moon.

Note especially the frequency with which these space objects are reported in pairs. Mrs. Murphy saw *"two meteors."* Arago saw two meteors. Watson and Swift saw two objects in 1878. And so on, for many sightings of two objects crossing the sun.

Weidler records a friend's report of bright bodies seen long before and after totality at the eclipse of 1738. In *Monthly Notices* (volume XII, page 38) a letter from Rev. W. Read records luminous objects seen September 4, 1850, at a total eclipse; a similar reference by Dawes appears on page 183. In some instances, these bodies appear to be numerous and small. It is unfortunate that we do not have more details in the light of our conclusions as to objects inhabiting space near the moon.

In the *Philosophical Transactions* for 1715 (page 249) Halley says ". . . there were perpetual flashes or corruscations of light which seemed for a moment to dart out from behind the moon on all sides now here, now there . . ." This relates to the total eclipse of 1715. According to a similar notation in the memoirs of the French Academy, De Louville saw flashes lasting only an instant on the surface of the moon during totality.

Weidler reported in the *Philosophical Transactions* for 1739 (page 228) that his friends saw, toward the commencement of the eclipse, what resembled flashes of lightning upon the disc of the moon and again after more than an hour.

From *Doubt,* the Fortean Society magazine (issue number 47)

distant background, as seen from two different points. Hold up one finger and sight past it with first one eye and then the other. The apparent displacement of the finger against distant objects is parallax.

we have the first-hand report of a member of the society that a sighting through the Edinburgh observatory telescope on October 12, 1954, showed a "dark sphere move from the crater Tycho to the crater Aristarchus in a period of twenty minutes." This obviously is space-flight, because there is not enough atmosphere on the moon to support a conventional type of flying machine. The dark sphere could not have been a meteor, which would require only a few seconds to cross the entire lunar disc.

The distance from Tycho to Aristarchus is roughly two thousand miles. If that UFO was close to the surface of the moon, it was moving at a hundred miles per minute, or six thousand miles per hour, a speed commonly reported for UFO navigating the earth's upper air.

In *Celestial Objects*, page 96, Webb says that Schroeter noted singular changes among some rugged mountains near the east edge of the moon and attributed them to a lunar atmosphere. Beer and Madler attributed the same phenomena to variations of illumination. (Our comment: more and more we find that Schroeter saw certain types of variation while Beer and Madler did not, and emphatically said that these variations did not exist. Yet Gruithuisen saw them after Beer and Madler and some have been reported more recently.)

From later observations we conclude that there is a cyclic manifestation on the surface of the moon. The complete cycle covers eighteen to fifty years. In other words, things were going on in Schroeter's time, in the latter decades of the eighteenth century; there was a period of quiescence in the first three decades of the nineteenth century. Then another period of activity began.

Another example of this cycle, again from *Celestial Objects:* on the western edge of the moon, Schroeter delineated a crater called by him *Alhazen,* which he used as a point for measuring the librations of the moon. After a time he saw unaccountable changes in it. Later it could not be seen by Beer and Madler. But Gruithuisen saw it in 1824.

III

ECHOES OF HISTORY

◆ **Levitation** ◆

In the London *Times* (September 24, 1875) it is related that some inexplicable force lifted a fishing vessel so high out of the water that when it fell back it sank. There was no wind. Rescuers in nearby boats had to row, as they could not use their sails. The London *Daily Express* (June 12, 1919) reported from Islip a loud detonation that shot a basketful of clothes into the air. The London *Daily Mail* (May 6, 1910) reported detonations that sent stones shooting into the air for two hours, near Cantillana, Spain. The Niles *Weekly Register,* November 4, 1815, reported stones rising from the ground in a field in New York and moving sixty feet horizontally.

Thus, levitating forces are seen to act from time to time. The question of levitation is one of the most provocative in UFO research. One must bring to it as much knowledge of history and anthropology as he can acquire.

Oddly enough, as one reaches back into ancient history and studies the ruins or traces of ancient structures, one discovers that the workmanship, in stone walls, deteriorated steadily with successive buildings. The ramparts, if such they be, of Sacsahuaman in ancient Peru and other structures, were undertakings comparable to our great dams. Handling those vast blocks of stone, so accurately fitted, demanded vast controlled power. Yet those remains seem to have been the earliest. From that prodigious perfection the construction appears to have degenerated. In the later efforts smaller and smaller stones were used and workmanship lost its skill. A few buildings were marvelously well-built while later ones were crude. Eventually all the work declined to a low level. True, there are some fairly large stones in the structures of downtown Cuzco, such as the Temple of the Sun, but the largest weigh only a ton or two. True, also, there is superb workmanship in the Temple of the Sun and the House of the Virgins, where stones were almost perfectly squared before being worked into walls; but other walls built on the same principles showed progressively poorer skill, the later stones being scarcely more than large pebbles. One wonders how they stand up. Many are built as superstructures on the older more solid bases.

From this it appears that the original massive structures were erected by the earliest colonists in the pre-Inca era. They brought with them expert knowledge of stonework and a special source of power or levitating machinery. At least, this is our postulate. Then they must have lost the source of power and their descendants used hand labor, which couldn't manipulate really big stones.

The Black Pagoda of India, believed by some to have been built seven centuries ago, is 228 feet high. Its roof, twenty-five feet thick, is a single stone slab weighing 2,000 tons. A sizable chunk of rock to put on top of a 228 foot building which looks like a silo. Historians conjecture that the building was buried in sand, providing a ramp several miles long, up which the roof block was dragged. That is a possibility, of course, and the only method conceivable by any mechanical principle known to present-day engineers. But there might be another possibility. The structure might have been raised *under* the huge stone, pushing it up a tier at a time, with jacks of some sort. In some ways this looks simpler than building a ramp with hundreds of thousands of tons of sand to bring up and cart away.

That two thousand tons! I do not think modern engineers could put it on top of such a building without unlimited labor or funds to build the ramp. Even then I do not see how they could possibly get sufficient purchase on this thing to move it at all, or attach sufficient harness to apply the necessary force. This incredible stone is larger than those at Baalbek.

Levitating it into place seems as credible to me as any known mechanism including a sand ramp. Maybe this would require that it be more than 700 years old, since levitation would almost certainly have been recorded if employed as recently as 700 years ago.

If *you* were trying to move this thing up a ramp, no matter how gradual, how could you anchor your tackle in the loose sand to get a pull? How would you place enough men around it to push or pull; and how would they secure a toe-hold? Levitation is the lesser quandary.

◆ Fossils: Mysteries ◆

In the *Astronomical Register* (volume VIII, 1870, pages 11-13) are some letters discussing a piece of flint found embedded in chalk at Fawley near Southampton. Most of the correspondents protested that "it couldn't have come from space," and "if it did come from space, it could not have picked up fossils when falling." There were said to be several flint balls in stratified layers of the chalk; these were globular, although chipped. A Mr. W. B. Galloway postulates that the flint was molten hot when dropped and took on globular form in falling. Another correspondent doubts that it actually did fall. Antiquity is certain and space origin probable.

The largest drawing board in the world is probably the great sand-flat of the Nasca Valley of Peru. Here, intermingled with figures of beasts, birds and fish, some hundreds of feet across, are huge geometric symbols—triangles, spirals, lines, roadways, etc., which stretch for miles. The shapes cannot be distinguished from the ground, and were not reported until aviation developed. The *National Geographic Magazine* (Oct. 1950, p. 448) has reproduced some of them.

There are points of similarity in size and other aspects between these diagrams and the figures of the mounds in the Ohio flatlands, and also the giant effigies in southwest United States. (*National Geographic Magazine*, Sept. 1952) In both, the shapes are imperceptible to observers on the ground.

This writer has seen the Nasca drawings from the air, and to put it mildly, they startled him. Not only their magnitude, but the geometric accuracy of designs extending for miles, is almost unbelievable.

It is an almost inescapable conclusion that the project was directed from the air, at an altitude of several thousand feet. Some are best seen 1000 feet above the surface, but the largest are most advantageously observed from a mile high or more, about the cruising level of the DC-6's.

Even more inescapable is the conclusion that this vast drawing-board contains signs meant to last a long time, and to be read from a distance of from twenty-five to a hundred miles above the earth's surface. Whoever, or whatever made these designs was accustomed to doing things in a big way.

The vastness of these drawings make one think of the mighty stone constructions nearby Sacsahuaman and Tiahuanecu; of the colossal idols and ramparts of Easter Islands; of the 1,200-ton monoliths of Baalbek; of the massive geometry of the pyramid at Gizeh; the immense stone arches and roadways in Polynesia; of Angkor-Wat; of the scattering of huge non-volcanic craters of Mexico. One also remembers the reports of giants of prehistoric days. Bigness is the key, the common denominator . . . for *something!*

And we recall reports by astronomers about things which seem to abide in space near the earth, perhaps at gravitational neutrals where life's exigencies are minimal, things miles in diameter, exhibiting controlled motion, which share bigness with Peru, Mexico, Egypt, Easter Island, Baalbek, India and Angkor-Wat.

Buried deep in the archives of the U.S. Air Force film library in the Pentagon is a photo of something in Mexico which looks like a cross between an irrigation project and a rebus. Its area, stretching several hundred yards, is adjacent to a group of extra-terrestrial or artificial craters ranging in size from nearly half a mile to a mile and a half in diameter. It is a complex of spirals, crosses and human figures, laid out on an absolutely flat expanse partly covered by shallow ponds.

Numbers of fossils in the west and midwest of the United States indicate a tremendous antiquity for civilized man. These erratics confuse scientists who have not yet settled on a common denominator of archaic civilization which would explain them all. According to H. W. Splitter (*Fate*, January, 1954, page 65), a fossil human legbone *about a yard long* was found in 1877, near Eureka, Nevada, many feet below the surface, embedded in quartzite. Some bones, and the cast of a woman's body were taken from solid rock in a quarry at Zanesville, Ohio, in 1853.

In a block of solid feldspar taken from a mine, a thing resembling a two-inch screw was found near Treasure City, Nevada, in 1869.

Memoirs of Manchester Literary and Philosophical Society (2-9-306): Roundish stones, found embedded in coal, are deduced to have fallen from the sky ages ago when the coal was soft enough to have closed around them with no sign of entrance.

Proceedings of the Society of Antiquities of Scotland (1-1-121): On an iron instrument embedded in a lump of coal: "The interest attaching to this singular relic arises from the fact of its having been found in the heart of a piece of coal, seven feet under the surface. . . . The instrument was considered to be modern."

◆ Ancient Records and Lore ◆

Ethnology, archeology and related fields, not being among the exact sciences, are somewhat dependent on intangibles like imagination and intuition. But this permits them to make use of evidence supplied in tradition and folklore and permits them to explore misty areas of intellectual perception which are closed to minds shackled by scientific or religious dogmas.

The epic, *Rama and Sita*, by the ancient Hindu poet Valmiki (circa 1300 B.C.) is, according to Churchward, a paraphrase of an ancient prose history in India or Tibet. This account places the settlement of India and Burma at least 70,000 years into the remote past. We quote a passage in Romesh Dutt's translation, which indicates that mechanical flight was known to a civilization already hoary with age when dynastic Egypt entered history. Even after allowing for symbolic language and poetic license, there are sufficient corroboratory temple records, according to Churchward and other researchers, to make us take the references to flight as more than flights of fancy. In the following quotation, the italics are ours:

Vain her threat and soft entreaty, Raven held her in his wrath
As the planet Buddha captures fair Rokini in his path.
By his left hand, tremor-shaken, Raksha held her streaming hair,
By his right, the ruthless Raksha lifted high the fainting fair.
Unseen dwellers of the woodland watched the dismal deed with shame,
Marked the mighty armed Raksha lift the poor and helpless dame,
Seat her in his *car celestial, yoked to asses winged with speed,*
Golden in its shape and radiance, fleet as *Indra's heavenly steed.*
Angry threat and sweet entreaty, Raven to her ears addressed,
As the struggling, fainting woman still he held upon his breast.
Vain his threat and vain entreaty; "Rama! Rama!" still she cried,
To the dark and dismal forest where her noble lord had hied.
Then *rose the car celestial o'er the hill and wooded vale,*
Like a snake in eagle's talons, Sita writhed with piteous wail.

Still the doubtful battle lasted, until Rama in his ire,
Wielded Brahmin's *dreadful weapon, flaming with celestial fire.*
Winged as lightning, dart of Indra, *fatal as the bolt of Heaven.*
Wrapped in smoke and *flaming flashes,* speeding from the circle bow,
Pierced the iron heart of Raven, laid the lifeless hero low.

Colonel Churchward points out that Dutt, like other translators, had difficulty with the words before "yoked asses," for which there is no English equivalent. (Churchward, not an engineer, studied fifty years ago.) Here, the modern engineer immediately senses "horsepower" ("winged horses" . . . "winged horsepower"). And note how casually mentioned, as though an accepted part of the life of the times. Colonel Churchward reports that these, with one exception, are the most specific accounts of the Hindu flying machines of 15,000 to 20,000 years ago. But this *one exception* is a honey. He says:

. . . except one, which is a drawing and instructions for the construction of the airship, her machinery, power, engine, etc. The power is taken from the atmosphere in a very simple, inexpensive manner. The engine is somewhat like our present-day turbine in that it works from one chamber into another until finally exhausted. When the engine is once started, it never stops until turned off. It will continue on, if allowed to do so, until the bearings are worn out. The power is unlimited, or rather, limited only by what the metals will stand. These ships could keep circling the earth without ever coming down until the machinery wore out. I find various flights spoken of, which, according to our maps, would run from one thousand to three thousand miles. (*Churchward wrote this about 1925.*)

Colonel Churchward further states:

All records relating to these airships distinctly state that they were self-propelling; in other words, they generated their own power as they flew, and were independent of all fuel.

Colonel Churchward claims to have devoted some fifty years of his life to the study of the ancient temple records in India and Tibet. But we believe that he failed to appreciate that this was his greatest discovery, transcending even his translations of records, tracing the human race back 200,000 years. He gives it so little thought that he allots only two or three pages to it in all his three interesting volumes.

It must occur to one that the power to sustain flight may be drawn, in some way, from the gravitational field; also that something related to it may have been used to handle the great blocks making up the Great Pyramid, the stupendous works of Baalbek, the huge boulders at Sacsahuaman, the aqueducts and reservoirs of Ceylon and the monuments and building stones of Easter Island. *Something* other than a reasonable facsimile of modern machinery had to be used. Was it connected with the mysterious "perpetual" or "cold" light that recurs in South American mythology? (H. T. Wilkins, *Mysteries of Ancient South America*, Citadel Press, N. Y.)

Such types of flights, sources of power, and methods of control are from times so immemorial that available records are but faint reverberations down the corridors of time. The uses of sound, of color, of tuned vibrations, in connection with flight and levitation in general, have been listed and expounded. Not the least remarkable are some recent discoveries or "rediscoveries" in the field of vibrational power.

Easter Island traditions of lifting huge stones by a tune, shifting boulders by the spoken word, recall records which were crumbling before man appeared on the Nile. No matter how far one goes into the misty Past, there is flight; there is functioning civilization. From where? All along the path there is the hint, and sometimes the evidence, of life in space—not on Mars, not on Venus, not from Alpha Centauri, nor the Andromeda Nebula—but from space near and around the earth. Time, as an indication of the age of our little rekindled campfire, has become an illusion if not a self-imposed delusion.

You may have seen Oge-Make's rendering of the traditions of the Piutes. He could almost have taken the materials from Churchward's *Children of Mu*, so closely do they coincide. It was one of Churchward's major points that the southwest United States was colonized from Mu, as were Central America, India, Burma, Central Asia, Egypt, Asia Minor, Atlantis, and parts of Europe. What matter if Mu may be fiction? What matter that geologists say that Mu could not have been in the Pacific? It was somewhere—it was something—it was the common origin, the common denominator of all that we know as civilization today.

Churchward would have agreed that the archaic progenitors of the Piutes came in ocean-going ships, through seas and inlets now dry. It is as logical for other generations of civilization to have had flying machines; and in America as in Asia. We can go that far to reconcile our reason with our instincts, if we but revise our time scale. If the Andes were honeycombed with tunnels and caverns, now rent by glaciers—perhaps by the raising of the mountains—who are we to quibble over a thousand years, or to say that flight was unknown to a civilization flourishing a quarter of a million years ago, before it was overwhelmed by nature.

Of that which immediately follows, I am, as you will be, at a loss to know how much to believe. It is my guess that, like me, you will seek an intermediate ground.

TRIBAL MEMORIES OF THE FLYING SAUCERS *
by Oge-Make

Most of you who read this are probably white men of a blood only a century or two out of Europe. You speak in your papers of the Flying Saucers or Mystery Ships as something new, and strangely typical of the twentieth century. How could you but think otherwise? Yet if you had red skin, and were of a blood which had been born and bred of this land for untold thousands of years, you would know this is not true. You would know that your ancestors living in these mountains and upon these prairies for numberless generations had seen these ships before, and had passed down the story in the legends which are unwritten history of your people. You do not believe? Well, after all, why should you? But knowing your scornful unbelief, the storytellers of my people have closed their lips in bitterness against the outward flow of this knowledge.

Yet, I have said to the storytellers this: Now that the ships are being seen again, is it wise that we, the older race keep our knowledge to ourselves? Thus for me, an American Indian, some of the sages among my people have talked, and if you care to, I shall permit you to sit down with us and listen.

Let us say that it is dusk in that strange place you, the white man, call "Death Valley." I have passed tobacco (with us a sacred plant) to the aged chief of the Piutes who sits across a tiny fire from me and sprinkles corn meal upon the flames. You sprinkle holy water, while we sprinkle corn meal and blow the smoke of the tobacco to the four winds (compass points) in order to dispel bad luck and ask a blessing.

The old chief looked like a wrinkled mummy as he sat there puffing upon his pipe. Yet his eyes were not those of the unseeing, but eyes which seemed to look back on long trails of time. His people had held the Inyo, Panamint and Death Valleys for untold centuries before the coming of the white man. Now we sat in the valley which white men named for Death, but which the Piutes call Tomesha— The Flaming Land. Here before me as I faced eastward, the Funerals (mountains forming Death Valley's eastern wall) were wrapped in

* From the September, 1949, *Fate* Magazine.

purple-blue blankets about their feet while their faces were painted in scarlet. Behind me, the Panamints rose like a mile-high wall, dark against the sinking sun.

The old Piute smoked my tobacco for a long time before he reverently blew the smoke to the four directions. Finally he spoke:

"You ask me if we heard of the great silver airships in the days before white men brought their wagon trails into the land?"

"Yes, grandfather, I come seeking knowledge." (Among all tribes of my people, "grandfather" is the term of greatest respect one man can pay another.)

"We, the Piute Nation, have known of these ships for untold generations. We also believe that we know something of the people who fly them. They are called The Hav-musuvs."

"Who are the Hav-musuvs?"

"They are a people of the Panamints, and they are as ancient as Tomesha itself." He smiled a little at my confusion. "You do not understand? Of course not. You are not a Piute. Then listen closely and I will lead you back along the trail of the dim past.

"When the world was young, and this valley which is now dry, parched desert, was a lush, hidden harbor of a blue-water sea which stretched from half way up those mountains to the Gulf of California, it is said that the Hav-musuvs came here in huge rowing ships. They found great caverns in the Panamints, and in them they built one of their cities. At that time California was the island which the Indians of that state told the Spanish it was, and which they marked so on their maps.

"Living in their hidden city, the Hav-musuvs ruled the sea with their fast rowing-ships, trading with faraway peoples and bringing strange goods to the great quays said still to exist in the caverns.

"Then as untold centuries rolled past, the climate began to change. The water in the lake went down until there was no longer a way to the sea. First the way was broken only by the southern mountains over the tops of which goods could be carried. But as time went by the water continued to shrink, until the day came when only a dry crust was all that remained of the great blue lake. Then the desert came, and the Fire-god began to walk across Tomesha, the Flaming land.

"When the Hav-musuvs could no longer use their great rowing ships, they began to think of other means to reach the world beyond. I suppose that is how it happened. We know that they began to use flying canoes. At first they were not large, these silvery ships with wings. They moved with a slight whirring sound, and a dipping movement, like an eagle.

"The passing centuries brought other changes. Tribe after tribe swept across the land, fighting to possess it for a while and passing like the storm of sand. In their mountains, still in the cavern city, the Hav-musuvs dwelt in peace, far removed from the conflict. Sometimes they were seen at a distance, in their flying ships or riding on the snowy-white animals which took them from ledge to ledge up the cliffs. We have never seen these strange animals at any other place. To these people the passing centuries brought only larger and larger ships, moving always more silently."

"Have you ever seen a Hav-musuv?"

"No, but we have many stories of them. There are reasons why one does not become too curious."

"Reasons?"

"Yes. These strange people have weapons. One is small, a tube which stuns one with a prickly feeling like a rain of cactus needles. One cannot move for hours, and during this time the mysterious ones vanish up the cliffs. The other weapon is deadly. It is a long, silvery tube. When this is pointed at you, death follows immediately."

"But tell me about these people. What do they look like and how do they dress?"

"They are a beautiful people. Their skin is a golden tint, and a headband holds back their long dark hair. They dress always in a white fine-spun garment which wraps around them and is draped upon one shoulder. Pale sandals are worn upon their feet . . ."

His voice trailed away in a puff of smoke. The purple shadows rising up the walls of the Funerals splashed like waves of the ghost lake. The old man seemed to have fallen into a sort of trance, but I had one more question. "Has any Piute ever spoken to a Hav-musuv, or were the Piutes here when the great rowing ships first appeared?"

For some moments I wondered if he had heard me. Yet as is our custom, I waited patiently for the answer. Again he went through the ritual of the smoke-breathing to the four directions, and then his soft voice continued:

"Yes. Once in the not-so-distant-past, but yet many generations before the coming of the Spanish, a Piute chief lost his bride by sudden death. In his great and overwhelming grief, he thought of the Hav-musuvs and their long tube of death. He wished to join his bride so he bid farewell to his sorrowing people and set off to find the Hav-musuvs. None appeared until the chief began to climb the almost unscalable Panamints. Then one of the men in white appeared suddenly before him with the long tube, and motioned him back. The chief made signs that he wished to die, and came on. The man in white made a long singing whistle and other Hav-musuvs appeared. They spoke together in a strange tongue and then regarded the chief thoughtfully. Finally they made signs to him making him understand that they would take him with them.

"Many weeks after his people had mourned him for dead, the Piute chief came back to his camp. He had been in the giant underground valley of the Hav-musuvs, he said, where white lights which burn night and day and never go out, or need any fuel, lit an ancient city of marble beauty. There he learned the language and the history of the mysterious people, giving them in turn the language and legends of the Piutes. He said that he would have liked to remain there forever in the peace and beauty of their life, but they bade him return and use his new knowledge for his people."

I could not help but ask the inevitable. "Do you believe this story of the chief?"

His eyes studied the wisps of smoke for some minutes before he answered. "I do not know. When a man is lost in Tomesha, and the Fire-god is walking across the salt crust, strange dreams like clouds, fog through his mind. No man can breathe the hot breath of the Fire-god and long remain sane. Of course, the Piutes have thought of this. No people knows the moods of Tomesha better than they.

"You asked me to tell you the legend of the flying ships. I have told you what the young men of the tribe do not know, for they no longer listen to the stories of the past. Now you ask me if I believe. I answer this. Turn around. Look behind you at that wall of the Panamints. How many giant caverns could open there, being hidden by the lights and shadows of the rocks? How many could open outward and inward and never be seen behind the arrow-like pinnacles before them? How many ships could swoop down like an eagle from the beyond, on summer nights when the fires of the furnace sands have closed away the valley from the eyes of the white man? How many Hav-musuvs could live in their eternal peace away from the noise of white man's guns in their unscalable stronghold? This has always been a land of mystery. Nothing can change that. Not even white man with his flying engines, for should they come too close to the wall of the Panamints a sharp wind like the flying arrow can sheer off a wing. Tomesha hides its secrets well even in winter, but no man can pry into them when the Fire-god draws the hot veil of his breath across the passes.

"I must still answer your question with my mind in doubt, for we speak of a weird land. White man does not yet know it as well as the Piutes, and we have ever held it in awe. It is still the forbidden: Tomesha, Land-of-the-Flaming-Earth."

The author of that story is a Navaho Indian.

◆ Fireballs and Lights ◆

In classifying UFO into different types for analysis we must provide for a category of lights which seem to lack material substance. These may be related to nebulous clouds observed by astronomers which also have the characteristics of moving in formation.

An example appears in *Notes and Queries* (series 5, volume 3, page 306, April 17, 1875):

> A gentleman writes from Pwllheli, a coast town in Caernarvonshire, Wales, to the Field newspaper of February 20, as follows: "Some few days ago we witnessed here what we have never seen before—certain lights, eight in number, extending over, I should say, a distance of eight miles; all seemed to keep their own ground, although moving in horizontal, perpendicular and zigzag directions. Sometimes they were of a bright blue color, then almost like the lights of a carriage lamp, then like an electric light, and going out altogether in a few minutes would appear again dimly, and come up as before. Can any of your numerous readers inform me whether they are will-o'-the-wisps, or what? We have seen three at a time afterwards on four or five occasions."
>
> Surely we are not going to have a repetition of the "Fiery Exhalation" mentioned in *Evelyn's Diary*, April 22, 1694, and fully discussed in Gibson's continuation of Camden. These "Mephitic Vapors" as they were called occurred on the same coast.—A. R. Croeswylan, Oswestry.

This is so typical of certain types of saucer reports that it might have been written yesterday. Note the number "eight," common in such reports both before and after Arnold started the present "saucer" excitement. Compare it with Barnard's "numerous" cometary masses of 1882, of which six are shown in "V" formation; and the four in formation shown in the Coast Guard photograph. (*The Case for the UFO*)

The "foo" fighters were lights of a peculiar maneuverability seen by military pilots in both the European and the Pacific war theaters in World War II. They have been generally considered a type of UFO, but they differ from the structural types.

In many cases where UFO lights have been reported they appear as bluish-white, like an electric arc: hard, brilliant, flickering, functional. The "foo" lights on the other hand, apparently entities in themselves, are usually reddish or yellowish, soft or diffused, unattached to any tangible object and extremely mobile. My impression from the descriptions is that the "foo" lights are almost pure energy. They certainly are not to be associated with ordinary flying contraptions, even those of the saucer type.

That the "foos" either *have* intelligence, or are remotely *directed* by intelligence seems inescapable. It is only another step to say that they *are* intelligence. We can compromise on *a manifestation of intelligent activity.*

Both in Europe and over the Pacific, American pilots found these puzzling lights pacing their planes but usually keeping out of gun range. British and American flyers in Europe thought the "foos" were German weapons, but after Germany was defeated intelligence investigators found that the Germans had considered "foo" fighters to be allied weapons.

During the air battles over Japan, there were no such objects seen in the daytime; and those seen at night did not cause blips on radar screens.

There were entirely too many proven instances to permit accusations that pilots were having hallucinations. To this day there has been no satisfactory explanation; and few cases have been recorded of similar lights following civilian or commercial planes.

The unidentified flying lights which maneuvered over Washington, D. C., to the consternation of both military and civilian authorities in the summer of 1952, may be related to the "foo" fighters. But they, at least, were observed by radar. It is also to be noted that they appeared in groups of six or eight, whereas the "foo" fighters were usually seen singly. We also remember that the lights seen over Virginia by William Nash and his co-pilot appeared as six objects in linear formation and were joined by two more, *making eight.*

Many of these objects have been called fireballs, an unfortunate term. The word fireball usually denotes something like a meteor or bollide entering the atmosphere from outer space.

Mysterious lights, apparently under control, have appeared in many times and places. Their descriptions have been rather similar over a period of centuries. For instance, globes of light were observed high in the air over Swabia, Germany, May 22, 1732.

On September 19, 1848, Inverness, Scotland, saw two starlike globular lights which were sometimes stationary, and sometimes moved erratically at high speeds.

You will remember that 1877 marked the beginning of the "incredible decade" which saw many unexplained occurrences. In March 23 of that year dazzling balls of light appeared from a cloud over Venice, in Italy. They moved slowly in the sky for more than an hour. Similar balls of light had been seen in that area some eight years previously.

On October 5 of the same year mysterious illuminated spheres were seen over the coast of Wales. They moved at high velocity, appeared and disappeared with erratic suddenness.

On July 30, 1880, three luminous spheres, one larger than the rest, appeared in a ravine near the city now known as Leningrad. They were seen for about three minutes, then vanished without a sound.

Captain Norcock, of H.M.S. *Caroline,* saw globular lights on the China Sea on the night of May 25, 1893. They were visible about two hours between sunset and midnight. They were seen the same night by the captain of H.M.S. *Leander,* but for seven and a half hours! The ship's course was changed to approach the lights, but, as we would say today, they took "evasive action" and fled.

To the omniscient astronomer who would say that an ignorant ship captain was chasing the deceptive planet Venus, we can point out that the lights were seen against the backdrop of a mountain range. Therefore, they were neither in distant space nor on the surface of the sea.

You will think of the "devil's footprints" found in Devonshire, England, during the middle of the nineteenth century, when you learn that two bluish balls of light appeared over Devon, England on October 30, 1950, between 10:50 and 11:00 P.M., moving north to south at terrific speed. They came inland from over the Bristol Channel. Eyewitnesses included Naval officers at Devonport.

John Phillip Bessor published a detailed report of mysterious lights in *Fate* Magazine (August, 1953, page 87). Sightings in Australia are reported in the same terms as sightings in the western United States. Animals will not pass through gates or along roads over which the balls of illumination have hovered. They usually appear singly and take evasive action when approached. They seem to have a localized range of operation. The qualities of acceleration, evasion, color, erratic movement, and apparent purposefulness shown by these entities isolates them from the field of the purely mechanical.

I do not know what they are, any more than you do. But we must distinguish between true flying saucers and maneuverable lights. Both may be called UFO; but they certainly differ in nature and function, although they may be under identical control.

The "foo" fighters seem to belong in a special class because of their preference for accompanying military planes on fighting missions. In this, and in their control, selectivity and, at times, evasive action, they exhibit intelligent operation.

If we postulate some fourth-dimensional continuum, these glowing spheres might represent the diffusion of a ray of energy passing through our space—just as a searchlight dissipates energy and light in passing through a thin film of smoke—a kind of cross-section of something from a higher plane of existence.

◆ Disappearing Planes and Crews ◆

Certain "enemies" of UFO research question the use of old records to support hypotheses. They especially question old reports of ships vanishing and crews disappearing en masse. "Why doesn't it happen today?" they ask.

I therefore doubly appreciate the following letter, and ask especially that you note the date.

Mr. M. K. Jessup
c/o Citadel Press
222 Fourth Avenue
New York 3, New York

Dear Mr. Jessup:

On November 13, 1955, an Air Force jet fighter radioed McClelland Air Base in Sacramento that it was preparing to land. It has not been heard from since. The whole area of our Central Valley is fairly thickly populated, and it seems highly unlikely that a crashed plane could go unnoticed.

A burned-out area, about thirty miles from here was investigated, but yielded nothing. The plane simply vanished. This seems to follow along with other cases cited by you. Like the ones you have given, it disappeared after asking for landing instructions, and usually very close to its landing point.

Sincerely,

(*Signed*)   DAVID BELL

Rt. 1, Box 82
Linden, Calif.
November 18, 1955

And we continue to have ghost ships!

A report in the New York *World-Telegram and Sun*, November 11, 1955, describes a most mysterious disappearance of twenty-five people.

Pago Pago, Nov. 11 (UP)—Seafaring men said today a long-missing island trading vessel had become sister ship of the fabled *Marie Celeste*, a ghost ship drifting aimlessly across the sea without passengers or crew.

The 70-ton cabin cruiser, *Joyita*, disappeared five weeks ago. It was carrying twenty-five passengers and crewmen when it left Apia, Samoa, for a two-day voyage to Fakoafe in the Tokelau Islands. When the ship became overdue, planes and ships searched for days over a 100,000 square mile area.

Yesterday the steamer *Tuvalu* came upon the waterlogged *Joyita* drifting far off its course, ninety miles north of the Fijian island of Vanua Levu. There was no trace of the twenty-five persons who had been aboard.

Further information indicates damage to the funnel and rigging. Nobody has any explanation why the vessel escaped a systematic search, yet suddenly appeared as an abandoned hulk. Nor why all hands disappeared with the logbook but left no messages. Suddenly—as usual, and without trace—as usual.

People, singly as well as in groups, continue to disappear. H. T. Wilkins, in *Flying Saucers Uncensored*, cited the example of Isaac Martin, a young farmer of Salem, Virginia, who disappeared while working in his field. Other people in this area have disappeared, among them a farmer who dematerialized before the eyes of five people. Wilkins reported thirteen children missing on August, 1869, in Cork, Ireland, and in the same month Brussels was similarly afflicted.

On January 1, 1888, five *wild men* and a *wild girl* appeared in Connecticut. Was this teleportation by UFO? In 1883 (the "incredible decade") many people disappeared in Montreal. In one week in August, 1912, five men vanished without a trace in Buffalo, New York.

On November 27, 1954, a British lightship was driven from her anchorage and all on board disappeared without a trace. She was equipped with radio and signalling devices. *Why did she not communicate with anyone?* What destroys, or "takes" (remember there are never any bodies) these people from their vessels; and why is there never any radio signal?

Add to these the disappearing colony in the early days of Virginia; the disappearance of thriving and populous centers in Greenland, hundreds of years ago—with a few remains and runes several hundreds miles *northward toward desolation.* And what became of the miners of Zimbabwe? The Easter Islanders? And, just to show you that there is no especial geographical preference, we have the following story of a disappearing Eskimo village.

In late November, 1930, Joe La Belle, a lone trapper in the North Canadian woods, was returning to trading posts and civilization when he came upon an Eskimo village which astonished

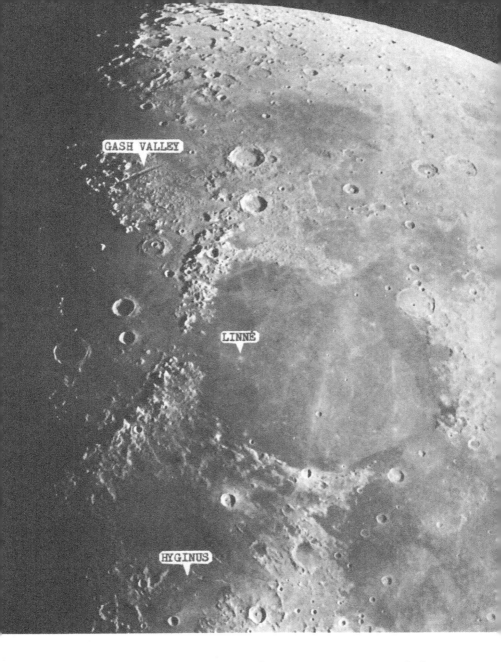

GASH VALLEY

LINNÉ

HYGINUS

LUNAR REGION OF MARE SERENITATIS *showing Crater Hyginus and the white cloud covering Crater Linné since about 1865. Note also the great gash made in high Lunar Alps by an object from space.*

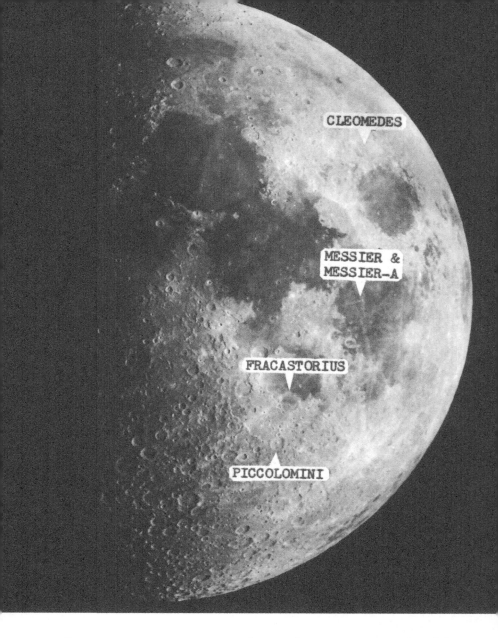

THE MOON AT FIRST QUARTER, *showing location of mystery-shrouded craters Cleomedes, Messier and Messier-A, Fracastorius and Piccolomini.*

THE MOON AT THIRD QUARTER, *showing locations of mysterious craters Plato, Ptolemaeus, Alpetragius, and Schickard.*

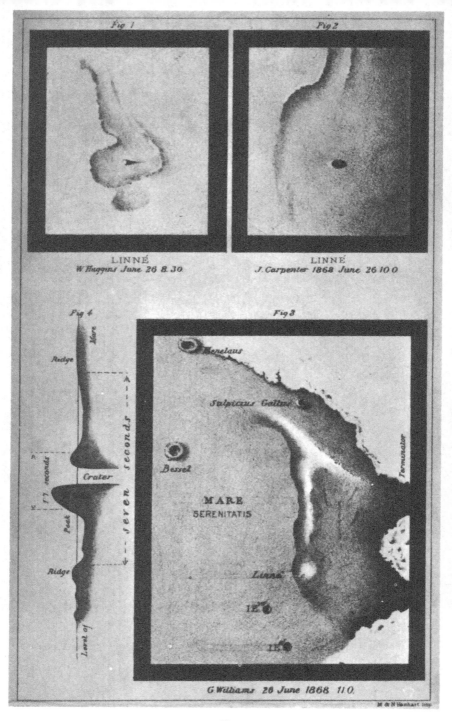

Fig 1

LINNÉ
W. Huggins June 26 8.30

Fig 2

LINNÉ
J. Carpenter 1868 June 26 10 0

Fig 4

Mare

Ridge

seven seconds

Crater

Peak

Ridge

Level of

Fig 3

Menelaus

Sulpicius Gallus

Bessel

MARE
SERENITATIS

Linné

IL

IL

Terminator

G. Williams 26 June 1868 11 0.

May 11th, 1867.

W   E

8h. 45m.

The White "Cloud" Occupy-ing Crater Linné, *with the minute deep "pit" on top, as seen in 1867. Contrast this with the usual type craters as seen in lunar photographs. Linné was such a crater before the "in-vasion."*

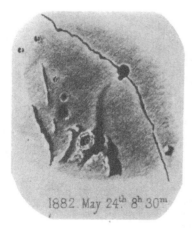

1882 May 24th. 8h 30m

Two Drawings of Hyginus Region *by the same observer, 24 hours apart. Note disappearance of large ring-shaped object near Hyginus-N and the sudden appear-ance of two others; also the fluctuation in Hyginus-N.*

1882 May 25th 8h 45m

HYGINUS. N.

Drawn by John Mc Cance

(*opp. page*) Three Drawings of Linné *made in one evening.* (*Fig. 1*) *A mountain casting shadow.* (*Fig. 2*) *A large definite crater casting a shad-ow.* (*Fig. 3*) *A large hazy white spot.*

69

(top) CRATER LA CALDERA. Extra-terrestrial double crater on Mexican plateau, 3 miles in circumference, made by objects from space. The letters are about 80 to 100 feet high. Same size and shape as small lunar craters where changes occur. (Compañía Mexicana Aerofoto, S.A.)

(bottom) CRATER PEROTE. Extra-terrestrial crater on plateau of Mexico. Lake is 1½ miles in diameter, village on opposite side being dwarfed almost to vanishing point. Identical in shape with lunar "half-craters." Note resemblance to lunar landscape. (Compañía Mexicana Aerofoto, S.A.)

CRATER XICO. *Extra-terrestrial crater on Mexican plateau, about ¾ of a mile in diameter, exactly the size and shape of small lunar craters where activity of UFO nature is observed. Note hundreds of acres of farm land inside the great ring. (Compañia Mexicana Aerofoto, S.A.)*

him by its silence. No dogs were barking. An Eskimo village without barking dogs is a phenomenon.

La Belle entered the silent village, but not without a few goose pimples. Shelters made from caribou skins were still erect and in good condition. Inside were the necessities of Eskimo life, including cooking utensils, hides and clothing, and even that essential of wilderness living—rifles!

At some distance from the camp La Belle found the bodies of seven dogs, but that was all. It was obvious that the settlement had been without human inhabitants for some time.

Abandonment of this village, which had housed at least twenty-five of the wilderness folk, had been sudden and unpremeditated. Where had they gone? They had not "moved." There was no evidence of an intention to break camp, for such an operation would have required packing their equipment. If they had fled in the face of danger they would certainly have taken their rifles and their dogs, if nothing else.

La Belle saw nothing to explain the absence of the villagers as he retraced his steps throughout the little settlement. Nothing was disturbed and there were no signs of violence.

At the edge of the camp, La Belle found an Eskimo grave with the usual cairn of stones. For some reason the grave had been opened and the stones had been carefully moved to one side. The grave was empty and there was nothing to indicate when it had been opened or what had been done with the body. Prowling animals could not have done it for the stones had been placed too neatly and there were no scattered bones.

Who are *we*, to blame Joe La Belle for taking a somewhat precipitous departure? He made his way to the nearest Royal Canadian Mounted Police post and reported his discovery. Officers who investigated for months found no clue to the mysterious disappearance. Autopsies on the corpses of the dogs showed that they had died from starvation. Their state of preservation indicated that the abandonment had taken place after the warm summer months. There was no indication as to why the seven dogs had all died at the same time and in a group, and just outside the village, for starving animals are not selective of their final resting place. Nor is there any indication of why they remained in the village to starve, in an area containing much small game, or why they didn't turn cannibalistic. Had something terrified them and made them huddle together?

The case remains unsolved. Maybe the Mounties always get their man, but are they *now* dealing with a marauding UFO?

Far from diminishing, the number of crashing and disappearing planes seems to increase. This is particularly true of jet planes, mostly fighters.

In the November 4 issue of the CRIFO *Orbit*, published at 7017 Britton Avenue, Cincinnati 27, Ohio, its editor, L. H. Stringfield, asserts his conviction, citing the losses of jet planes and other data, that *the earth is already engaged in interplanetary warfare, and we are on the defensive!*

What happened to Hunrath and Wilkinson, electronics technicians, who, on November 16, 1953, disappeared in a small plane hired for a short "hop around the airport"?

Peculiar hieroglyphs appeared on the house and garage, which H. T. Wilkins says resemble those of pre-Deluge civilizations. We are most forcibly reminded of the megaglyphs on the Nasca Desert, Peru.

Do you remember that, a year or two ago, five RAF jets all force-landed at exactly the same time, from a cloudy sky—because they "all ran out of fuel simultaneously"?

Do you remember that six USAF jets had exactly the same experience at Wright Field, only a short time thereafter? Out of gas?

This from the New York *World-Telegram and Sun*, November 4, 1955, makes a fitting close to "Echoes":

London, Nov. 4 (UP)—It was like the ten little Indians when the four jet acrobatics team of the Royal Air Force zoomed up to the post for a U. S. Air Force photographer and a television cameraman yesterday.

Everybody lived, but it was rough on the planes.

There were four Hunter jet fighters piloted by RAF aces and a Vampire jet carrying U. S. Air Force Captain R. G. Immig, and an older Meteor jet with the TV crew.

A thick black cloud suddenly clamped down on the six planes. One Hunter exploded after its pilot bailed out

The Vampire crashed in flames after Captain Immig and his pilot parachuted and then there were four!

A second Hunter buzzed down for a wheels-up crash landing, and then there were three!

The third and fourth Hunters, running out of fuel, made forced landings at the Farnsborough Air Base where the jet acrobats are famous for the performances in the annual Farnsborough Air Show.

And then there was one—the old, outdated Meteor jet. It landed safely!

IV

SELENOLOGY SPEAKS

THE SATELLITE

◆ The Silly Little Satellite ◆

The brilliantly negative antics of the United States government anent UFO were again illuminated in July, 1955, by a press release, the build-up of which must have cost the taxpayers a handsome penny. I refer to the fanfare about the silly little satellite. There was little real news value, as you will see.

When you review those satellite reports, everything about them gives you pause—in addition to the lengths to which the press went in stimulating public belief that *once again* we are getting there "fustest with the mostest."

To a man, the press writers tackled the canned government data with a sobriety as obliging as it was unexpected—in the columns and columns of discussion, though *not* in the headlines. (One in a New York paper read: AROUND EARTH IN 90 MINUTES. U.S. TO LAUNCH "SPACE SHIPS" IN '57. Another: EXPERTS HERE SEE NEW VISTAS. SATELLITE TO CIRCLE EARTH AT 18,000 MPH. Another: MAN SEEN ON HIS WAY "OUT OF THIS WORLD."

Here is a typical news lead. I quote from the New York *Daily News,* the story datelined Washington, July 29, 1955:

The U.S. will launch earth-circling satellites, tiny man-made "moons," in 1957-58 for the benefit of science all over the world, it was announced today.

The satellites, about the size of basketballs, will speed around the earth, 200 to 300 miles up, at 18,000 miles per hour. Delicate instruments are expected to pick up data on cosmic rays and other phenomena of outer space, relaying it to earth by automatic radio.

The spectacular venture will be part of the U.S. participation in the International Geophysical Year. This is a joint effort by the scientists of 38 nations, including Russia, to gather more information about the earth and universe.

Which I find tremendously interesting in view of the contention that UFO which dip and dive at fantastic speeds are pinnacle-secret devices of some government or other. Here is a significant paragraph (italics mine) from the *Daily News* article:

If successful, it will also be a long step toward fulfillment of man's long dream of space conquest—travel to the moon and planets. For the tiny satellites will have crashed through the barrier of gravity for the first time.

If this means what it says it is an obvious misstatement. The satellites do not crash through any barriers; they reach a state of equilibrium between gravity, speed, and distance.

The Washington *Post and Times-Herald,* July 30, 1955, among other papers, carried a long article enumerating the satellite's characteristics: size—that of a basketball; distance—200 to 300 miles from earth; orbital speed—18,000 mph, etc. But this paper included on the front page with the satellite story an item captioned: RUNAWAY ROCKET MAY BE OUT THERE.

United States experimenters already have pierced outer space with guided missiles and there is a wide belief that at least one such projectile may already be circling the earth as an "uncontrolled satellite."

Announcement of the plan to launch a satellite program took the lid off highly competent reports that one rocket "worked too well" and shot out into outer space. According to these reports, this test rocket generated such enormous energy and unexpected thrust that it burst free of the earth's atmosphere; that it is 800 miles out in space with its fuel long since expended, but still whirling at the rate of about 16,000 miles per hour.

But it is possible the "runaway" slipped back into the earth's atmosphere, where high friction would have disintegrated it quickly.

Except for the varied ways the newspapers reworked the government release, all breathed the prescribed exhilaration, and presented substantially the same conclusions.

Newsweek, August 8, 1955, quoted rocket expert Willy Ley, whose words, to my mind, emphasize the silliness of this project. Speaking for the "rockets-will-get-us-there" group, he said: *"This is the beginning of space flight."*

The government is using several German scientists. The one most repeatedly mentioned was Professor Hermann Oberth. Remember his name, for he is important—not only as an experimenter, but as one who is intellectually courageous.

In the *American Weekly*, October 24, 1954, in an article called "Flying Saucers Come from a Distant World," Professor Oberth wrote:

I think that they possibly are manned by intelligent observers who are members of a race that may have been investigating our earth for centuries. I think that they possibly have been sent to conduct systematic, long-range investigations, first of men, animals and vegetation, and more recently of atomic centers, armaments and centers of armament production.

I have examined all of the arguments supporting the existence of flying saucers and denying it, and it is my conclusion that the "Unidentified Fying Objects" do exist, are very real, and are visitors from outer space.

Now, once again, there is a hint of relationship. Oberth wonders why the UFO operators have not communicated with us. This takes my thinking to the megaglyphs of Peru, Mexico, and southwest U.S.A. Regarding efforts on our part to communicate with the UFO, Oberth says:

We might try to communicate with them by radio signal. Mathematical symbols might be interpreted by them. A mutual mathematical understanding might be the forerunner of written words and sounds.

Finally, because I'm suspicious about the news explosion across the land, I will point out that 18,000 mph, the hypothetical speed of the yet-to-be-launched, silly satellite is a speed frequently reported of the UFO. Why is the little satellite to have the same velocity?

I smell odors of a dead rodent from the whole publicity campaign about the silly satellite.

The true, uninflated value of this monstrously juvenile enterprise was demonstrated several months before the newspapers were tipped off to start the ballyhoo and feed readers the puréed Pentagon pap. As early as February and March, news commentators cried the tidings that we not only could, but almost certainly would, launch a satellite within a very few years at most—but got no public response.

And yet, all hail! When Washington pulls the strings, assuring the public that the world will have an artificial satellite, a thousand reporters spring into action.

On March 10, 1955, the Washington *Post and Times-Herald*, in an Associated Press feature by Frank Carey, reported the American Rocket Society's request to the National Science Foundation to make a definitive study of the possibilities and practical value of launching a small unmanned satellite. Some of the scientific applications would be.

1. Gather information on the upper atmosphere.
2. Study the effects of outer-space radiation on experimental animals carried aloft.
3. Serve as a relay station for radio communication and perhaps aid in making TV telecasts across oceans.
4. Help in more detailed mapping of the earth.
5. Furnish additional information on whether space flight will eventually be possible by man.
6. Obtain new data for meteorology and astronomy.

On May 26, 1955, news commentator Stewart Alsop announced a debate on the satellite (Miami *Daily News*, May 26, 1955). He said:

With a determined, but not very expensive, effort it should be possible to launch an artificial satellite into space about this time next year . . . contention of technicians in the missle field who have submitted plans to the Pentagon . . .

Alsop announced that the object would be about nine inches in diameter, containing no instruments except a radar-response gadget which could hardly be expected to yield much scientific information.

Scientific purists have objected to the name "satellite" and want the object called "orbital vehicle." It was suggested that the experiment could be carried out relatively inexpensively as a sort of side issue to an extended Intercontinental Ballistic Missille (IBM) program.

But the most cogent reasons were related to the Soviet developments. Alsop pointed out two significant recent headlines: SOVIETS CLAIM SUCCESSFUL LAUNCHING OF EARTH SATELLITE; and US RADAR CONFIRMS EXISTENCE OF SOVIET SATELLITES.

Alsop further states that satellite detection stations had been established at White Sands, New Mexico, and on Mt. Wilson, California. It is stated that not one, but two satellites were discovered, but turned out to be natural rather than artificial. Readers of *The Case for the UFO* may recall the description of two UFO seen by astronomers about eighty years ago, evidently controlled objects closer than the moon.

Further, according to Mr. Alsop, the Russians, in April (1955), installed a high-sounding governmental agency called Permanent Interdepartmental Commission for Interplanetary Communication, which included their greatest scientist, Peter Kapitsa.

This book is not primarily concerned with the military use of space flight, but it is, however, important to realize that space flight questions have been taken much more seriously by foreign countries. Have we become blasé gadgeteers?

To return to the great blast-off by the press on the satellites: as a *sporting* event, it may have been a bit of news. But as a challenge to Russia? Well, the Russians started working on such things a while ago. But we *did* beat Russia *to the announcement!*

Or—*did* we?

In the Washington *Post and Times-Herald,* Thursday, November 11, 1954, almost a year before the announcement of the satellite launching, the following article appeared under a United Press dateline from Santa Monica, California:

The Soviet Union is rushing plans for an interplanetary space ship, and unless America awakens to this real danger, the West may lose its margin of power, an aircraft company executive said today.

"Building of a space-ship by the Russians would have a far-reaching effect on the West," said William P. Lear, head of Lear, Inc. "We know they're working hard at it, too."

Lear said the Russians "recruited" several top German scientists, chiefly from the Nazi Missile stations at Peenemunde, after World War II for the purpose of exploring the possibilities of interplanetary warfare.

"The Germans were thinking in terms of space ships as early as 1939 . . . *It will be possible to build a space ship within another year."* he added [Italics mine, because it is now more than a year since that prediction was made.]

Now, I am inclined strongly to the belief that there may be another purpose behind the furor over the Minimum Orbital Unmanned Satellite of the Earth, otherwise known as MOUSE, otherwise as the silly satellite. Sharp readers suspected that the whole fanfare was part of a not-so-subtle build-up toward a major announcement about Unidentified Flying Objects.

In fact, one of the best-informed American UFO reporters stated in August, 1955, that he expected something significant to break within a period of months. Independently, I had then come to the same conclusion.

Is our government getting set to claim the invention of the the UFO? Or, while we wondering, is Russia? Who will be the first to "invent" the UFO which people have been seeing for at least 3,500 years?

The silly satellite was kept in the public eye by the major news release of October, 1955. I refer to the release from the boys with security clearance, that UFO just naturally *ain't*. This strikes me as protesting overmuch and we suspect that this October denial of UFO was directly related to the satellite smokescreen.

The October release not only denied UFO, but said that the government was just about to spring some aircraft on us that will *look like* UFO. (Ask your Congressman how the government *knows what a UFO*—and they do mean flying saucers—*looks like!*)

But many would like to know what the Pentagonian troglo-
dites' next step will be in "breaking it gently to us." What kind of
public education is it which confuses the public on such a grand
scale? And if this gentle approach is defended as a means of preventing public panic, then to where can I panic when the first
UFO anchors to the Empire State Building?

I am trying to make clear the danger of the silly satellite's
confusing the public. Because the satellite has been heralded as
a stepping stone to space travel, many UFO devotees have been
misled into believing it little short of a veritable UFO.

Let's get one thing straight: neither rockets nor freely revolving* man-made moons are true stepping-stones to space
travel, much less relatives to UFO.

True, rockets fired up and erupting like boils in the outer skin
of our atmosphere and the rising volumes of hot air about the
artificial satellite all stimulate that upward look toward UFO.
But what a costly way of introducing us *subtly* to UFO.

I can go along with the rocket and satellite experiments only
as an expression of pioneering desire to see what's on the other
side of the mountain . . . but not what's on the other side of the
moon. Its scientific or military value is dubious; and as a stepping-
stone to space travel or UFO activity, the value is nil.

Those who have spent lifetimes promoting rocket power as
a solution to space flight have been backing the wrong horse.
Rocket power is not the answer to sustained space flight. If we
have had civilizations on earth, or around the earth, which developed space flight experimentally or through accidental discovery

---

* Two types of rotary motion are dealt with in celestial mechanics:
(1) a body "revolves" around its primary, as for example, the moon "revolves around the earth; or the earth revolves around the sun. (2) A body
"rotates" about its axis, as the earth rotates once in twenty-four hours, or
the sun is about twenty-six days. A third type of quasi-rotary motion is
the special indulgence of the galaxies or spiral nebulae. It is still a somewhat unsettled question as to whether the components of the great spiral
conglomeries are in true revolution about the gravitational center or whether
they move *along* the spiral arms. If we assume gravity to act inversely as
the fifth power of the distance instead of inversely as the square of the
distance, we end up with spiral motion instead of elliptical or circular
orbital motion.

(which seems probable), they certainly used some source of power other than rockets—cheap power.

A commentator who has access to special information, writing in the *Weekly Review*, August 26, 1955, a British non-profit intelligence sheet, expresses a dim view of space-conquest:

> Encouraged by scientists of first importance, public opinion thinks that, somehow or other, man is now so clever that what he could not solve when circumscribed by this planet, may be solved by mastery of interplanetary research. . . .
>
> It is rather odd that we should think that if we could not stop the encroachment of the Sahara, let alone reclaim it, nevertheless we can colonize the moon; and very likely, somehow or other, bring Mars and Venus into our service . . .
>
> Some may think that this is extreme escapism. How far people accept all this one cannot say; but certainly many do. . . .
>
> This mood (encouraged by some scientists) makes us ready to spend immense sums of money—billions in fact—in an effort to reach the moon. . . . It is odd that, when a few paltry millions are refused for better roads and land reclamation, billions are to be spent in trying to reach Mars. Can this be serious inter-government policy? . . . .
>
> The American, British, and Russian governments are not quite so moon-struck as it would seem . . . these experiments are largely for military purposes and do not go beyond an attempt to circulate a projectile a few hundred miles above the earth's surface. *Your services reported such projects in Russia long ago. They were and are in the military context.* [Italics mine]
>
> . . . different ideas are emerging and [I paraphrase] interplanetary travel is not in the picture. . . . I have heard things which lead me to think that what is now considered the summit of scientific knowledge is about to be drastically changed and, while this may not affect the high altitude projectile observations, it will affect anything approaching visits to Mars.
>
> I am sure of two things: first, that many will disagree with me. Second, that we are on the verge of revolutionary thoughts on interplanetary questions, which will change our present ideas. This may advance our thinking in certain respects but the signs are that it will exclude interplanetary travel by inhabitants of this planet.

I agree with much of this comment, though I think *we are on the verge of space travel in the neighborhood of the earth,* or at least of apprehending such activity. There is more than a mild hint in this report to indicate that new vistas are opening in *qualitative* science—a discovery (probably not an invention) of new principles of locomotion in space. But this will be *new* only to our present racial generation. It was probably known to our predecessors of thousands of years ago.

Therefore, without wishing to decry the effort, we can say that an attempt to push basketballs through the ionosphere is not UFO activity or a stepping-stone to space travel. The UFO is a horsepower of another tint.

◆ The Man-Made Moon ◆

Willy-nilly the human race is growing up and reaching toward maturity. Now with adolescent brashness it is beginning to imagine that it has all the answers.

It has been in the process of intellectual development for many, many centuries. During those centuries, it has consistently looked towards, and reached for, the stars.

Our race has been in a state of generation and re-generation since before the days of the Flood. Many times the youthful and growing race of mankind felt frustrated, thinking its goals were too distant for attainment.

Perhaps resurgent mankind passed through puberty and reached adolescence—probably during the Renaissance. At that time there was a tremendous increase in man's racial capacity for learning, and the major accumulation of his knowledge began. Within our time, our own life span, this accelerating accumulation of knowledge has reached frightening proportions.

Today mankind is in the difficult position of an army whose mechanized advanced elements are moving at an ever-increasing pace, with which its main forces cannot keep up. The vanguard is composed of our young engineers, scientists, researchers and independent thinkers, who are moving forward at an awesome pace.

Man is setting out on one of the greatest conquests in his

history. The mastery over space is an accomplishment of a higher order than anything he has previously undertaken. It is only within our own lifetime that he has begun seriously to consider jumping off the surface of the earth to explore space. Only within the last decade have sober calculations been made toward this accomplishment.

Within this decade, man's conceptions of space have changed in an astounding manner. Today, even governments express confidence that man, or his agents, will leave the surface of the earth on reconnaissance trips within a very few years. The conquest of space is before us. It is for us, the people, to decide whether we have the mature judgment to take this venture whose risks include mankind's self-destruction.

The part played by Russia in the race for space, like everything else about that vast curtained land, is a mystery. However, there have been some significant hints.

For example, *Intelligence Digest* (October, 1946) said:

The Soviets have ordered the building of a special center of astronomical research in which will be a number of institutes, observatories, and special air fields where flying observatories, special balloons and airships are to be based for carrying out protracted studies at high altitudes.

Little, if anything, appeared in the public press about this. The Russians were said to have procured special machinery, the inference being that this machinery came from abroad. There were reports that work was going on with monster mirrors, and that the Russians were busy on a highly secret project involving cosmic rays.

At that time, atomic development was in every mind and (without much evidence) it was surmised that the secret Russian project was related to atomic development. However, the Russians were reported to have made some significant post-atomic discoveries.

What the *Intelligence Digest* reports is well worth listening to. It has proven remarkably accurate on other occasions. For example it announced, many months in advance, that the Russians would explode an atomic bomb the following spring. The detonation occurred close to the predicted time.

One thing is certain, fear of our stockpile of atomic and hydrogen bombs plays very little part in Russian policy. I wonder why?

In *The Case for the UFO* it was postulated that this secret development in Russian might involve some kind of UFO. However, these reports and the equipment described could just as easily have been applied to the development of a satellite.

Both possibilities involve aspects of space flight. We usually think of space flight as involving a contraption which may contain a crew of operators. A satellite, on the other hand, is merely a special type of missile and may not even be, in the full sense, a "guided missile."

There is the further possibility that all this secret research by the Russians merely envisions a method of guiding missiles by astronomical controls. Similar work has been done by Britain and the United States in which the stars are used, by means of photoelectric devices, to keep missiles on their courses. It is questionable whether such a project would have involved all that reported equipment, or have been so jealously guarded. More likely it dealt with either a satellite or a UFO. In any case, if the Russians do beat us in establishing a satellite in the ionosphere, or in space beyond, we could not honestly say that we were not warned. It is inconceivable that our government took no notice of these news items.

A comment by Robert N. Webster, in *Fate* Magazine, September, 1949, has a bearing on artificial satellites. He says that, according to reports from the rocket-proving grounds at White Sands, New Mexico, one high-altitude rocket did not return to the earth! Excitement about this was so great that the story leaked out before radar operators could get together and censor their stories for publication.

This rocket, like others, was monitored by radar for the purpose of triangulation. All the operators claimed that at the peak of its trajectory, about 250 miles above the earth, it just vanished. This may very well be the highest altiitude attained by any instrument of modern man.

The rocket simply disappeared as though it had disintegrated or de-materialized. A movement by the rocket into an orbit would have been detected by at least some of the ground radar.

There was some mild speculation at the time associating the disappearance with possible activities of UFO. It was known from previous reports that UFO joined some of the experimental rockets in their vertical climb and had practically flown circles around them in spite of their tremendous speeds.

The report cited in *Fate* Magazine is only one of several not officially confirmed by the United States Government but taken as fact by American experts. Some assumed that the rocket, for some unknown reason, generated an enormous and unexpected thrust at the last moment, which carried it free of the earth's atmosphere. This is not exactly in conformance with the radar reports that the rocket simply disappeared. In the absence of candid government statements it is difficult to determine the facts.

If this rocket really did escape, it may be about 800 miles out in space, completely beyond the earth's atmosphere, and coasting on its momentum. At that distance, if it is moving with a speed sufficient to balance the pull of gravity from the earth, the artificial satellite would be moving at about 16,000 mph, and circling the earth about thirteen times every day, or roughly once every hour and fifty minutes.

A Pentagon spokesman maintaining the olive-drab cloud of bureaucratic secrecy, denied any knowledge of a runaway rocket. However, every statement coming out of Washington must be examined for "gobbledegook." Take note that this statement applies only to "runaway rockets." Nothing is said about disappearing rockets.

It is unlikely that this experimental rocket powered to go 250 miles contained enough unanticipated power to take it to a height of 800 miles. What did, in fact, become of it? Since radar reported not a movement into space but a disappearance, and since these rockets have been accompanied by UFO, may we assume that this rocket was carried off by some space-craft?

Or is this the "satellite" for which Dr. Tombaugh is searching so arduously at the behest of the Military?

Perhaps it is only recently that even *natural* satellites were understood or comprehended. Very few people understood their nature before Copernicus. Our moon was then the only known satellite, and its relationship to the earth was not thoroughly understood.

About the turn of the sixteenth century, Jonathan Swift wrote his satire *Gulliver's Travels*. We can skip over many of the fictional accomplishments of the Laputian astronomers, including the excellence of their telescopes and the fact that they had already catalogued 10,000 stars and calculated the motions of comets. We can ignore the account of the flying island on which their capital was built and on which their astronomers conducted observations. We can also skip the fact that the flying island of Laputa is the first example of a true flying saucer to be found in literature.

More significant is the fact that Swift must have had some kind of prescience about astronomical data not yet discovered.

Referring to the astronomers of Laputa, Gulliver has this to say:

They have likewise discovered two lesser stars, or satellites, which revolve about Mars, whereof the innermost is distant from the center of the primary planet exactly three of the diameters, and the outermost five; the former revolves in the space of ten hours and the latter in twenty-one and one-half hours, so that the squares of their periodical times are very near in the same proportion with the cubes of their distance from the center of Mars, which evidently shows them to be governed by the same law of gravitation, that influences the other heavenly bodies.

Now this is one of the most remarkable predictions ever made. Nothing but some type of extra-sensory perception can account for it.

The satellites of Mars, two in number, were not actually discovered by telescopes until almost two hundred years *after* Swift wrote *Gulliver's Travels*. The sudden discovery, or appearance of these bodies was one of the strange events which ushered in the "incredible decade"—1877-1886.

Satellites so close to the surface of their parent planet and revolving in such short periods were completely unknown to the formal science of Swift's day, and except in the case of Mars, are unknown today. In Swift's time the period of rotation of Mars, that is, the length of its day, was unknown. Is it not truly remarkable, therefore, that the two Martian satellites almost completely fulfill the description given by Swift nearly two centuries before?

These little moons are abnormal in almost every respect as compared to other satellites. There appears to be no way of integrating these two objects into the systematic placement of planets and satellites set by Bode's law. Their size, also, is unusual. These two satellites are too small to be seen except with the largest telescopes. Even then it is impossible to make accurate direct measurements of their diameter, and indirect estimates have to be used. The smaller is thought to be seven to ten miles in diameter, and the larger about fifteen.

Their appearance in the skies of Mars must be truly unique. The movement of one of these tiny moons is so rapid that it makes more than one complete circuit a day (as planned for our silly satellite) and therefore rises in the west and sets in the east. The other has a period so close to the rotation or day of Mars, that this little globe stays in the sky continuously for days at a time— an ideal scanning or take-off platform.

There is more! These suddenly appearing moons are about the size of the disturbances involved in crater Linné and the "bowler hats" now increasing in numbers on our moon. And they were discovered shortly after the disappearance of Linné!

◆ Mars and Its Satellites ◆

The description of these two satellites, and particularly of the innermost one, *almost duplicates descriptions of artificial satellites.*

In most physical characteristics these, and again particularly the inner one, are *anomalous* to the general set-up in the solar system. Serious students have suggested that at least one and perhaps both Martian satellites are artificial, *created and placed relative to Mars by intelligent beings.*

Until very recently, astronomers have scoffed at any such notion. But today our government proposes an artificial satellite to be in place within two years, as the first step in the establishment of a large artificial satellite to circle the earth as a laboratory site. If we can be so close to building such a contrivance and maintaining it in space, there seems to be little reason to question the ability of some older civilization on another planet such as Mars to do so.

Add to this the mysterious flashes and beams of light seen on and near the planet Mars within the past seventy-five years. This is what we may anticipate after our own establishment of a space way-station.

We can only conjecture why a space station should have been set up over the planet Mars. Conceivably the surface of Mars became uninhabitable, through dessication or artificially generated radioactivity. If conditions on the surface became intolerable, an intelligent race might retreat into space and set up a new frontier for life. This is not to say that the Martian satellites are UFO. But there is reason to believe that they are artificial.

Mars is considered to be geologically older than earth. If a civilization exists or has existed on Mars, it probably reached a higher intellectual development than ours.

It may be, then, that the concept of artificial satellites and space-stations is not without precedent and man can take encouragement from what he sees on a neighboring planet. At any rate, the size of the satellites is not so great that artificial construction is to be considered impossible.

There have also been some peculiar appearances over the planet Jupiter. Sometimes, *more shadows of satellites have been seen on Jupiter's surface than the number of its visible satellites!* And sometimes the shadows have appeared elswhere than the places where a shadow should have appeared, and we are not altogether certain these extra objects *were* shadows. They may well have been maneuverable creations *between* us and Jupiter. Admittedly some of these happening were recorded many years ago in the period of the mysterious 1880's. Later, in the second quarter of the twentieth century, some extremely small satellites were discovered near Jupiter through our powerful new telescopes. Conceivably some of these shadows or extra satellites were the tiny ones recently discovered.

These minute satellites of Jupiter are probably larger than those of Mars. But compared with Jupiter's four major satellites they are insignificant.

Observations have been made, particularly in the nineteenth century, of small objects near the planets Venus and Mercury. No astronomer could make any reasonable explanation of what they were. On at least one occasion an object was seen *leaving* Venus, or at least appearing to leave; on another occasion it seemed to be *returning*. Yet no verified object moving in an orbit around either Venus or Mercury has been discovered.

Our hypothesis is that these objects were *artificially created and intelligently controlled*.

This assumption may be challenged, but in the light of the announcement by government and other reputable scientists it is no longer ridiculous to make such assumptions nor to interpret observational data from the viewpoint that artificially created, maneuverable structures may exist in the solar system.

Contingent upon the establishment of a space-station moving in an orbit around the earth large enough to contain observational equipment and laboratories, we may be able to determine more definitely the nature of the satellites of Mars. We may also learn whether there are small satellites accompanying Venus and Mercury. Observations from such a space-station may likewise reveal a larger number of satellites accompanying Jupiter and Saturn. Once we establish broadcasting and observational facilities outside the earth's ionosphere, the possibilities of interplanetary communication become enormously enhanced.

It is incorrect to speak of an "artificial" moon, for the word moon is properly the name for our satellite. True, it is customary to speak of the "moons" of a planet—newspapers do it all the time, but textbooks seldom do. Satellite is the correct generic term.

Any artificial satellite which we may place in space by means of rockets or any other type of power will have little resemblance to our moon. First, it will be far closer to the earth; second, it will be much smaller than the moon. In fact, within any foreseeable time, such a satellite will likely be so small as barely to be seen by the unaided eye.

Because the artificial satellite is functional, it will not necessarily share all the characteristics of the moon or other "natural" satellites. But, of one thing we are certain: once it attains an orbit, defined by its velocity around the earth, the little object will have to obey the laws of gravitation and celestial mechanics. Consequently its artificiality would be difficult to determine, once it settles into a definite orbit . . . *unless it were subject to intelligent control: remote or internal.* Therein lies the difference between any small satellites, natural or artificial, detected in the earth-moon system, and the true UFO observed by such men as Watson, Harrison, and Swift. *These* objects seemed to defy the laws of gravitational motion and thus disclose their intelligent nature.

◆ Before Rockets ◆

Most of the radical developments of engineering and science were taken as jokes until put into operation. The flying machine was a joke, particularly to mathematicians, until just about the turn of the century, when Langley and the Wright brothers got such machines up into the air. The local plutocrats of my hometown ponderously stated in 1917 that there was no future to this ridiculous thing called wireless.

People laughed (or trembled) at the first notion of a balloon carrying people aloft. But ballooning, then called "aerostatics," did not point the way toward mechanical flight, even to intelligent and thinking people. Why?

Because ballooning made use of the principle of flotation,

while mechanical flight is a dynamic phenomenon. The former has not been very successful, but flight by dynamic thrust has conquered distance and time to a degree. However, just as areodynamic flight superseded balloon-flotation, so will the new principles, which will give us space flight, supersede aerodynamic and rocket flight.

The development of the little satellite is the last, farthest reach of dynamic, or thrust-powered flight. Its limitations are comparable to those of aerostatics. It must give way to the emerging concept of space flight through gravity control.

Our present probing of the upper air with rockets is comparable to the experiments of our forebears of a hundred years ago. They were first afraid to ascend in balloons. They experimented by sending birds and animals up in balloons. When nothing happened to *them,* a few brave *men* went up. Even then, only one hundred years ago, science did not associate the rarefied air on mountaintops with the atmosphere entered by a soaring balloon. But science was then still debating the reality of meteors from space.

That timorous beginning of flight surprises us by the lack of comprehension and analytical ability of that time. Today we are so conditioned by the seemingly unlimited strides in engineering, and particularly in aviation, that we accept the thought of an artificial satellite without hesitation and consider it a step towards UFO and space flight.

Gradually the public mind has become conditioned to accepting without question almost anything in the nature of high-altitude ascensions either within our atmosphere or beyond. But caution is needed. The soaring rocket experimenters are having a field day—besides holding down interesting and well-paid jobs.

We cannot hope that a metallic basketball, carried to the upper reaches of our atmosphere by rockets, will be either space flight or the answer to the problem of UFO—even if the little ball does follow a conventional orbit set by conventional minds.

I do consider true space flight as being related to the mysteries of the UFO. I believe the UFO will be found to be using the same types of power and controls. I do not believe that aerodynamics or rocket power will produce space flight or UFO.

What bothers me is that the blind and gullible confidence of the twentieth century has displaced the equally blind fear of those earlier days. Where we previously feared to tread, however softly, we now rush pell-mell up a blind alley.

As I write these words, I wonder again what frustration, or what frightening knowledge prompted the suicide of Secretary Forrestal of the Department of Defense. We do know that, in 1948, he officially reported that the department was considering the military possibilities of an artificial satellite.

We know, further, that his department has maintained continued researches in space flight. So seriously is this taken that a department of space medicine has been established, in the School of Aviation Medicine at Randolph Field in Texas, to conduct research on what would happen to passengers under conditions of space flight.

In 1953, a Philadelphia newspaper announced that the government was letting a contract for determining whether algae, grown in tanks abroad space craft, could produce oxygen for a crew, or convert carbon-dioxide into usable oxygen.

Today, we are asked to believe that all of this is suddenly news!

Satellite-building is considered by most authorities to be an important step in the development of astronautics, a term coined by the French novelist Rosmy for navigation in outer space. We've already had international congresses on astronautics.

Many flying saucer societies are in the act, generally accepting without question that preliminary steps to space flight must include the building and launching of satellites and their maintenance as space way-stations.

Some experts have stated, within the past five years, that given a sufficient amount of money they could produce a space station or artificial satellite to move around the earth forever and serve as an observation station, or as a springboard to further probing into space.

The idea of an artificial moon is not especially new. Dreamers and "astronauts," as they call themselves, began to give thought to such things more than twenty-five years ago. The writers of science fiction were envisioning such a space station in the twenties. Satellite enthusiasts considered it a necessary step toward the launching of interplanetary space-ships, postulating a quick visit to the moon, and a takeoff there in the general direction of Mars. The purpose of the space station is to establish a launching platform at such a distance from the earth that gravitation would be weakened, with a corresponding saving in fuel. The initial speed of departure would approximate escape velocity.*

It is doubtful if Army, Navy, or Air Force is seriously interested in visiting Mars. But in view of the unbridled intrusion of government into every conceivable activity, it would be brash indeed to say that no part of government is so interested. When one thinks of the enormous range of do-goodism, interplanetary point-four plans and give-away programs are not inconceivable. The military is more practical and believes in the advantages of an observation platform, however small, in very high altitudes or even outside the atmosphere. As things stand, however, the scientists have most to gain from a small artificial satellite.

At present, no means other than rocket power has been considered for hoisting the necessary material into space for building a satellite of any appreciable size.

Some responsible writers assert that it will never be possible to leave the earth for a long period in anything but a rocket ship. This naive assumption is based on over-simplification and ignorance. True, rocket power is the only kind we know capable of moving a mass in space *once we are outside a tangible atmosphere.* However, this ignores the fact that a rocket is effective *only* because it can kick material out from a jet, and that this reaction is as important as the power generated.

Theoretically, an artificial satellite or man-made moon can be planned for any convenient altitude above the earth, pro-

* Escape velocity: The speed at which a rocket or other body will completely defy gravity and continue its course in space without further application of power. This is about 6¾ miles per second at the earth's surface.

vided it is directed into an orbit at that altitude and at a speed exactly sufficient to offset the earth's gravitation at the required height. At 350 miles this orbital velocity would have to be about four and one-half miles per second. At a little less than 1100 miles, an altitude favored by rocket specialist Von Braun, a speed of something more than four miles per second would be needed and a complete revolution would be made around the earth about every two hours. The higher the missile, the slower the speed needed to stay at its orbital altitude.

At a distance of approximately 22,300 miles, an artificial satellite would revolve around the earth once every twenty-four hours. If this satellite revolved directly above the equator eastward, it would remain directly over a fixed spot on the earth's surface for an indefinite period of time.

◆ Goddard's Rocket Experiments ◆

Official thinking now fixes on rocket power to launch a space satellite. But only a short time ago official opinion did its best to stifle the development of rocket power. Do you know the part Dr. Robert Hutchings Goddard had in making the satellite a possibility?

Few people do.

He is the forgotten man of rocket power. He died in 1945, after living to see the Germans exploit his designs in the devastating V-2 rocket. Just as the Wright Brothers pioneered the airplane, Dr. Goddard pioneered the rocket.

Some responsible newspaper commentators, realizing the injustice of ignoring Dr. Goddard in the recent announcements, have brought out biographical material on this remarkable man.

Dr. Goddard labored for decades to develop rockets, hoping ultimately to send one into space. It was Goddard who developed liquid fuel for rockets and thereby multiplied the efficiency of rocket propulsion.

Goddard began in New England in the early part of this century; then, with meager funds, he carried on in the desert country of New Mexico, at a site not far from the now famous White Sands proving grounds.

Now there is a rocket exhibit in the aircraft building of the National Air Museum on the grounds of the Smithsonian Institution. Here the visitor can follow Goddard's work. It is said that the largest and last of Goddard's rockets, intended for peaceful research, inspired the German V-2 with which Hitler's diabolical experts came close to demolishing London.

Dr. Goddard was born on October 5, 1882, one of the years of the "incredible decade." More cosmic and terrestrial events of unexplained and seemingly inexplicable nature, happened in that decade, than in any other like period in recorded history. In that year the great comet of 1882 was in the skies, awesomely visible to the naked eye. In November of the same year, a weird object of indeterminable size sailed majestically through the skies of northern Europe and England. It has been described variously as an aurora, or a UFO. This "thing" crossed over England, heading southwest, at a height of *one to two hundred miles*. To this day it remains unidentified.

A few years before Goddard's birth, but still within the memorable decade, the astronomers Watson of Michigan and Swift of New York saw two spherical, clearly defined, objects near the sun and moon during a total eclipse. These completely fill the requirements and description of *artificial* satellites or navigable space structures.

We cannot say for certain that Dr. Goddard was influenced by this cosmic condition. Still it cannot be denied that there was something of the auspicious in the timing of Dr. Goddard's birth.

This we do know, however: at about the age of thirty-eight, Dr. Goddard became a professor at Clark University at Worcester, Massachusetts. His first rocket study began soon after.

The first known flight of a liquid-fueled rocket was Dr. Goddard's accomplishment. It lasted only a few seconds and attained a speed of only about 60 mph. The date: March 16,

1926. Dr. Goddard was forty-four and had spent approximately twenty years in study and experimentation. He was a persistent but reticent man. Only two brief reports were published during his lifetime, but he left voluminous notes when he died in 1945.

I happen to be old enough to remember and to have been interested in this initial drive towards space. Even in the twenties there was something inspiring about the attempts of a quiet scientist to reach outer space. And Dr. Goddard was doing this singlehandedly and without fanfare. As I remember, Dr. Goddard was considered something of a crackpot. A rocket, after all, had no use except for Fourth of July fireworks, or at best, for shooting ropes to foundering ships.

Dr. Goddard certainly was not a salesman. He may have been that reprehensible human being, an introvert, but today, after having had the brashness to write something serious on unidentified flying objects, I have come to believe that Dr. Goddard was reticent to avoid becoming the public laughing-stock of orthodox science, government, and engineering.

Goddard was handicapped by trying to operate on the meager income of a professor in a small college, but he was scientifically thorough and meticulous. He made the best possible use of data accumulated from his successful and unsuccessful rocket flights, of which the latter were in the majority. As for official opinion, at one time Goddard was arrested for disturbing the peace; and ultimately he was forbidden to fire more rockets in Massachusetts.

But Goddard was not altogether without the attention and interest of progressively-minded people. Charles A. Lindbergh, while serving as an adviser on aeronautics to the Guggenheim Foundation, interested Daniel Guggenheim and his son Harry in financing the rocket project. Guggenheim funds, joined with those of the Smithsonian Institute, enabled Dr. Goddard to get his plans off the drawing board and into the sky. Funds were taken from the somewhat obscure Hodgkins' Fund set up years before to promote exploration of the air.

Even in such things there can be a note of humor. It appears that one of the grants made by this ponderous fund was three miles of silk thread to the inventor of a high-altitude kite!

Government officials, with characteristic apathy for anything new and with customary high regard for bureaucratic decorum, took a dim view of Goddard's rocket. If the reader thinks this is funny let him try to interest government officials in any scientific project not originating within the bureaucratic compounds. The fact that the taxpayer is now putting up many millions of dollars to subsidize rocket developments is neither here nor there, for the government waited until it was almost too late and is now backing a horse unlikely to place in the final heat.

However, other governments, as has been the case in all matters pertaining to aviation and to aerial exploration, were more interested. The German Military Attaché in Washington became the best customer for the pamphlets issued by the Smithsonian Institution, describing Goddard's liquid-fuel rocket.

But let us go back in the history of rockets before the time of Goddard. After all, the rocket is a very old appliance.

Though one of the oldest forms of self-propulsion, its nature was understood by very few people prior to this century. Believe it or not, within the current month of writing and of the government's announcement of the satellite program, I have heard, from people considering themselves well-informed, completely mistaken notions of rocket propulsion.

The rocket is a powerful but very inefficient mechanism. The Chinese are almost universally accredited with the invention or discovery of gunpowder. We believe discovery is the better word. Somehow or other, rockets were developed at about the same time, and it is not difficult to think of an ancient Chinese experimenting with gunpowder, setting off a charge which caused a powder container to whiz up like a rocket.

Gunpowder and rockets appear to have been brought to the Arabs by the conquering Mongols. The intelligent Moslems, against whom they were used, soon found out how to make their own gunpowder and rockets, and so the art spread to Europe.

Despite centuries of use the rocket was not fully understood until Newton developed the basic laws of physical motion.

During the conquest of India, the British were awed by the force of rocket missiles which the Indians had acquired through contact with the Chinese. Their effectiveness impressed a young officer named William Congreve. Beginning about 1801, Congreve set out to improve the rockets for military purposes, applying the scientific methods available at the time. He produced a much improved military rocket. When used in 1806, in the bombardment of Boulogne, rockets devastated the city by the fires which they caused. In the year after, 1807, Copenhagen was practically destroyed by means of rockets. During our war of 1812, the British used rockets in the bombardment of Fort McHenry at Baltimore. From them came the phrase "rockets' red glare" in "The Star Spangled Banner," written by Francis Scott Key at that time. However, rockets were displaced by other missile weapons and did not stage a comeback until the Second World War, when the Germans took up where Goddard had pointed the way.

Though rockets fell out of favor as military weapons, interest in them continued for other purposes. The sky-rocket became an indispensable adjunct to celebrations.

Rockets found peacetime applications of a more practical nature. They were used in maritime life-saving operations for carrying ropes or lifelines from the shore or from rescue craft to ships in distress. In this capacity, rockets were reported to have saved more than 12,000 lives on the coast of England.

Since the original discovery, there seems to have been no qualitative improvement in rockets. There have been many quantitative improvements and today's rocket is incomparably superior to its predecessors, *but the principle of its propulsion remains the same* although we have a better understanding of it than the Chinese, Arabs, and Hindus. The early Chinese rockets appear to have been made by filling bamboo stems with loose powder, the natural divisions within the bamboo serving as pockets for the explosive. A hole was bored through one of the ends of the bamboo section and the crude, loose, black powder was painstakingly pushed through the hole until the section was filled. With a modern black powder such a contrivance would have blown up before it could have risen into the air; but with the old slow-burning powder made by the Chinese, the expelled gasses could lift the rocket before internal pressure became great enough to rupture the rocket's shell.

From the time of Congreve to the time of Goddard, rockets were powered with powdered or solid fuel, the latter being simply compressed gunpowder.

◆ Bagby's Satellites ◆

Already there may be one or more artificial satellites travelling in orbits around the earth. On February 18, 1955, the Washington *Evening Star* carried a story by the North American Newspaper Alliance about the discovery of small satellites close to the earth seen by an amateur astronomer of high standing, John P. Bagby. Mr. Bagby disclosed his findings in a paper read at the Adler Planetarium at Chicago. Mr. Bagby, an electronics engineer, is an amateur astronomer, which means only that he does not make his living thereby. He has the optical equipment and the technical knowledge to make important discoveries and to evaluate them. Mr. Bagby made his discovery with a six-inch telescope which he built himself. He has, associated with him, a team of skilled amateur astronomers who work together in the identification of objects in the sky. In reporting his discoveries he asked professional astronomers to check his observations.

Mr. Bagby began his search two or three years ago when another amateur reported small spots crossing the moon singly and in groups. His friend, Mr. Holpuch, a skilled observer both of telescopic meteors and bird migrations, was not without some skill in identifying objects in the sky. He reported that the procession had continued for *an hour and a half* with more than fifty objects observed, *some of which glowed dull red occasionally.*

Mr. Bagby made his first observation of the phenomenon in February, 1954. The observation is of such a startling nature that Mr. Bagby began checking through the world's astronomical literature. He found scattered reports of similar objects over the years.

Mr. Bagby and Mr. Holpuch have seen these objects on several occasions and believe they are periodic in their appearance. If this is true, it rules out anything of the nature of meteors or migratory birds.

The objects observed in 1954 and early 1955 appeared to be at a distance of about 475 miles from the earth. This lies within the extreme limits of the earth's atmosphere.

Remember that similar flights of objects have been reported during the past 200 years, some of them by professional astronomers. A flight of objects, moving singly and in pairs across the face of the sun at intervals of a minute or so was observed at Zacatacas, Mexico, August 12, 1883. In two hours, 283 crossed the sun, and 1,100 more were seen by noon next day. Photographs were taken and one was reproduced in a French astronomical journal a few years later. More were seen the next day, but no evidence has ever been offered to indicate that they were definitely satellites of the earth.

Mr. Bagby suggested that the "moonlets," as he called them, may be traveling as fast as 18,000 mph. If true, and if they are natural, then they are either closer than 475 miles from the earth's surface, or else not moving in a circular orbit. They could, perhaps, have been moving in an elongated elliptical orbit, but we have to consider that the speed is greater than that required by the laws of gravity. Therefore artificial speed and control are suggested. Most of them appeared to be less than one hundred feet in diameter, but he warned that this data was not based on sufficient observation for him to consider it accurate.

This description is so close to that of the proposed artificial satellite as to be startling. We certainly do not believe any other nation has forged so far ahead as to launch dozens of artificial satellites up to one hundred feet in diameter. Yet this description almost precisely fits the forecast of the satellites we propose to launch in 1957.

Strangely enough, also, these descriptions match sightings made in the past which would seem to indicate UFO in space.

The professional astronomer Dr. Clyde W. Tombaugh, who discovered the planet Pluto in 1930, has been searching under

U. S. Army auspices for just such satellites as those Mr. Bagby reported.

We agree with Mr. Tombaugh's statement:

It is strange that with all the thousands of years man has been studying the heavens, he has almost ignored space right around the earth. What I am doing is exploring this unknown area between the earth and the moon.

This is just what I have been recommending in the search for UFO in space.

Recently there have been other reports of the discovery of small satellites, and considerable debate as to whether they are natural or artificial.

I have pointed out previously that these objects, considered by most astronomers to be small planets or satellites, may not be moving in orbits around either the earth or the moon, but may be existing at a gravitational neutral between the earth and the sun. To be maintained in such a position, without circling around the earth, they would have to be artificially controlled. If so, they fall into the category of UFO.

Such objects, located at a gravitational neutral towards the sun, would seldom be seen crossing the face of the moon, since they would line up with the moon only at the time of a new moon. The fact that they are seldom seen is easily explained by their being almost in line with the sun and practically invisible because of its glare. I think it possible that both Mr. Bagby and Mr. Tombaugh err in their assumption of orbital motion around the earth. If they would look in the vicinity of the sun they might make some startling discoveries.

Although other reports from Mr. Bagby were expected, nothing further has appeared. Persistent inquiries of publishers of some small magazines have been ignored. Again, as in the field of flying saucers and UFO, we run into mystery if not deliberate secrecy. Why no announcements from professional astronomers in this field? Have the Russians then, actually beaten us to the launching of an artificial satellite, and is this fact being concealed by both Russia and the U. S. A.?

Stewart Alsop pointed out that the possibility of the Soviets eventually launching a satellite was taken so seriously that a satellite detection project was established at White Sands and another at Mt. Wilson.

This agrees with other statements made about various searches for satellites. There was a big stir at the Pentagon when not one, but two satellites were identified; but it was eventually announced that both were natural, although never before detected. Yet, nothing more about these two satellites in the public press *nor in the astronomical publications,* so far as this writer knows. If, in fact, two natural satellites were discovered, the entire astronomical press would be agog *unless* for some reason astronomical announcements had been throttled.

Second, so Alsop pointed out, the Russians had announced in April (1955) that they had created "A permanent Interdepartmental Commission for Interplanetary Communication," with their greatest scientist, Peter Kapitsa, on its staff.

Here again, our government appears to have underestimated the Russians. What is this blindness in our national character which refuses to allow us to admit any superiority in any other nation? When will our omniscient pundits in the Pentagon stop considering themselves the only informed group of people on the face of the earth? It is high time some of the "boasting" of the Soviets be taken seriously. Perhaps, at last, the Pentagon is doing so.

In closing his comment, Alsop stressed the enormous military value of such satellites for reconnaissance and missile-guidance. He also said that the news of such a feat on the part of the Russians would have far-reaching effects on an impressionable world. If the Russians have beaten us to the launching of a satellite it is a vast gain for them in prestige and a vast loss of face for us. It may even indicate a decisive Russian lead over the Americans and the West in general in the race for what may be called "The Ultimate Weapon."

The question is, then, have the Russians actually beaten us, and has our government been forced to predict our own launching to save face? Is the U. S. Satellite announcement of July 30, 1955 merely a step toward breaking the unpalatable news that Russia has had a satellite for some months, or even years? Is this another result of the absurd craze for secrecy which has engulfed Washington, D.C.? Is this erratic secrecy part and parcel of the program of concealment which has prevented the government in general and the military in particular from issuing a candid and factual statement regarding the UFO? Is not this kind of secrecy, defended as a means of preventing panic, itself a form of panic?

On September 5, 1954, two amateur astronomers named Peter Bartkus and Theodore McColm were watching the moon through a six-inch reflecting telescope, using magnifications of 150-200. Between 10:35 and 11:15 P.M., they observed an astonishing phenomenon. The moon was in the first quarter, and they saw what appeared to be a spherical object moving away from the northern section of Mare Humboldtianum.

The object was not glowing or brilliant, but (and this is important) it seemed more like a planet's dull, reflected light. The same appearance might apply to a satellite. Whatever the object was, it moved up from the moon in approximately forty minutes. The observers checked every possibility of reflection or other illusion and tried different eye pieces and also traversed the telescope. They were forced to conclude that the object was definitely in space and in the same telescopic field with the moon. It was not moving with the moon, for the moon was going down in the sky or setting in the west, and the object was moving upward. There was no way of saying for sure how big the object was or how far from earth.

◆ Newton's Laws and Space Flight ◆

Sir Isaac Newton, born in 1642, was first to generalize the mechanical laws of the universe into mathematical form. The earth, and the rest of the universe so far as we know, operates, at least approximately, on his three basic laws of motion.

These laws represent as much genius as do the advanced equations of Einstein, because Newton had to begin with uncoordinated materials of dubious accuracy. To him must go the credit for making the first broad basic conclusions regarding universal mechanics, at least in the racial generation of man which has arisen since the Flood.

Newton's laws are particularly applicable to rocketry and equally so to the launching and establishment of an artificial satellite. They may be summarized as follows:

1. Inertia

Every object continues in a state of rest or of uniform motion in a straight line unless influenced by some outside force. Unfortunately, to the average reader of today, the word inertia, like many others loosely used, has been weakened by additional meanings. Commonly, we think of inertia as lethargy or sluggishness. But in its scientific sense, inertia is that characteristic of matter which causes it to resist changes in its velocity or position.

2. Acceleration

This defines the result of applying a force to a movable mass. Like any other natural law of physics—including UFO phenomena —this is a generalization from observed data. Acceleration, it states, is directly proportional to the force which produces it, and the change in motion takes place in the direction in which the applied force acts.

Here we become involved in still further definitions, which call for some very fine distinctions. We must distinguish between speed and the more technical term, velocity. Technically, in the language of physics, speed is the rate at which distance is traversed, while velocity includes both speed and direction. Speed alone cannot be conveniently represented by a vector in graphs, but velocity is readily represented by an arrow whose length represents speed and whose head points in the direction of the acting force. In other words, if a force is applied to a mass, its speed and direction are changed, and the change is in proportion to the force applied.

Since any mass resists, through its inertia, any attempt by a force to change either its speed or its direction, it is possible to say that acceleration is proportional to force divided by mass. This law is beautifully simple in application.

One of the least understood applications of this law of acceleration is the phenomenon of curvilinear or circular motion. A ball swinging around your finger at the end of a string, although its speed may be constant, is undergoing acceleration because its direction of motion is being forced to change continually. It may be covering a uniform number of inches per second in the air around you, but it is constantly diverted from the normal straight line on which it seeks to move. The continuous diverting force is exerted by the string attached to your finger. This ball, revolving at any speed you choose, is changing its velocity, but not its speed; covering a uniform number of inches per second, but in a constantly changing direction. Technically, the change is acceleration, just as if the speed itself varied.

This is of the greatest importance in studying the possibilities of artificial satellites. The moon is moving around the earth in a path which is almost circular and with a speed which is practically constant. However, it is constantly changing direction like the ball you swing at the end of a string. The string is replaced by gravitation, possibly the least understood of all known physical forces.

The greatness of this force of gravitation may be conceived by the following. If the gravitational force, compelling the moon to circle the earth, were replaced by a steel cable it would have to be several hundred miles thick. The calculation needed to compute it would wear out your pencil simply writing down the number of zeros involved.

In contemplating the establishment of an artificial satellite, it is necessary to give thought to Newton's second law of motion. It is necessary to calculate a velocity, or rather a speed, of the satellite, just sufficient to balance the earth's gravitational pull *at the predetermined altitude* above the earth's surface.

3. Action vs. Reaction

While the second law of motion can apply specifically to the satellite, the third law can more directly apply to the rocket or other means by which the satellite is lifted to the altitude of the predetermined orbit. It defines the relationship of action and reaction, stating that to every *action* there is an equal and opposite *reaction*.

It may come as a shock to you that you cannot exert any force unless it is opposed by an equal and opposite force. Have you ever tried, for example, to step on a stair which was not there? If you did, you attempted to exert a force against which there was no equal and opposite force and you will admit that the results were disconcerting. If you strike a baseball with a bat, the ball resists the force applied by the bat with an exactly equal force; but since the ball is quite small and of comparatively little weight or mass, as compared to the bat and your arms, the ball takes on a very rapid motion because of the impact. Since acceleration is proportionate to force divided by mass, the large force exerted by the heavy bat produces a large acceleration on the small mass of the ball, and a high speed or velocity is the result. It is something like this which we have to contemplate in launching a rocket.

To lift a rocket from the earth we have to apply a continuous force to the structure itself, and this force cannot be obtained except through reaction against some mass other than the structure of the rocket. Accordingly the fuel of the rocket must be ejected through a nozzle at great velocity, and it is the inertial resistance of the fuel to the expelling force which creates the driving force, or 'power" of the rocket. The burning gas, of comparatively small mass, moves through the jet at many thousands of feet per second, whereas the much greater mass of the rocket and the unburned fuel starts at a velocity of only a few feet per second. It is the continuation of the force which accelerates the rocket to high velocities.

By this time you are asking yourself: "What has all this to do with the UFO?"

Unfortunately it has been necessary to clear the air clouded by the government obfuscation about rocket power and astronautics, and therefore I have had to take a negative approach. I hope you have gained a clearer picture of rocket power and its inadequacy to power UFO. The little basketball which will weigh fifty pounds, more or less, will require a two-stage, or possibly a three-stage rocket to lift it to its destined orbit. This means many tons of rocket in stages one and two which will be dropped as the fuel, tons of expensive liquid, is exhausted. The basketball is the payload; all the rest is expendable. The ratio of payload to total weight? Well, about one to eight hundred!

This may strike you, rightly enough, as poor efficiency. Worse yet, with all that heroic effort we place a fifty-pound ball only two hundred or three hundred miles above the earth, not even outside the atmosphere!!!

Before you whistle, remember that we have no control over the widget when it gets there. To put one ton of usable material into a space station will require some 800 tons of expendable materials. As yet we have no assurance that a rocket can be built sufficiently large and sufficiently well-powered to carry aloft pieces of assemblies big enough to be serviceable.

An intermediate space station, to be used as a launching platform, could, of course, facilitate other rockets in their departure into space. The space platform is already moving at a speed more than half the velocity of escape. A rocket starting from the platform would only have to generate the difference to overcome the drag of gravity.

Secondly, the drag of gravity is slightly less at the higher altitude, though this is not a major consideration. The platform is only about 4,200 miles from the center of the earth as compared (roughly) to the 4,000 miles at the surface. The advantage, then, in percentage of gravitational drag is insignificant. Together, however, these two factors reduce to a fraction the fuel needed for taking off from the platform, as compared with the fuel requirements for a takeoff from the surface.

Conceivably, a rocket trip can eventually be made to the moon —at a cost of some billions of dollars. But this is not astronautics, nor is it in any sense UFO-activity. For sustained space existence something must be thought of which does not depend upon rocket power with its wasteful expenditure of materials.

That something is controlled reaction with gravity or the gravitational fields.

UFO do not use rocket power. They are not limited to a

mathematically fixed orbit. They can undertake tremendous, erratic accelerations.

UFO are astronautical craft, or entities. If they have a fixed base of any kind, that base is likely the moon. They may have bases (past or present) on the earth, possibly in mountainous areas where there are craters suitable for landing cradles—such as are on the moon.

Such areas exist in Mexico.

The silly little satellite does not appear to be a potential parent either for space-craft or UFO-craft.

To sum up, *the Bureaucratic Mountain has labored—ponderously—and brought forth an M—O—U—S—E. . . .*

THE MOON

◆ A Case to Consider ◆

In *Fate* Magazine, August, 1955, Cassens points out that nowhere in the Bible is it implied that *man* is God's only creation of a race possessing intelligence and personality. His hypothesis is that the moon may once have been inhabited and that the space travel hinted in the book of Genesis may have originated there.

In our unending search for evidence of a pre-cataclysmic, or pre-flood civilization, we must consider the theme of lost continents, e.g. Mu and Atlantis, and lost civilizations on the mainlands of Asia, Africa and South America. We ponder not only *where* these lost worlds may have been, but also *what* they may have been. One possible location is the moon. Some life forms on the moon might have grown to giant stature, because of the low lunar gravity which would permit bone structures to carry much larger bodies. There are many Bible references to giant races which hint (e.g. Genesis 6) that some such race of giants arrived from space.

Early English explorers reported a race of giants in Patagonia and H. T. Wilkins in his *Mysteries of Ancient South America* (Citadel, 1956) cites Andes Indian records of men eighteen feet tall who came from a source unnamed and killed women with whom they attempted intercourse. The isolated remains of giants have been reported in graves in various parts of the world, particularly the American southwest and other parts of the great Cordilleras, extending the full length of the American continents.

Cassens posits that these giants may have come from the moon.

On the other hand, the reverse of this theory is perhaps more acceptable. If a very ancient civilization arose on the earth and discovered space flight its people may very well have colonized the moon at a remote age when it may have been more habitable.

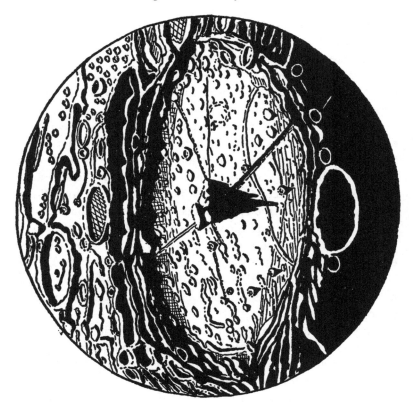

MAGNIFICENT PETAVIUS: *Complex interior of lunar crater.*
(From *Our Moon*)

Under the influence of lesser gravitation, the colonists may have evolved into a race of giants.

After all, the Pygmy races are shown to have been on earth in the Miocene Age, more than thirty million years ago. A civilization may have thrived and perished during that long span of time. We must remember that the little iron meteorite from the Austrian coal-beds is a very old artifact. Through a peculiarly repeated error, the age of this tertiary coal bed was stated to be 300,000 years in my book *The Case for the UFO*. Fortunately, Willy Ley, in a TV broadcast with me on May 16, 1955, pointed out that these tertiary coal beds are more than 30,000,000 years old instead of 300,000. Thus we have the antiquity of intelligently made iron and steel artifacts established at millions of years ago. Either a native terrestrial race dropped a little "erratic" into the incipient coal bed or it came from space. No other explanations are tenable.

If space travel was common in the remote times when the moon may have been habitable, there may be indeed some factual basis behind the story of invading giants who suddenly appeared in the Andes mountains.

Having less gravitation to cope with, it would have been easier for the Selenian moon dwellers to have developed a device for getting off their small planet and beyond the control of its gravitation. If at the same time they developed, as we appear to be doing, vast destructive powers without the capacity for rational restraint, they may have caused uncontrollable explosions on the moon's surface. Such explosions may have caused some of the still unexplained great crater rays or splashes which stretch almost entirely across the face of the moon, as from the crater Tycho.

As might be expected, the few items observed on the moon which seem to have been constructed by intelligence are of a cyclopean nature.

Possibly if the moon was, in fact, captured by the earth instead of developing simultaneously with it from primordial materials of the solar system, then it may have brought civilization and possibly giants with it from some other part of the system.

Mr. Cassens has also proposed that these giant Selenians may have been the ancestors of Mt. Everest's "abominable snowmen." We may smile at this, but after all, if giant Selenians were dropped on mountain ranges of South America, why not in Asia? And if these have no discernible connection, is this any more unacceptable than a similar distribution of isolated Pygmy races from contacts or crashes of UFO?

Was (is) there then a race, human or semi-human, on the moon? If so, were (are) they the descendants of our race, or are we the descendants of theirs? After all, our notorious missing link has yet to be established with finality.

The moon has been under telescopic observation from the earth for almost 350 years, but it is only from the time of Schroeter, before the beginning of the nineteenth century, that records and drawings of the more minute features have been secured.

The question of changes on the surface of the moon is perennial. Diehards deny them, but painstaking observers, such as Moore and Wilkins in our day and Birt, Neison, Schroeter, Klein and others in past decades, insist that changes do take place.

In looking for such changes on the moon as would signify life or the result of intelligent action, we have been, and still are, handicapped because even our largest telescopes will not clearly show anything under 300 to 400 yards in diameter; although long cracks of 300 to 400 feet width may be seen if they are quite long and contain dark shadows.

Thus, unless the effects of intelligent action on the moon are on a grand scale, it will be difficult to become aware of them. Yet, there *are* some evidences of such large-scale action. We must be alert and open-minded enough to apprehend events or phenomena which might ordinarily be overlooked because of their large size, or a very slothful and slow-acting time cycle. It may be something like looking for a name on a very detailed and cluttered map, and being chagrined to find that one has missed it because it was the biggest thing in sight and spread over a broad area.

We cannot assume that life as we know it—that is, animal life —can exist on an airless and waterless moon; but we must be prepared to accept evidence of "life" or "intelligence" of a different nature. Such entities and their works may be on a far vaster scale than we would anticipate on the basis of our own structures.

The lunar surface is extremely rugged. The larger the telescope and better the definition, the rougher it appears. In most lunar districts, travel from place to place would be virtually impossible for animals moving on the surface; and wings would do them no good on an airless planet. We can be reasonably sure that wings have not developed on the moon unless in very early geological times when the moon may have had an atmosphere.

Lunar changes, for the most part, have been on a comparatively small scale and are barely detectable with our telescopes. Certainly there are no new craters on the scale of Plato, Copernicus, or Aristarchus. So-called "minute" changes may actually cover several square miles of area and involve craters up to three, four or five miles in diameter. Changes have also been observed in the lights and streaks within some of the larger craters.

Schroeter was one of the first observers to announce evidence of changes and artificial structures on the lunar surface. He thought a small crater had formed inside of one of the larger craters during the period of his observations and that changes were in progress in other areas.

Some recent observers attribute most of Schroeter's changes to his imagination, defects in his instruments, or to changing illumination on the surface of the moon. But there is a trend toward accepting some of Schroeter's observations.

The two classical illustrations of changes on the moon, and the hassle which goes on between the conservatives and the open-minded observers, are those of the craters Linné and Hyginus-N. Observers today are conceding that Linné has undergone major changes, while maintaining skepticism regarding Hyginus-N.

In 1866 Schmidt of Athens suddenly announced that the well-known crater Linné, repeatedly drawn by Lohrmann, Madler and himself over a period of about forty years, had disappeared. He declared that Linné had turned into a whitish cloud. Other observers have noted either a pit on the upper surface of this cloud, or something which looked like a hill or protuberance. There has been much disagreement as to whether the "pit" was in the center or near the edge. Furthermore, it appears to be moving around.

Somewhat later than Schmidt's announcement, Goodacre in England described Linné as a cone on the edge of a shallow depression. Today, Linné appears to be a low dome, with a pit on the summit and practically in the center of a large white area. If Lohrmann, Beer and Madler, Goodacre, Neison, Birt, or any of the other observers in the nineteenth century have correctly described what they saw—namely a deep crater in the case of Lohrmann, or a cone in the case of Goodacre—then major changes *have* taken place in this limited region.

As evidence accumulates, there are indications that the changes in Linné are repetitive or even cyclic. Whether or not something actually moves in and out of a crater-like depression in the Mare Serenitatis is something perhaps which the reader will have to decide for himself, but I propose to present a large quantity of observational data and the personal expressions of a number of honest observers. I believe that this presentation is important to the study of UFO.

In the *Selenographical Journal* (April 17, 1882, opposite page 26) are comparative—and confirmatory—drawings by Hyginus-N by Neison and Green made on March 26th. Neison describes it as resembling a deep, blackish-grey rounded spot with softened edges, about two-thirds the diameter of Hyginus. To the south-west was a somewhat smaller, somewhat lighter spot of similar character, *the two being connected by a short, narrow band.* (The dumbell formation, again.) It was remarkably distinct.

Green says:

The two views of Hyginus-N at the lower part of the plate were added as confirmation of Mr. Neison's drawings. On both occasions Hyginus-N was a most conspicuous object and could not possibly have been everlooked by anyone making a drawing of the locality. It is visible at sunrise long before the nearby small craters which are frequently drawn.

The many drawings of the region of Hyginus made by the sharp and persistent Gruithuisen fail to show Hyginus-N.

The reactionary Proctor claimed, in the *Selenographical Journal* (volume II) that he had identified Hyginus-N on some photographs, but nobody else seems to have done so, and this would be a most difficult object to photograph even with large modern equipment.

Madler and Gruithuisen noted variable tints near Hyginus—an indication that something was happening. On March 22, 1879, the appearance and disappearance of the dark spot at the location of Hyginus-N was reported, but no crater. On March 1, he saw the spot. On March 2, *nothing*. The whole region around Hyginus seems to be unsettled and Neison speaks of remarkable changes in tint and appearance. It seems obscured at all times, and occasionally crossed by a fine network of dark streaks.

On October 17, 1879, Gaudibert reported having seen two small, darkish spots near Hyginus-N. The previous year, on September 18, he had seen a *low, rather large mound,* somewhat *elliptical* (oval, or spindle), and with *a minute white spot at its center.*

On February 17, 1880, Capron described Hyginus-N as a very marked feature resembling an inkspot, not misty or dull as on other occasions. He calls it a deep hole, although others have been reporting it as shallow or of no depth at all. He saw two dark markings nearby. Here are Capron's observations:

1878, Nov. 2: Faint dusky spot, not well defined, crater-like, slightly oval, somewhat nebulous.

1879, Dec. 4: Large and conspicuous, but soft and no defined margin; had all the appearance of an elevation with appropriate shadings.

1880, Jan. 19: Faint dull spot, with faint light-border shaded obscurely as a depression.

1880, Jan. 20: Very faint, misty greyish-black spot, looking like an *elevation* with a bright ring around it.

1880, Feb. 17: Apparently a deep *depression.*

Capron, a good observer, says:

It may seem strange that the same object should be seen . . . sometimes as a depression and sometimes as an elevation, but *I have no doubt* as to the accuracy of my observations.

In 1879, Nathaniel E. Green made a series of observations of Hyginus-N. On one occasion he saw it first as a "large black crater filled with shadow" and later as a "large black spot surrounded by a vaporous border." On March 29, he watched the sun rise at this location and saw nothing but a dark spot—no crater.

The question of Linné is perennial. Doubts have been expressed as to whether Lohrmann, Madler, Schmidt and Schroeter can be relied upon for accurate descriptions of the appearance of Linné in their time. But we must also reckon with Goodacre, who saw Linné as a small cone on the edge of a shallow pan, a condition not reported by any other observer. Dr. H. P. Wilkins repeats, for emphasis, that Linné today is a pit on the summit of a dome which is itself at the center of a whitish area.

To quote a recent newspaper report:

> It is said that in July a whale gave up a lump of ambergis weighing 926 pounds. The market was $9.00 per ounce, so this was quite a trove. The account says two other lumps of ambergris were said to have exceeded the latest weight of 926 pounds, *but the reports date from the last century and are considered unreliable.*

Why is it always universally considered that our predecessors did not know what they were talking about?

In *Celestial Objects for Common Telescopes* (page 68) Webb says, while discussing the possibility of life on the moon:

> It is, in Beer and Madler's words, no copy of the earth; the absence of seas, rivers, atmosphere, vapors and seasons bespeak the absence of the "busy haunts of men;" indeed of all terrestrial vitality unless it be that of insect or reptile. Whatever may be the features of the averted side on which, as Gruithuisen and Hansen have suggested, other relations may exist, we perceive on this side merely an alternation of level deserts and craggy wildernesses. The hope which cheered on Gruithuisen and others, of discovering the footsteps of human intelligence must be abandoned. *If it should be thought probable, as it very well may, that the lunar surface is habitable in some way of its own, we have reason to suppose, that where the conditions of life are so extremely dissimilar its traces would be undecipherable by our experience as a brief inscription in a character utterly unknown.*

This philosophical observation falls short of being entirely adequate. We do have to consider gigantic size and peculiar design, but there is more to be pondered. We know that speed of movement generally decreases with size. We also know that vegetative life moves with great deliberation. But speeded-up motion pictures of plant movements show almost as much dexterity and purposefulness as animal motion.

If, then, we are contemplating entities that *may* be a mile or more in diameter, we must expect movements which appear to us grotesquely slothful. They may require several of *our* days to complete even simple movements. Unless we can find a way to compress the time scale, we may easily fail to recognize such manifestations of intelligence when we see them.

It has been reiterated that no "high form of life" can exist on the moon. If by "high form of life" we mean only mammalian life, or the even more restricted human life, then, of course, we must agree (unless such life is housed in protective structures). But since we are continually faced with phenomena which seem to demand intelligence for their behavior, we must contemplate intelligence incorporated in some other type of physical organism, different from ours.

Consider the reports of changing color on the moon, particularly within some of the larger craters. The crater Eratosthenes has sometimes been called "the crater of insects" because of the American astronomer W. H. Pickering's speculations of insect life there. This selenologist pointed out, what anyone who studies the lunar details can verify, that during the lunar afternoon dark areas can be seen spreading over part of the interior and even spilling over the walls. These cannot be shadows, because the sun has moved to such a high altitude that shadows are impossible; and frequently the patches move in directions other than those which spreading shadows would take.

Now, daylight on the moon lasts fourteen of our days; therefore an afternoon lasts one of our weeks. We do not say that these dark smudges can actually be seen to move, but they do slowly change their position; and if these ponderous movements could be speeded up by slow-speed movies the results might be astonishing.

Professor Pickering was one of the earlier observers to recognize the fact that non-systematic motion on the moon or anywhere in the universe, implied intelligence or at least an equivalent of life, no matter how low an order it might be. Because of his open-mindedness on this subject and his willingness to interpret his own observations as well as those of other selenographers in an open-minded and objective manner, Professor Pickering was the object of many snide remarks within the American astronomical profession. In fact, he was considered by many to be a little bit peculiar. However we are now coming to realize that the pioneers in this field were rendering a great service.

Pickering stated that since we could not predict the speed and direction of these moving spots, they must be caused by some kind of life. He considered vegetation, but also postulated insects. (So far as I know, he did not suggest what these boundless hordes of bugs were eating.)

Although the floor of the crater Plato sometimes displays a wealth of streaks, white spots and craterlets, at other times nothing can be seen there. On April 31, 1952, H. P. Wilkins and Patrick Moore looked at Plato with the 33-inch Meuden telescope, and each made a drawing independently of the other. When compared these drawings agreed throughout, particularly in the fact that nothing whatever was shown on the far, eastern side of the interior of Plato.

Yet a small object, which has been called a crater, has been seen there by observers many times.

Also a few hours afterwards an American observer named Craig, using a good telescope, *could not see anything at all within Plato,* not a trace of craters or spots. Craig could not even see the four other little craters in the center which were plainly visible to the European observers. Certainly this little object on the eastern wall did not disappear permanently, for it was seen again in October of the same year, and in April, 1953, at both Cambridge and Meuden. This is a modern and current report of the sort of thing that takes place within Plato, but identical phenomena were happening seventy-five, eighty and ninety years ago.

There is a complex region of craters and hills to the north, beyond Plato, extending to the edge of the "Sea of Cold," another area of mystery. As noted elsewhere, Madler drew and described a small bay in the Sea of Cold as an almost perfect square, with a perfectly shaped cross, formed by white ridges, within. Today there is no such thing; one side of the square no longer exists; and the cross is gone. These features were assiduously sought by Wilkins and Moore with the best optical equipment of today, and so it is reasonable to assume that they have been altered or moved.

We are going to have a great deal more to say about the object or "thing" called Hyginus-N, near the well-known crater Hyginus. This object was reported as a newcomer in 1878 by Klein, and the ensuing excitement raised a controversy which has not yet entirely subsided. Dr. H. P. Wilkins says that the "N" stands for the Latin word *nova*, meaning new, so that what we have here is literally a "New Hyginus." The peculiar, smoky-colored appearance of this region led Schroeter and other early observers to believe there was actually smoke hovering about. This, they speculated, might be an area of industrial activity on the moon, the Pittsburgh of the Selenites.

It has been thought that other craters were new, indicating that the moon was not truly a dead world. Changes were usually attributed to natural, perhaps tectonic, causes, but we have reasons to believe that this is not always the case.

The accompanying drawing shows the location of Hyginus-N. It is a strange landscape; but many astronomers (not lunar specialists) believe that "N" has always been there, and was merely overlooked by earlier observers. I cannot agree with this.

H. P. Wilkins admits that dark patches appear from time to time in this area, and that, if they are not vegetation, then they may well be due to some kind of clouds. He suggested the possibility of dust shot from the interior. We cannot accept the dust theory because there is not sufficient atmosphere to support dust even for a few hours. Regardless of the cause, dusky areas are sometimes seen on what was previously a bright patch. Such shades have also been seen along the edges of the great Hyginus crack, which shows up so sharp in the drawing. There is a dark patch to the west of Hyginus which varies in size but *appears to be flush with the plain.* Surface activity?

Between the lunar Caucasus and the Alps there is an intriguing crater called Cassini, which contains two minor craters and a few hills. The larger of the two has long been known to have something within it; but not until April, 1952, was that "something" seen with any certainty. With the giant Meuden telescope Wilkins discovered an "'extraordinary" appearance within "the washbowl," as he christened this crater, very white and shallow, perfectly circular with a minute pit like a plug hole.

The "washbowl" is approximately two miles in diameter, but the pit is only 500-600 feet across, and cannot be seen except with the very largest of telescopes and at certain phases of illumination. While this may be what geologists would denote a *cauldron* on earth, it is difficult to believe that a cauldron would have such a smooth concave interior. This reminds us of the white patches like Linné which have these little pits in them, about which there is always some doubt, apparently, as to whether they are actually depressions or domes.

Bill Raub, who spreads UFO news in Southern California, told me about a recent sighting on the moon. He was using a 7 x 50 binocular about 9:00 P.M. on April 15, 1954, when he suddenly noted a light about as bright as one of Jupiter's satellites. It pulsated and finally flickered out.

It was definitely over the moon's surface, near the edge of the disc. It was not a star in occultation,* for Bill is familiar with that phenomenon. The light behaved as if guided by intelligence. He reported the event to several agencies, but none deigned to reply.

Raub's observation is only one of many, old and new. I believe they substantiate persistent UFO activity of varied types. I believe that these UFO are large, and that their movements are correspondingly sluggish, judged by our standards. I hope some means of observation may be devised to speed up the appearance of the motions or activities so as to make them intelligible, as recent speed-ups of seismological shock waves which require min-

---

* Occultation: an event similar to an eclipse. In fact it may be considered an eclipse. Occultation is said to occur when a large body such as the moon passes between the observer and a smaller object such as a star, or distant planet. Or, an occultation takes place when the satellite of a planet, Jupiter for instance, passes behind the disc of the planet.

utes to complete a cycle, have made earthquakes audible in all of their awesomeness.

◆ Beaten to the Moon? ◆

W. J. B. Richards listed in *Astronomical Register* (volume XVII, 1879, page 100) eighteen lunar objects suspected of change, and asked for consistent observation. Birt divided these into three classes: 1. Objects that have changed appearance and form since they were noted by earlier observers. 2. Objects more strictly variable, changing in tint, shape, outline, because of variable angle of illumination or causes unknown. 3. Objects seen as bright points on the unilluminated part of the moon.

This means that the reality of changes on the moon has been recognized by top authorities for at least a century.

Richards offered another list of possibly variable objects on the moon, in the *Astronomical Register* (volume XIX, 1881, page 43). Here are fifteen of them:

Object	*Variable Feature*
1. Posidonius Gamma	Brightness
2. Paludes Amarae	Curved dark streaks; tint
3. Linné	Form, color, size
4. Hyginus-N	Tint, size, shape, density
5. Gruithuisen's "City"	Form, permanence
6. Floor of Archimedes	Streaks
7. LaHire	Tint and form
8. Neighborhood of Mont Blanc	Bright spots sometimes seen in the dark beyond terminator
9. Neighborhood of Carlini	Same as above
10. Plato	Tints and streaks; bright spots, lights
11. Aristarchus	Bright spots as in 8; also other variations

Object	Variable Feature
12. Crater rings of Chichus	Size
13. Floor of Billy	Tint
14. Spot on west side of Werner	Brightness
15. Messier and Messier-A	Relative form and size.

Professor Thury of Geneva reported a change in the center of the crater Plinius, in September, 1889. With his six-inch refracting telescope he saw, instead of the usual two hills in the interior of the crater, *a circular, chalk-like spot in the center, which had the appearance of the orifice of a mud volcano.* (Why do selenographers have to relate everything to volcanoes?)

Clearly this was a UFO. We are getting used to "something of a temporary nature with a little spot in the center," which fills or replaces craters, and whose numbers have increased from two in 1865 to about 200 today. Something of the sort was in the center of this crater and temporarily obscured its two known large hills. Linné was covered by one. What is this little pit or nipple on top of the hazy white spots?

According to *Nature* (volume 12, October 7, 1875, page 495) Loftus, an experienced observer, was aboard H.M.S. *Coronation* at Kopongsom Bay, in the gulf of Siam, in July, 1875. Together with Mr. C. E. Davidson, he reported two remarkable protuberances on the moon. On July 13, about midnight, they noticed on the moon's upper limb a projection visible to the naked eye and similar in color to the illuminated part of the moon. On July 14, at 8 P.M., the moon was observed perfectly clear without a vestige of the projection seen on the previous night. However, a small one was noticed in a different position on the limb and which disappeared before the moon rose on the 15th. Visibility to the naked eye implies a diameter of several miles.

Note that these protuberances were on the smooth circular edge of the moon, called the *limb,* not on the *terminator,* the borderline between night and day on the moon, where detached spots of light are frequently seen because of sunlight on mountain tops whose bases are in shadow. Our observers saw a mobile or temporary object as large as a range of mountains.

In the *Intellectual Observer*, (volume II, 1867, page 201) we read an almost prophetic phrase. The writer and diligent observer, Webb, was the author of a textbook for observers called *Celestial Objects for Common Telescopes*. Describing the craters Aristillus and Autolycus, Webb said:

> The character therefore of extreme relative depth—the goblet-like impression—which might be easily received in such cases from the appearance of the shadow near the terminator, is thus shown to be somewhat deceptive when checked by actual measurements. *But though our lunar cups may thus be said to be turned into saucers, enough remains in their proportions to fill us with astonishment.*

Webb was discussing the traits of craters like Linné, which seem to change their appearance from deep cup-like to very shallow saucer-like depressions, or white spots having no apparent depth. This, one of the strangest phenomena of the lunar landscape, has never been explained satisfactorily. I believe it has significance in the study of UFO on the moon.

Let us next examine a description of physical changes on the moon, published in the *Journal of the British Astronomical Association* (volume 48, 1937-8, pages 347 ff.). The report is by Robert Barker, who firmly believes that lunar changes are taking place, particularly vegetation with a very short life cycle.

On March 16, 1932, Barker was observing the Copernicus region which had just appeared over the terminator. From Copernicus to about latitude S. 20°, the terminator was misty and hard to define. Outside this area it presented its usual sharp definition. This phenomenon lasted about three quarters of an hour. The night was clear.

Barker suspected his equipment and his own sanity, so to speak. He cleaned the lenses of his eyepieces and telescope but the indefiniteness persisted. This reminds us of the great shadow on the moon seen by Russell and Hirst from the Blue Mountains of Australia.

There is no question in my mind but that cloud-like things are moving around in the space not far from the moon, whether considered UFO phenomena or not. They may be cloud-satellites, moving in orbits. *This* cloud may have been just above the surface of the moon.

Barker wrote his article comparatively recently—1937. He staked his reputation on the reality of vegetation in some craters.

Barker avoids astronomical dogmatism as nearly as a professional astronomer can. He is practically defying the science of astronomy to deny his conclusions that the changes take place and vegetation exists on the surface of the moon.

The *Astronomical Register* (volume XXII, 1884, page 93) contains a discussion about small craters which many observers of that era considered volcanic. In this article, Elger cited two examples on the floor of the crater Atlas. Other observers saw only one, yet Elger insisted that it could not be missed.

Such little craters seem to appear occasionally, and astronomers have not been able to agree on reasons for their origin. Meteoric impact *or the action of UFO* must be invoked to explain them.

Elger mentioned several drawings he had made in 1870-71 showing small dark patches, under various conditions of illumination. In comparing his drawings with previous observations, he found discrepancies hard to account for, unless change had taken place in the intervening thirteen or fourteen years. For example, one form had become triangular in that time. (A geometric shape suggests intelligent construction.)

Elger attacked dogmatists who denied change. He said:

In many quarters opinions are so pertinaciously wedded to the gratuitous notion that the moon is an exceptional body devoid of any form of life or activity that nothing short of a paroxysmal catastrophe involving the destruction and complete obliteration of Tycho, or of some equally familar formation, would settle the question of change.

Elger easily saw clefts on the floor of Mersenius, which had been seen by the French astronomer Gaudibert, while Schmidt, observing constantly over a period of years, had missed them. Elger commented: "Except on the supposition that it is either a recent formation, *or is frequently obscured from causes other than*

terrestrial, I cannot account for this discrepancy in observation."
(Italics mine.)

Consider the reports of the amateur astronomer, Proctor, author of popular books and many articles on astronomy, one time editor of a prominent English popular scientific journal. In 1878 he wrote a violently reactionary article in the *Echo* of London, berating astronomer Russell in Australia for saying he had seen a huge shadow on the moon. Perversely, in two other articles written the same year, he had taken a liberal and open-minded attitude regarding changes on the moon, even while questioning the validity of much of the evidence presented by other observers.

Proctor doubted the reality of changes in Linné and Hyginus-N, but admitted the unreasonableness of expecting the moon, with one and a half million square miles of visible surface, to continue in unchanging stillness century after century. He said: "But it must be confessed that the evidence of change is not satisfactory, while the evidence of such systematic changes as we associate with the existence of life seems wanting altogether." Elsewhere, discussing Linné and Hyginus-N, he observed that: "Changes may possibly have occurred, but if they did, they must be volcanic."

In his book, *The Moon,* he says: "So far am I from considering it unlikely that the moon's surface is still undergoing changes, that, on the contrary, it appears to me certain that the face of the moon *must be undergoing changes of somewhat remarkable nature,* though not producing any results which are readily discerned by our imperfect telescopic means." (Italics mine.)

Fauth categorically denies all changes on the moon, yet postulates a deep cover of ice on the moon. This is inconsistent, for ice, being amorphous, cannot possibly maintain itself indefinitely in any rigid outline. Fauth admits unexplained discrepancies in the maps of various areas. For example, Madler omitted seventeen craters of such dimensions that they ought not to have escaped him. He included 337 small ones that Fauth could not find! When Fauth failed to find a twelve-mile crater mapped by Schmidt, he dismissed Schmidt (one of the best lunar observers of all time) as one who did not know what he was doing. He dismissed many other observers similarly and even denied Hyginus-N completely.

Can one avoid questioning the basic accuracy of a man so opinionated, so apparently afflicted with a mental block?

In the *Astronomical Register* (volume XXIII, 1885, page 144) Elger reported a very dark rectangular formation, southwest of the crater Menelaus. Schroeter showed this as a large crater designated as "a," inserted a somewhat smaller crater "b" to the north of it. In Elger's time there was no trace of it beyond an ill-defined white spot, never seen as a depression by Elger. Elger also commented on two very curious *square* depressions of great depth near by.

Question: Are these rectangular formations surface mines or strip mines by any chance? If so, by whom are they worked?

The crater Posidonius is always coming in for notations of changes and variability. Schroeter found repeated changes in the small inner details during the latter part of the eighteenth century, but Beer and Madler, in observations during the first quarters of the nineteenth century saw nothing unusual. Yet, on Feb. 11, 1849 Schmidt found this crater to be *shadowless,* as had Gruithuisen on April 7, 1821. *The phenomenon of one crater out of thousands suddenly appearing without shadow defies all explanation unless you invoke intelligent control.*

The undeniable changes observed in the pair of craters called Messier and Messier-A still remain to be explained by astronomers. Some attribute these changes to chemical deposits which alter their size and visibility with the cyclic change in heat and illumination from the sun. However, if this is true, we must have two different substances, for the Messier reaction to heat and light is the reverse of that observed in Linné.

As we shall see, their real changes in shape are even more significant.

The interior floor of the crater Archimedes was found smooth as a mirror by Beer and Madler early in the nineteenth century; but it was not so in 1860. Grey, in 1880, observed changes; Gruithuisen saw a small crater; Knott saw seven.

Just north of the crater now called "Schroeter," Gruithuisen discovered, in 1822, a "regular" formation known now as "Gruithuisen's City," consisting of gigantic ramparts, visible only when near the terminator. They extend about twenty-three miles along each side of a central rampart, from which they slant away southeast and southwest, about 45°, like the ribs of a leaf. The pattern appears obscured by clouds at times. Later, the pattern changed, and Gruithuisen sometimes had trouble making it out. Beer and Madler could not find it until 1838. Some of the other observers who have seen it do not consider it "artificial." It needs most careful study.

The nature of Archimedes-F has been seriously questioned because records, by independent observers, have variously shown it as a bright spot, a hillock, or a projection on the inner slope of Archimedes. Between April, 1880, and June, 1881, in the "incredible decade," it was seen as a crater. Its observers then considered their notations as final, and deprecated the "unreliable" work of their predecessors. We have the same attitude today toward *them*. If variations are ruled out, then all previously observed reports must seem the work of idiots. Defying critics, Mr. T. P. Grey upheld variability in Archimedes-F of which he had made a special study.

In the *Selenographical Journal* (October 15, 1879) Dr. A. von Bienczwski of Jaslo, Poland, reported mysterious appearances and disappearances of certain clefts in the neighborhood of Hyginus, which he related to the constantly changing appearance of Hyginus-N and "the possibility of similar occurrences with *other craters which come and go.*" He said: ". . . It may be possible that local occurrences, of a kind we are not acquainted with, may cause temporary obscurations of these objects."

He pointed out that Hyginus-N is not always seen with equal distinctness and comes very close to suggesting, outright, operations on the moon not accountable by "natural" activity. Gruithuisen maintained throughout his life that he had seen evidences of habitation on the moon, which is to say of "intelligence." Mentioning a little crater in Marius, von Bienczwski insists that Beer and Madler could not have overlooked it had it been there in their time. Gruithuisen saw it with a 3½" telescope on March 31, 1825.

Patrick Moore notes that close to the western rim of the crater Fontenelle, on the border of the Mare Frigoris, Madler drew a regular *square enclosure* with high mountainous walls. Denning, in *Astronomical Register* (volume VIII, page 86) comments on it as "a strange formation west of the crater Fontenelle." The conservative Beer and Madler commented that this would "throw the observer into the highest astonishment."

This is how Neison described it: "*A perfect square, enclosed by long, straight walls about sixty-five miles in length and one mile in breadth; from 250 to 350 feet high.*

"*Today the enclosure is incomplete. Current observers note that the southwest wall is no longer there, but there is a very noticeable mountain-mass some twenty miles southeast of Fontenelle which Madler and Neison have 'conspicuously misplaced'* (sic)."

Selenologists have, from time to time, called attention to a general element of parallelism or geometric shape, in this region. This is another way of saying "artificiality," a naughty word in astronomy. The most curious example is Madler's square.

Webb describes the ramparts as being very unequal in height, one being little more than a light streak. "*Yet,*" he says, "*they are so regular that it is scarcely possible to imagine them as being natural—until we find that they are sixty-four miles long, 250-300 feet high and one mile or more thick.*" (Italics mine.) Unfortunately, as Webb points out, this significant object, like so many others, lies in such a position that years may pass without a really good view of it. Why are artificial objects generally limited to lunar areas out of the line of direct and easy observation?

In Webb's discussion of this rectangle in his *Celestial Objects,* we have clear evidence favoring the case for the UFO. Webb, a conservative but open-minded observer, says forthrightly that only the size of this "thing" prevents it from being considered artificial.

But consider the Chinese wall which is *1500 miles long,* and of a size that could be seen from the moon at times when shadows were long. And what are we to say of a rock bridge on the moon with a span of twelve miles?

Why should we reject construction, merely because it is somewhat (and only somewhat) larger than we are accustomed to seeing? True, this structure would be a major undertaking today—larger by far than any unit structure made by *modern* man. But the "ancients" had ways and means beyond our ken. The forces and "men" that erected the colossal structures at Sacsahuaman, Tiahuanaco, Angkor Wat, Easter Island and the great Pyramid of Gizeh could have built walls, or halls, a mile thick and 250 feet high. They could have done it even on the earth where gravity is much more intense than on the moon.

In UFO-selenology we deal with entities which fit into craters of one to four miles diameter. Surely Madler's "square" does not represent in detail anything that could be considered disproportionately large in comparison.

The stones at Baalbek weigh about 1,200 tons; and there was a monolithic structure at Tiahuanaco which must have weighed at least 8,500 tons. These were moved, fitted, and placed, as were the colossal statues, walls and blocks of Easter Island, Sacsahuaman, and others. Sacsahuaman, in fact, is large enough as a *single structure* to be seen from the moon with an average telescope. A levitator which could lift these terrestrial megaliths could easily lift far greater objects on the moon, where they would weigh much less.

Possibly the stone citadels of earth were but outposts of those greater ones on the moon; smaller outposts, merely because the earth's gravitational pull is more difficult to overcome. Many thinkers have postulated an indigenous civilization on the moon.

To return to our subject: the geometrically artificial shape of Madler's "square" is significant, but there is even more significance in the changes recorded in serial observations covering almost 200 years. This "now you see it, now you don't" element cannot be ignored. Something moved these huge walls, picked up a part and dumped it twenty miles away. I am forcibly reminded of the wreckage of the intra-mountain construction at Sacsahuaman, above Cuzco, Peru. The manner in which chunks of rock thirty to forty feet in diameter were torn out of the solid mountain is hardly less awesome than the building of Madler's "square" and Gruithuisen's "city" on the moon.

Just for spice, add the numerous impact craters of Mexico, some of which are "half-craters" like some noted on the moon. *And* they are accompanied by megaglyphs on the scale of those at Nasca in Peru.

But there is also a cyclic element in these movements on the moon.

"Strangely enough," says Moore, "the difference between Madler's representation and the modern aspect was unnoticed for many years, and it was *only in 1950* that Dr. Bartlett directed attention to it." On the other hand, Moore finds data indicating that the formation was about the same in Schroeter's time as it appears now. Moore, unlike Wilkins, seems categorically against change on the moon.

Time after time, in the history of selenography, we find that something was distinctly seen by Schroeter and Gruithuisen, missed by Madler and Beer, and then again seen around 1865-1880 or later, by Neison, Birt, Williams, and others. Then, around mid-twentieth century, still other changes are noted. There is more than merely hints of activity from 1780 to now. This strongly suggests that the activity is cyclic. At least there was an upswing around 1790 and a downswing in the first half of the nineteenth century, and another upswing around 1865-80. Many reports confirm this.

By capable work, Moore, Barker, Wilkins, and others are contributing currently to our heritage of moon lore. Their writings seem vibrant with restraint, for they do seem to believe that significant changes *are* in progress on the moon.

The region south of the crater Picard was shown as featurless by all selenographers up to the first part of the twentieth century. About 1930, Barker found a conspicuous *quadrangle* of prominent craterlets connected by low ridges, where Madler had shown nothing at all. Examination of old drawings showed that parts of this quadrangle had been seen from time to time, but never complete or conspicuous.

Moore says it is now visible through a very small telescope and the whole region is dotted with craterlets and white spots which cannot be mists. His chart published in 1949 showed over seventy. Yet Goodacre, one of the best observers in England, did not see them in 1910. Either this large number of craters and other markings are new, or they were previously hidden by mists or other obscurations. A thin haze would do it, but the question arises how such a haze would be maintained in the very thin atmosphere of the moon. We have to give some thought to obscurations by mists, however, because they have been reported dozens of times.

Schroeter on one occasion drew four deep pits in the interior of the crater Ptolemaeus which he had never seen before, although he had maintained continuous observation of the area. Compare this with the period of Webb's and Birt's observations when there were only two minute craterlets.

These descriptions remind one of "surface mining" in the midwestern coal fields. Many "spoil banks" are extensive enough to be clearly seen from the moon and some would look like "Gruithuisen's city." Would mining on the moon account for the geometrical shapes, the occasional mists and the ambulatory walls of Madler's "square"?

I wonder who has beaten us to the moon—by hundreds or thousands of years?

◆ "Let There Be Light"—on the Moon? ◆

No single indication of UFO activity on the moon is more intriguing than the unexplained, intermittent lights. They have attracted observers for many years, but are not seen with sufficient regularity to be called normal features of the moon. When they *are* noted there is generally some abnormality that indicates intelligent control. Sometimes they fluctuate in a manner unlike the steady glare of reflected sunlight. Sometimes they appear suddenly, shine a few minutes or hours, and as suddenly disappear.

Lights on and near the moon have been seen for centuries— ever since telescopes were first used—and are still seen. Charles Fort listed hundreds of sightings of lights on the moon, but his reports mingled bright spots with lights.

Astronomers make a distinction. What an astronomer calls a "light" is a star-like, glittering point or gleam. When he refers to a light spot or bright spot, he means an *area* that is bright as compared to the surrounding surface but does not have the appearance of a lamp, arc light or blast furnace. Both are pertinent to our UFO investigation.

On June 12, 1865, Charles Grover wrote (*Astronomical Register*, volume III, 1865, page 189):

> On January 1, 1865, I had the good fortune to pick up one of these curious objects. At 6:00 P.M., I directed my telescope to the moon, and saw the dark side with its usual markings very distinctly, and my eye immediately caught sight of a little speck of light, very distinctly seen like a considerable star, a little out of focus. I most carefully studied its position and found it to be just at the east foot of the alps and very near the wedge-shaped valley. It appeared tolerably well-defined and very distinct, and was well seen with a power of fifty in my telescope of 2 inches aperture. I consider it the more interesting as Schroeter picked up a similar object very near the same place in 1768 (September 26), though Mr. Birt does not consider them identical. I believe the floor of Plato to be variable after years of observation.

Now, Birt's opinion is quite pertinent. There *is* other activity in this region, and his opinion that the two sightings are of different phenomena is indicative of the erratic and artificial character of this locality.

In the *Memoirs of the Astronomical Society of London* (volume VI, pages 157-8) William Olbers reported a bright speck in the crater Aristarchus. The sighting was on the night of February 1, 1821. The light differed from the usual faint brightness of that crater when seen on the dark side of the moon. The latter had been seen by many observers, including

Herschel; but the *speck* looked like a star of the 6th magnitude, the faintest to be readily seen in the moonless sky by the unaided eye, but a bright object in a small telescope.

The *Memoirs* (volume VI, pages 159-60) carries a discussion by M. Ward of changes in color inside the crater Aristarchus—from red in 1644 to white in 1821, the year he made his observations.

From *L'Astronomie* (volume VI, page 312): On the 11th of May, 1887, the astronomer A. Fauchier, observing at the Marseilles observatory, was startled to see two bright points of light on the moon. But this is one of many such observations. Astronomical literature fails to offer any explanation better than UFO activity.

Then, in *Monthly Notices of the Royal Astronomical Society* (volume VIII, 1848, page 55), this description of a self-luminous spot on the moon:

On the 11th of December, last, at 6:00 P.M., while Mr. Hodgson of Fir Grove, Eversley, was observing the dark body of the moon, "a bright spot" about one quarter the angular diameter of Saturn, was perceived, which, though it varied in intensity like an intermitting light, was at all times visible. On this occasion, Mr. Hodgson used an achromatic telescope of 5 feet focal length and powers of 50 and 80. The bright spot was best seen with the higher power, probably as he suggests, because the field was darker, but it was instantly visible to the most uninitiated eye when the bright part of the moon was excluded from the sky. On the following day glimpses of the same spot were caught between the passing clouds with a Newtonian reflector; power 40.

This is typical of transitory lights seen on the moon—except for its intermittent quality, which indicates intelligent control, and it may have been "beamed" toward earth.

The following note is from Denning's *Telescopic Work* (page 120):

On June 10, 1866, Temple noticed a remarkable light appearance located on the dark side of the moon in the known position of the crater Aristarchus. The entire area was faintly illuminated by earth shine, but this object did not exhibit the faint white light analogous to that of other craters which are occasionally seen to be luminous on the dark side. On the contrary, it was star-like, somewhat diffused, reddish-yellow in color. It was evidently dissimilar to ordinary bright spots. Temple called it a "chemical brightness."

Throughout all lunar literature, there are constant references to erratic activity in, near, or over the crater Aristarchus.

The *English Mechanic* (volume 25, page 89) reports Mr. C. Barrett as saying that on the night of March 21, 1877, he saw the interior of the crater Proclus entirely lighted, and without shadows. Is it possible to conceive of any "natural" cause for such an event? Since the entire surface of the moon is bathed in sunlight, where there are elevations there must be shadows. When one of these elevations fails to cast a shadow, then man's logical mind requires an explanation.

In the same volume (page 432) Frank C. Dennett writes:

. . . On June 17, 1877, at 10:00 P.M., I fancied I could detect a minute point of light shining out of the darkness which filled the crater Bessel." And ". . . on April 19, 1877, at 10:00 P.M., I thought that Linné had the appearance of a bright, conical peak, *surrounded by a circle of flat needle points* clustering close to it.

This is clearly a description of a peculiar object surrounded by some type of activity too small in scale to be identified. UFO is indicated. The "flat needle points" could be searchlight beams.

In his *Celestial Objects*, Webb says of crater La Hire:

There is nothing striking in its usual appearance, but it was twice seen by Schroeter under very different illuminations, so brilliant as to glitter like a star; and he also noticed changes in its form—I once found it on the terminator—the brightest object in sight and radiating as described by Schroeter. On another occasion I noticed a similar hill about one third of the distance from Lambert to Timocharis, glittering on the terminator like a star with rays.

Hunt says that he saw a striking exhibition of this phenomenon on November 19, 1863. Its brilliant glow was accompanied by flashes of singular brightness. Later it faded somewhat, but remained the brightest object in sight for some hours. Clearly an indication that some intelligently operated mechanism was producing these lights. Note that this is not routine on the moon but is definite and rare enough to occasion comment in technical publications.

James Short, observing an eclipse at Aberdour Castle, Scotland, on July 14, 1748, saw "a remarkable large spot of light of an irregular figure and of considerable brightness, about seven or eight seconds of arc within the limb of the moon next to the western cusp." The Reverend Mr. Irwin, at Elgin, also observed it. Clearly this is abnormal activity and belongs to our lore of UFO on the moon. The description could be applied to photographs taken at Ottumwa, Iowa, of the eclipse of 1869, where a similar bright patch was "explained" away as a reflection of light from a drop of water adhering to the back of the photographic plate.

In any discussion of UFO in space, the eclipse of 1869 deserves a prominent place. It had more unexplained phenomena than any other eclipse on record . . . and a UFO was clearly seen near the moon.

W. O. Williams wrote to the *Astronomical Register* (volume IV, 1866) that on November 24, 1865, observing the moon at about 6:00 P.M., he found the dark part unusually clear and distinct. His eye caught a "very pretty speck of light near the lower limb, towards the northeast and very much like a star of 8th magnitude but very distinct and clear." This sighting lasted an hour and a half, and was verified by other observers. These little self-luminous points of light cannot be ignored— and note that an ardent professional lunar map-maker was so impressed that he spent 90 precious minutes studying it.

Also recorded (volume IV, page 132): During an eclipse of the sun, Schroeter, Harding and Kohler saw a small luminous spot on the dark disc of Mercury. Some observers attributed this to volcanic action. Obviously this was not volcanic action since it would have certainly been too faint to be seen from the distance of Mercury. Nor was it an inter-Mercurial phenomenon, since it was seen against the planet as background. This was a UFO of great brilliance, operating in space, and similar to those seen over the moon.

In *Astronomical Register* (volume XXIII, 1885, page 64), A. S.

Williams called attention to a variation in the brightness of the interior of the crater Boscovich, normally one of the darkest. It brightened very noticeably, then faded. The variations took place in a manner unrelated to the diurnal passage of the sun. He thought these changes were unquestionably due to some "physical" cause. "Physical" is astronomical gobbledegook for UFO!

Several times Mare Crisium has been speckled with minute dots and streaks of light—reported by Schroeter and Beer and Madler; by Webb, who saw them in 1832; by Slack and Engle in 1865. The head of the comet of 1882 was speckled like that *for one night!*

A curious observation of something that looked like a red lamp on the moon was made by Lorenzo Kropp in Uruguay, and reported in *L'Astronomie* (volume IV, page 227).

The following items of things seen and unseen are from Webb's *Celestial Objects,* a most reliable astronomical text book. In the lunar Alps there is a peak 12,000 to 14,000 feet high called Mont Blanc. Close to its eastern foot Schroeter, on September 26, 1789, saw a *small speck of light* on the dark side of the moon as bright as a 5th magnitude star to the naked eye. The light remained in view for fifteen minutes. Normally there is a round, small shadow there which is *sometimes black, sometimes grey.*

Undeniably some kind of activity takes place at this point. Notice that the time of this observation is almost *identical with the time of Schroeter's first observation of the obscuration of* Linné. And this is the first such obscuration of Linné on record. On January 1, 1865, close to the time when the *disappearance* of Linné was first observed by Schmidt, Grover saw this same spot again as a 4th magnitude light, but larger than that seen by Schroeter and unchanged for thirty minutes.

All this drives one to the conclusion that the peripatetic lunar dark spots are UFO or evidence of UFO activity. They seem to occupy and vacate craters, produce lights, come and go, change size, shape, color, etc.

Webb reports that *Mare Tranquilitatis,* at times of full moon, is sometimes covered with small *bright specks* or points.

Schroeter once saw a minute point of light on the dark side of the moon near the crater Agrippa. And in *Astronomical Register* (volume V, page 114) Elger reported a *light spot of 7th magnitude on the dark part of the moon.* He watched it for an hour and during the last fifteen minutes the spot grew fainter. Returning half an hour later, he noted it was gone. He says he has seen similar phenomena several times.

The editor of the *Selenographical Journal* (August 17, 1879, page 62) discussed bright spots on the dark part of the moon:

It is well known that under certain conditions of illumination, Aristarchus appears as a bright point on the dark side of the moon. It is curious, however, that during the present century it has uniformly appeared white, while Hevelius was so struck with its red hues when on the unenlightened (sic) side, that he describes it as being formed "*rupe, rutra, aut sabulo, sive terra rubicunda.*"

In the philosophical transactions for 1792, the unimpeachable authority, Sir William Herschel, states that with a power of 360 on his big reflector, he perceived some 150 "very luminous spots scattered over the surface of the moon during the total eclipse of October 22, 1790." [Again a timely coincidence with the first-recorded disappearance or obscuration of Linné.]

On April 25, 1844, Schmidt saw a bluish glimmering patch of light southeast of crater Pico, within the dark part of the moon, although there are no elevations there to catch the higher rays of the setting or rising sun. There were similar sightings by Gruithuisen and Madler, and, in 1871, by several English observers.

◆ Ice ◆

Fauth, in his comprehensive book on the moon, sets forth a determined case for the moon as being completely covered with ice. He is convinced of the existence of meteoric ice in space, of which there is evidence aplenty in ice falls on earth. Fauth writes that he is "acquainted with some cases where flattish eminences lie *much like thin discs* on the floor of the moon. They generally have a little 'crater' inside them." This description is typical of the features of the variable and unpredictable crater Linné.

As for changes of the lunar landscape, Fauth is "agin" them, like a hard-shelled preacher "agin" sin! He overlooks the fact that ice, being amorphous, tends to flow under continued pressure, as do our glaciers, and that it would be above thawing temperature during the long lunar day. However, his reactionary stance almost proves the case for the UFO, as did C.H.F. Peters' bigoted tirade against intra-Mercurial planets.

We can agree with Fauth that there is ice in space and that it does, perhaps, strike the moon as well as earth. We can agree that the size of an ice-covered spot on the moon will fluctuate when surface temperature rises above freezing during the lunar day.

We cannot agree that the entire surface of the moon is ice. We conclude that some mists seen on the moon are caused by ice meteors when they strike and vaporize and that it is only natural that some UFO activity seen at these points is that of UFO using the water. This explains *some* of the moon's white spots, their periodic changes in size, and their eventual disappearance.

In this way, temporary mists can be explained in spite of lack of lunar atmosphere. Reflection and refraction from them would explain some of the anomalously illuminated interiors of craters. Thus we can thank Mr. Fauth. In taking his unreasonable stand, he provided useful data for us. The circumstances which Fauth cites as being opposed to change actually explain the changes seen.

◆ **Atmosphere** ◆

In *A Guide to the Moon*, Moore has this to say about its atmosphere:

Despite the statements so often met with in textbooks, there *is* a little air left on the moon. However, the atmosphere is extremely thin and no earth-born creature could possibly breathe it. If the moon was once a part of the earth, it is reasonable to assume that it took a small share of the atmosphere with it when it broke away.

As indications of a rarefied atmosphere, lunar twilight has been noted as well as thin extensions of the crescent horns. Also filaments, connecting the tops of lunar mountains, are reported on the dark side of the terminator. These all indicate, to Moore at least, a remnant of atmosphere around the moon—but are not these phenomena merely local nebulosities such as are seen in the craters Plato, Aristarchus, Schickard, and others?

Moore concludes after an excellent analysis that the moon's atmosphere at the surface is about 1/10,000th as dense as that at the surface of the earth. However, because of the relatively lower gravitational pull, the moon's atmosphere at fifty miles altitude should be as dense as that of the earth at the same height. Above fifty miles, the moon's atmosphere may be denser than that of the earth at corresponding levels. So, if there is any space life depending on air in such altitudes, it might find more hospitable conditions at high altitudes over the satellite than over the planet.

In the levels at which meteors become visible over the earth, they should also be visible over the moon. Numbers of lights have been seen moving over the moon, but not as many as theory would indicate, and they have not always been identifiable as meteors. Small meteors such as we see in *our* atmosphere would not be readily seen over the moon, because of their faintness and short arc of flight. A few flashes, lasting one to three seconds, have been seen on the dark side of the moon, which may be the result of meteors striking the surface.

The few known observations of lunar meteor-trails indicate a length of about seventy-five miles which is in agreement with theory. Since meteoric velocity ranges from fifteen to forty or more miles per second, a lunar meteor, seen telescopically from the earth, would appear slow-moving, crossing about one minute of arc of the lunar surface in two or three seconds of time. The very rarity of lunar meteors is indicative, however, of weakness in this whole concept. With our modern telescopes there should be thousands of sightings of lunar meteors, if they were comparable in number to terrestrial meteors.

Selenographers have reported shadows, especially in some craters which were not pitch black. This might indicate a minimum amount of atmosphere, serving as a light-diffusing medium; but it is difficult to explain these localizations on the basis of a generally overlying atmosphere. We face the fact that if any craters show this effect, then all should show it. On the contrary such grey shadows are exceptional. If gas is the cause, the gas is strictly a local phenomenon. Yet it is unthinkable that local clouds could maintain themselves in the presumed vacuum of the moon, unless deliberately controlled.

Sometimes penumbra are seen with lunar shadows, which Moore considers an indication of atmosphere. But the assumption would be sounder if the atmosphere were denser than it has proven to be. The point is, these shadows are very long—hundreds of miles in some instances—and considering the size of the sun, relative to the objects and their shadows, there should be thin penumbras in any case. But none are seen as a rule, and an isolated case does not indicate a widespread atmosphere, but rather a locally controlled lighting arrangement.

On March 29, 1939, Dr. H. P. Wilkins saw the central mountain of the crater Copernicus faintly lit against the black shadow of the floor, for about a quarter of an hour.

There is UFO significance in this. If it were due to atmospheric effect, the phenomenon would have lasted much longer. If it were due to atmospherically refracted light, then it should have appeared all over the surface of the moon. As we have already seen, any number of reported cases of similar abnormal illumination have been wrongly attributed to atmospheric action.

None of these explanations, however, can rationalize the local nature of the observed phenomena. The conclusion becomes inescapable: some type of highly localized "control" is being exercised. And by "control" we mean, in the last analysis, UFO action.

De Fonville pointed out that not only would water vapor freeze on the moon, but the air itself would freeze where the sunlight had been withdrawn for any considerable length of time. This precludes any extensive atmospheric blanket around the moon and emphasizes the restricted nature of clouds and of all phenomena dependent on the action of mists and fogs.

◆ Action ◆

While it is no longer possible to doubt activity on the moon, it is not yet feasible to appraise its exact nature. The resolving power of our telescopes is too limited and our own atmosphere too disturbed. Activity *originating* from sources too small to be readily analyzed through our lenses does, nevertheless, spread into our range, or at least creates by-products which spill over into our cognizance. We will have to make careful deductions based on them, in addition to continuing direct observations in search of basic phenomena.

On earth fog, clouds, mists, etc., are usually considered to be made up of water vapor, or some other volatilized liquid. But on the moon, we have to give thought to other kinds of clouds.

Patrick Moore, after a lifetime of studying the moon, doubts that lunar fogs are water vapor. He suggests that they may be carbon dioxide whose vapor, he deduces, would dissipate more slowly in the rarefied lunar atmosphere; its weight would hold it more closely to the surface, and for longer intervals.

But the probability is remote that *any* gas could maintain itself as cloud, unless controlled, without expanding explosively. Moore points out that these mists or fogs are local and do not prove a moon-wide atmosphere. But I take exception. I cannot believe that, if mists exist, they do not eventually expand and spread uniformly over the surface, unless artificially controlled. Therefore, until it is proven otherwise, I must suppose there is UFO significance in local clouds or mists—in other words, *control.*

Or that these localized things (when very temporary) are dust, which does not have an explosive tendency.

Schmidt, in the early years of the last century, twice saw the innermost cavity of crater A-399 feebly shining at sunrise as though it contained partially illuminated mist, partially obscuring the underlying shadow. A larger crater near the south pole has also shown internal twilight. According to Webb, obscurations in general have been confirmed by reliable observers. In crater Schickard in 1939, Moore saw a dense mist covering its entire 14,100 square miles and billowing over the walls, indicating expansion from a blast or explosion, since the rarefied lunar air cannot support high winds. H. P. Wilkins saw another mist on August 31, 1944, which had disappeared next day.

The crater Plato is noted for mists and clouds, and, for at least twenty years, mists have been seen also in the craters Timocharis and Tycho. Birt repeatedly noted mists in Tycho between 1870 and 1880, the years of the "incredible decade." Klein, who first noted the new crater Hyginus-N, reported something like fog seen several times in the eastern part of Plato in 1878. This has been repeatedly confirmed, particularly by Neison and Elger. It was 1878 when Russell saw a shadow, fifteen hundred miles in diameter, on the moon.

Obscurations of variable density and size are often reported in Plato and seem usually to originate in the same spot near the eastern edge of the crater floor. In A Guide to the Moon (Norton, 1953) Patrick Moore says (page 112): ". . . there are many records of mists inside the crater Plato, and obscurations undoubtedly take place there." His own observations and the recorded observations have convinced him of activity in Plato. He points out that A. S. Williams observed a white spot at the base of Plato's eastern wall in 1892, which Birt, reporting a few years earlier, had not seen. In 1920, Stevenson saw this spot as a small crater with inner shadow, while observing with the great 28-inch Greenwich refractor.

Both Wilkins and Moore failed to see this spot with the 33-inch Meuden refractor in France on April 3, 1952, though most of the remainder of the floor of Plato was clearly defined at the time. Four hours later, the American T. A. Craig could see nothing of the floor with a 12-inch reflector. Moore thinks a mist *or other obscuration* spread over from east to west. This phenomenon in Plato has been seen by many others.

W. H. Pickering, American lunar expert, observing in the wonderfully clear mountain air at Arequipa, Peru, found that changes had taken place since Plato was systematically observed around 1869 to 1880. Moore states unequivocally that changes do take place in Plato. The obvious inference is that the changes in Plato are erratic and non-permanent, which we expect from mists—and UFO.

Such obscurations, in view of the almost total absence of lunar air, make us think of the nebulosities seen in space above the earth's surface, apparently controlled, or directed, or exhibiting volition. I also think of earth's "dry fogs."

In 1892, Barnard saw the crater Thales filled with a pale luminous haze, although all surrounding features were sharp and normal. In 1902, Charbonneaux, with the Meuden 33-inch, witnessed a small white cloud actually forming close to the crater Thaetetus. Mist—dust—smoke? . . . or UFO?

On March 27, 1931, Barker saw the central mountains of Tycho as a curious grey, as if they were phosphorescent, or artifically illuminated, although within a usually pitch-black shadow.

The best example of a lunar cloud was seen by F. H. Thornton, on February 10, 1949, near the "Cobra Head" in Herodotus Valley. Under good observing conditions, and using his 18-inch reflector, he saw a puff of whitish vapor obscuring details for some miles, while the surrounding surface details remained sharply clear.

Mists seem to prefer certain localities, which may be, although not necessarily, an indication that they arise from certain local features of a fixed nature.

On July 26, 1881, the *Selenographical Journal* reported the interposition of a thin cloud over a streak, and that Williams saw an "obscuring medium" spread over a *portion* of Plato. (See also *Astronomical Register*, July 1881, page 181). Consider this along with Gudibert's report of January 18, 1880: "The whole of Mare Nectaris was foggy so that, with the exception of crater Ross, and a *black patch to the east,* no detail whatever could be seen. The fog reached *midway into the floor* of Fracastorius." Here, in the very middle of the "incredible decade" was a definitely limited nebulosity not attributable to a fault in the telescope.

We have accounts of mysterious clouds *passing over the earth.* One was the rapidly moving thing seen over New York by Harrison in the 1870's. Barnard saw a "comet" on May 12, 1881, which *remained two days* and disappeared.

The astronomical descriptions of these nebulosities tally almost exactly with the descriptions of mists and fogs on the moon. Since both manifest UFO characteristics, we cannot but wonder if they are not the same thing. They may be indigenous to the moon . . . what are they?

◆ Obscuration ◆

In the *Siderial Messenger* (volume III, 1884, page 252) Haywood of Otterbein College, Westerville, Ohio, stated that on September 16, from 3:30 to 4:00 A.M., he found a bright glow covering, nearly uniformly, the dark part of the moon. Professor Haywood considered it an electrical manifestation because it was too bright for earthshine, and *it obscured the features of the moon's surface.* The professor said, "This latter fact is puzzling and unsatisfactory." Telling *us?*

Here is the undoubted counterpart or identical cloud that caused Russell's shadow on the moon"! Here it is between the earth and the moon, illuminated by sunlight!

On March 24, 1882, at 10:00 P.M. the Rev. W. J. B. Richards noticed that a part of the dark limb of the moon was considerably brighter than the remainder (A.R. 1883, vol. XXI, page 18). He checked what he saw with several eyepieces. The eastern part of the limb was brighter than the northern and southern parts. This irregularity of illumination is significant as an indication that shadows are occasionally cast on the moon by *partially transparent things in space,* or that these clouds reflect sunlight to local areas.

On page 176 of *Light Science for Leisure Hours* Proctor speaks of the effect of "the earth in meteoric shadow," and suggests that shadows cast by meteor swarms in space may cause erratic cold spells on the earth by shutting off the sunlight.

This would appear to be quite a concession from Proctor, who was so caustic regarding the 1,500-mile shadows seen on the moon, in daylight, by Russell and Hirst. Yet Proctor admitted that the earth may experience cold spells from what he calls meteoric shadows.

Here again is *something:* In the *Astronomical Register* (volume XVII, 1879, page 38) the selenographer Neison reported that ". . . the sky had been too cloudy for the purpose except one night in August, and then a shadow came over the place where the new crater Hyginus-N ought to be." Now—what can we make of that? Wasn't something moving above the surface of the moon at the site of Hyginus-N? One observer, while trying to prove the existence of Hyginus-N, reported something moving about twelve miles per hour at that place.

And the night of the "Maunder Object"! You will find in the *Astronomical Register* (volume XXI, 1883, pages 139-140) that Williams reported an unusual view of the head of the great comet, as seen on the night of November 17, 1882. It seemed to be a large luminous mass surrounded by a much greater envelope. "On closer attention the whole of the large luminous mass was resolved into numberless points of light and looked exactly like a resolvable, globular star-cluster."

Williams was also reminded that, on July 1, 1881, the great comet of that year was preceded by "a bunch of lights" which looked like a star-cluster. Both these comets appeared in "the incredible decade."

Brooks and Barnard saw strange cloud-like organisms in space accompanying the comet of 1882. Schmidt, in Athens, confirmed some of these phenomena and also observed a number of such large entities moving at right angles to the comet, but apparently accompanying it in its forward course. Schmidt, a serious professional, thought this so significant that he published elaborate diagrams of the bodies and their interrelated movements. Viewed in retrospect, the entire phenomenon seems to reflect control of a gigantic and incredible kind.

There is solid significance in the fact that a number of anomalous wonders were seen contemporaneously, some the same evening. These various spatial "objects" have a striking similarity to the local, mottled bulks of glowing "haze" and undulating lights seen on the moon, particularly the "things" in the interior of Plato. They are certainly suggestive of intelligent manipulation on a scale of time and space indicating a different order of existence from ours. The tremendous and deliberate "Maunder Auroral Object" was one of them. (See *The Case for the UFO.*)

On November 20, 1878, (*English Mechanic*, volume 28, page 444) Hammes, an American astronomer, saw an uprush of something in a crater in the vicinity of Baco Barocius and Nicholi. His immediate thought was that it was a volcanic eruption, and he reported it as such to the U. S. Naval Observatory. The disturbance was easily seen for half an hour with a 6½-inch telescope. Was it, indeed, a landing or blast-off?

We may note in passing that 1878 was the year when the Great Red spot broke out on Jupiter; and that the disturbance seen by Mr. Hammes occured within a few days of Russell's 1,500-mile shadow on the moon. November, 1878, opened the "incredible decade" when a number of UFO were see in space.

We can assume that Mr. Hammes saw the dust raised by a UFO as it took off from its lunar crater lair. Throughout the history of such sightings, there is the suggestion that the entities may be several miles in diameter. Hammes' sighting recalls Schroeter's in the late years of the eighteenth century. He saw a swirl of dust or vapor and a crater formed before his telescopic eye.

Parenthetically, for researchers among my readers, the *English*

Mechanic (volume 27, 1878) issued at the opening of the "incredible decade," would repay a thorough scanning for material of UFO import. The subsequent volumes covering 1879-1886, inclusive, are also worth attention.

A remarkable description of the total eclipse of the sun that occurred on November 30, 1853, was sent by Dr. Mosta, Director of the Observatory at Santiago, Chile, to a Lt. Gillis. (*Astronomical Journal*, volume III, number 19, page 145, February 17, 1854.)

> . . . Twelve or fifteen minutes before the beginning of total eclipse, the space between the moon's limb and the bright limb of the sun was instantaneously covered by a dark rosy nebulous matter and I am sure that there was no kind of connection between them prior to the apparition of this matter. As the unobserved portion [sic: does he mean obscured?] of the sun became smaller, this nebula became of a darker color, as though compressed, and finally it became difficult to distinguish the limbs with satisfaction. As soon as the second contact took place, the clouds disappeared, leaving no trace behind.
>
> But from this instant the eclipse presented an aspect more glorious than I can describe. The moon was surrounded by a luminous corona of uniformally white light, *just as you have seen on clear evenings at Satiago, when the full moon chanced to be concentrically covered by a smaller and dark body which, for the instant, caused an annular eclipse.* (Italics mine)

Now what in the world does he mean? Have bodies the size of the moon passed in front of the moon, as seen in Santiago . . . ? That is certainly what he *says*!

Where can we find something more about this?

Almost all the more prominent selenographers have noted temporary obscuration. Clouds in such a rarefied atmosphere as the moon's would seem to be almost an impossibility—yet something does obscure *limited areas* on its surface.

We well know that a gas injected into a vacuum immediately expands to fill the container. On the moon the container is practically infinite in size and, therefore, no natural cloud would exist more than a moment.

Some scientists have suggested that the obscuration is caused by clouds of dust kept in motion by escaping subsurface gas.

While this is remotely possible, it is hardly an acceptable explanation.

On the other hand, dust particles do not tend to dissipate in a vacuum, like gas molecules. Clouds of dust may, therefore, be able to maintain themselves *in space*, perhaps in orbits, for indefinite periods of time.

The alternative we keep turning to is that some of these "space clouds" may have an intelligence incorporated within them which enables them to maneuver not only in space but also on the surface of the moon.

We are reminded of our "dry fogs," which appear inexplicably from no determinable sources. They sometimes maintain themselves over large but limited localities for a period of days or even weeks in spite of winds and other climatic deterrents. These "dry fogs" of ours are certainly as large as those that fill the craters on the moon. They have been known to blot out the stars and sharply reduce sunlight intensity; they are thought to have caused some of the phenomenal dark days of history. Even such conservative writers as Proctor have postulated that during unusually cold seasons vast space-clouds interposed between the earth and sun, especially during the very cold winters of 1878-1883.

Contemplate this: During the total lunar eclipse of May 18, 1761, the moon disappeared altogether for about half an hour and could not be found, even with telescopes. A total eclipse does not mean complete blackout for the moon. For the moon to so disappear is almost unbelievable because normally there is enough light during the eclipse to enable observers to distinguish many lunar surface features. In fact, there have been total eclipses, such as that of March 19, 1848, when the moon was so bright that many people did not believe an eclipse was under way. To account for its disappearance in 1761 we must consider some other cause than an eclipse. It is difficult to envision anything other than an obscuring medium between the earth and moon large enough to blot out the satellite. If this "cloud" was only a few miles above the earth, it would not have to be more than a few miles in diameter to obscure the moon. The fact that it remained stationary over the moon indicates control. Was it hiding in the earth's shadow?

In the *Selenographical Journal* (May 17, 1882) we read a remarkable report by selenographer A. S. Williams on what he describes as an "abnormal appearance," on the evening of March 27, 1882, "in connection with the shadow on the floor of Plato."

. . . the first thing that struck my attention was a long broad streak of light on the floor to the east, and somewhat to the north of the center. There were also some fainter and smaller streaks to the south but what struck me was that *nearly the whole of the floor in the shadow seemed to glow with a curious luminous, milky kind of light.* (Italics mine)

This milky appearance extended over the whole of the floor in shadow except for about one quarter of the diameter of the floor from the west wall, which *appeared quite black.* At 8:10 P.M., clouds intervened and when they had cleared at 9:00, not a sign of this remarkable phenomenon could be seen, the whole floor in shadow appearing uniformly black. It is possible that this is analogous to Schroeter's "kind of fermentation" in 1789 (the time of the first recorded obscuration of Linné) and of the late Mr. Birt's impression that a kind of sparkling or agitation played over the dark floor deep in shadow, on November 20, 1871. From my own experience I recall one instance similar to the above. This was at sunset on Plato on the evening of August 31, 1877, when . . . the crater was seen filled with shadow and over nearly all of the southern half of the floor there appeared a glow corresponding very nearly with the one forming the subject of this note. . . .

There we have several references to the "cloud" that frequents Plato, with evidence that it is self-luminous, or controls a source of light.

In the June 15, 1882 issue of the *Selenographical Journal*, Pratt commented on the "inexplicable" changes in the shape of the shadow of Bessel.

Webb says that Schroeter saw unaccountable, erratic variations in visibility of the crater Manilius.

There are many notes in the *Selenographical Journal* and elsewhere on the varying size of Hyginus-N, which often appears merely as a dark spot. On January 4, 1879, Capron saw it with a brighter border and larger than the reported crater. This is a characteristic shadow with umbra and penumbra. On November

3 and 4, 1878, Baxendale saw it as an irregular dark spot. On November 2, 1878, Noble could not see Hyginus-N, but later the same night it was described by Capron and Baxendale as being very distinct. These are rapid changes.

Remarkable changes have been reported in Posidonius-A. Madler, Schroeter and Gruithuisen all report that *sometimes* the inner shadow is not visible. On April 7, 1821, the small hills on the crater floor were sharp and clear, but there was *no* shadow and almost no darkening. Yet the next evening the crater interior was the usual sharply marked shadow. This disappearance of lunar shadows is one of the most mysterious of lunar phenomena.

◆ Hyginus-N ◆

In the *English Mechanic* (volume 28, December 20, 1879, page 369) Lord Lindsey exhibited a series of drawings, made near the crater Hyginus, *showing markings which changed their appearance completely in twenty minutes.* This is too rapid a change to be ascribed to changing altitude of the sun, which is only 1/28th as fast as on the earth. As we have seen, there have been many other reports of changes near Hyginus, particularly among the dark, ill-defined spots which are apparently flat on the surface, having neither height nor depth.

In the *Astronomical Register* (volume XVI, pages 35-37) there is a transcription of a report made by Neison to the Royal Astronomical Society describing the discovery of Hyginus-N. The area in which Hyginus-N lies was sketched ten times by Schroeter; ten by Lohrman; fifteen by Julius Schmidt, and many times by Neison, himself. All of these top ranking observers saw several craters in the immediate neighborhood but not Hyginus-N, now a prominent object. Yet conservatives insist that Hyginus-N was "there in the first place."

In the talk before the Royal Astronomical Society in 1879, during the "incredible decade," Birt called for a study of the region near Hyginus. He says that Goodacre was studying a

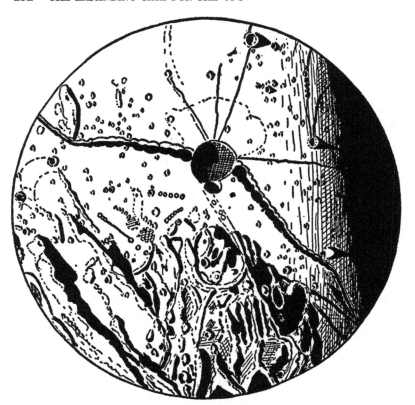

HYGINUS AND HYGINUS-N: *One of the most controversial areas on the moon, where smoky vapors have suggested industrial activity to expert observers.* (From *Our Moon*)

known dark spot southwest of Hyginus when he saw to or three bright spots. These, Birt indicated, were transient features.

In the *Astronomical Register* (vol. XVII, page 144) N. E. Green called Hyginus-N a spot rather than a crater and says that its brightness changed from night to night—"evidently no crater or hollow . . . but seems rather a spot of color instead of a crater, but this cannot be the case because it is lost when the sun rises."

In his recent book, Moore reports continuing activity near the crater Hyginus-N. On April 4, 1944, Wilkins found Hyginus-N much darker than usual, while the south edge of the Hyginus valley was bordered by a narrow dark band for about eight miles.

In the *English Mechanic* (volume 28, page 562) Birt said that there were strong indications of rapid change, *within the span of one evening,* in the area near Hyginus, and noted that *blackness in some areas increased noticeably in thirty minutes.* Variability was particularly noticeable at Hyginus-N which *became invisible between 6:45 and 8:00* P.M. This is very indicative of temporary activity.

In the same publication, (page 605) Capron reported great changes in the size of Hyginus-N on November 2 and December 4, 1878, and January 4, 1879. On December 4, Hyginus-N and the crater Agrippa were misty and hard to focus, although nearby objects were sharp. Three drawings published with this article showed changes. On November 2, 1878, Hyginus-N was depicted definitely as a crater, whereas on January 4, it was shown as a white ring, and much larger. Why?

There is still, seventy or eighty years later, disagreement on the reality of the sudden appearance of Hyginus-N, but the preponderance of positive evidence favors drastic changes, and an abrupt advent of the crater. Discussions are similar to wrangles about UFO. There is little disagreement on the reality of the changes in shading or tone in the immediate area of Hyginus. Dark spots, resembling shadows or fields of vegetation, come and go or change intensity and shape in rapid and unpredictable ways. Whatever may be said of the catastrophic arrival of Hyginus-N on the moon, variations at its site are established.

◆ Spots and Streaks ◆

The *Astronomical Register* (September, 1883) carries a discussion of small bright spots and streaks on the moon. These streaks, and particularly the spots, differ from the large patches such as Linné and those of Hyginus. In fact, these small luminescences almost always are confined to the interior floors of medium-size craters. They are usually, but not always, associated with small, fine, bright veins or streaks on the crater floors or, now and then, on the surface of the smaller seas.

The spots frequently seem to be connected with small craters and crater cones or crater pits. Among the regions where these "glows" are found are Plato, Fracastorius, Mare Imbrium, Mare Humorum, and Ptolemaeus on whose floor they are especially prominent, and where only four of one hundred and forty-five glows are *not* on streaks.

In contrast to the larger, fluctuating white spots which develop into domes, these are scarcely large enough to be clearly resolvable to our telescopes. They appear in considerable numbers, but not all can be seen at any one sighting. It is these, largely, that Charles Fort called lights, making no distinction between them and the glittering star-like lights on the other hand, which are much rarer.

The brighter the streak, the more and brighter the glowings on and near it. There is also a tendency for these glowings to collect in pairs and groups, and their separations range from one second to four seconds of arc, approximately one to four miles. The streaks seem to be elevated, with sometimes a shading on the side away from the sun. There is a tendency for the streaks to be parallel. When they cross, which frequently happens, it is usually impossible to tell which one is uppermost.

Occasionally a small streak can be seen to cross over a larger one and it is assumed that the upper one is newest. Birt tried to relate the streaks to glowing lava, but most of them appear to be mathematically straight which would not happen with flows of lava. The streaks tend to traverse the surface without much regard to local irregularities.

This discussion relates to minute streaks, mostly *within* craters, rather than to the great ray systems springing from Tycho and other large craters.

Drawings of the streak-spot systems in many craters look surprisingly like irregularly laid-out real estate subdivisions complete with street lights at the intersections. We cannot make such an assumption lightly, for such lunar streets would have to be several hundred feet wide. Yet . . . ?

In *Astronomical Register* (1882, page 288) Williams discussed bright streaks and indicated that many of them are double, and that the two components have glows on them, *opposite to each other.* He says the two halves of the streaks sometimes alternate in brilliance, which may make the combined streak appear to shift its position. There is a hint that changes do take place along the streaks involving the glows. Some streaks may be up to a hundred miles long. The central dividing lines are less than a mile wide. There appears to be some connection between streaks and spots, with spots occurring at intersections of streaks.

Webb writes (*Celestial Objects,* page 89) about Mare Crisium:

> On rare occasions it has been seen by Schroeter and in part by Birt and Madler, speckled with minute dots and streaks of light. Something of this kind I saw . . . on July 4, 1832, near [the time of] first quarter. A similar appearance was noticed by Slack and Ingall, in 1865. It would be difficult to say why, *if these are permanent,* they are so seldom visible; a suggestive, though at present unintelligible, phenomenon.

Unintelligible in 1865—before UFO were recognized as space phenomena.

In the *Astronomical Register* (1882, page 165) Williams maintains that these occasions are not particularly rare. He says well-defined bright streaks frequently appear. On May 9, 1881, he remarked that there must be nearly 1,000 streaks and light spots. On March 26, 1882, he remarked that Mare Crisium was one mass of light streaks and spots. These unusual appearances, he said take place once in every two or three lunations, or months.

On April 10, 1873, Schmidt found a small "grey spot" on the floor of Hipparchus. This "temporary object" was seen the next day—but never since although hunted by experts. Another UFO?

Near Pico, Madler showed a bright elliptical spot south of Mare Imbrium. Lohrmann did not show it. Neison, however, saw it at 5° bright, but fainter than in Madler's time. Schmidt could not find it on February 12, and March 12, 1851. Neison saw it several times. *Schmidt once saw a small crater nearby, not seen at any time by anyone else.* A bright spot was seen twice in the Mare Crisium, on May 15 and October 16, 1864. Such evanescent spots are puzzling unless we assume controlled activity of some kind.

In the *Selenographical Journal* (volume IV, February 28,

1881) T. P. Gray reported on a series of observations made by him and by F. B. Allison and T. G. Elger of a spot designated as "L" on the floor of Archimedes. These are important for the theory of UFO.

The first discovery was by Allison on April 19, 1880, when the spot appeared as a faint white patch. In successive observations, brilliance varied from a maximum between June and September and a minimum through October, November, December and January, when it faded to a white spot. Then, on February 11, 1881, in clear air and a good telescopic definition, it suddenly appeared as a *faint circular dark patch* with *two minute but brilliant spots on its border.*

Changeability of this type argues some kind of control, and usually occurs at about the limit of visibility of average telescopes.

◆ Vegetation ◆

There are many areas on the moon which seem to have changes of color as the lunar day advances, some within craters and some outside. These spots change size, spread and contract, or disappear. They move in a manner suggestive of amoebae seen in the field of a microscope.

As the day progresses, the spots darken and become brownish or greenish, as though some kind of quick-growing vegetation sprang up in the morning, and passed through a complete growth cycle in the course of one lunar day, which, it must be remembered, is equivalent to about fourteen of our days. For all practical purposes the moon's day is also its year, although the intensities of heat and cold vary considerably depending on the earth-moon orbital position in relation to the sun.

Interest in the problem of vegetation on the moon has been intense and continuous for more than a century, for vegetation means life. We have been so eager to find life on the moon that we have even developed a sort of brotherly longing for anything as much alive as a lichen. If there is vegetation on the moon, there is hope of higher life as well. *I am confident that there is something more.* The UFO are demonstrating it to all who wish to see.

In the *Intellectual Observer* (volume V, page 360) Webb discussed possibilities of vegetation on the moon. He assembled much favorable evidence, particularly in those patches of cyclic change. Gruithuisen, he remarked, had noted the changing tints so continuously and repeatedly that he was able to classify them into colors, shadings, and types of development. Gruithuisen was convinced that they indicated vegetation.

Webb and others belittled Gruithuisen for this, and for a correlative belief in activity on the moon. Now, in the light of modern work by Moore, Wilkins, Pickering and others, we are beginning to think that Gruithuisen may have been close to the truth. Gruithuisen's observations are now among the most valuable of all for the case for the UFO although repugnant to formal astronomers. He recorded whatever suggested life and intelligent action on the moon. His era *may* have included *another* "incredible decade."

Around the turn of the century, W. H. Pickering, who wrote and illustrated the finest book on the moon produced in America, came to the conclusion that life does exist on the moon, at least vegetable life. Pickering's observations were made in the clear air of the Andes, under unsurpassed conditions.

The floor of the crater Eratosthenes, which sinks about eight thousand feet below the average level of the plain, has cracks and rills seen intermittently, being interpreted by some observers as canals. This is doubtful, but if there *is* any lunar atmosphere, it would be very likely to flow into and settle in these depressions.

The deep floor of Eratosthenes has been found to darken with prolonged sunlight. The dark tint appears after about fifty to sixty hours of sunlight. Since, otherwise, the surface of the moon brightens with rising sun, a growth of vegetation is the simplest explanation of the darkening in the depths of Eratosthenes.

It may be that you and I, liberal thinkers though we are, are too limited in our thinking. After all, there is no reason for assuming that "life" is restricted to only the two forms, animal and vegetable. If changes of tint are definitely observed on the moon, under conditions at variance with what we believe to be requirements for "life," perhaps we have observable evidence here of a new "kingdom."

Tints possibly attributable to vegetation, have been frequently reported in the craters Plato, Atlas, Aristarchus, Grimaldi, and Alphonsus, not to mention the more extensive areas of the Mare Imbrium and Mare Serenitatis. The tints may be either green or brown, and usually retain the same color, though they change in size and density. In Atlas, at least, the "vegetation" has been associated with cracks, leading to tentative conclusions that these are vents for vapor exhalations. Incidentally, they seem to be increasing in number.

The crater Endymion has a long crack and some dark spots which become darker with prolonged sunlight. The areas expand from night to night, as lunar day progresses, and many observers think they may be a kind of moss.

The region of Hyginus, particularly Hyginus-N, has been subject to particularly acrimonious debate. Its many shifting dark patches or spots, which are associated with cracks, seem at best "unstable." They may be clouds expelled from the interior, or they may be growth of some kind. Actually they are so erratic as to arouse speculation that they are at times intelligently directed.

Pickering pointed out that it was impossible to predict the movements of the dark patches from night to night—proof of some kind of life. He thought it was vegetation, but admitted the possibility of masses of insects.

When we say that the spots move, we do not necessarily mean motion that one can actually watch in a telescope (although some such cases have been suggested). We mean that a spot shifts from one place to another overnight, and in unpredictable directions.

The extremely bright crater Aristarchus has been continuously changing over the last fifty to eighty years. Early observers depicted it as uniformly a glaring white, but by mid-twentieth century, dusky bands or streaks have appeared in a radical pattern over the eastern wall, with one or more traceable on the outside plain. Robert Barker and other modern selenographers believe that these are steadily becoming more conspicuous than twenty years ago. Using the greatest telescope in Europe, Wilkins found these "streaks" to be made up of a series of dots and dashes, the nature of which *nobody* knows. They may be alternate patches of bare rock and vegetation. But they are real and they are discontinuous.

Dusky bands on the moon are more common than most people realize. Lenham and Moore have both noted many. More systematic recent observation alone cannot account for their increasing numbers. Robert Barker, who is probably the most persistent student of such lunar phenomena since Pickering, has staked his astronomical standing on the assertion that the shifting dark areas in Aristarchus and Plato are caused by vegetation. Wilkins, noting that the bands are discontinuous and acknowledging that no one can prove Barker wrong, suggests that the vegetation grows in clumps.

Haas and Latimer Wilson made color photos of the moon with a 12-inch aluminized, parabolic mirror. These bring out, near the time of the full moon, an olive green tint in the Sea of Rains, and part of the Sea of Peace, and brownish tints elsewhere.

Color is not really pronounced on the moon. The casual sighting will likely miss colored patches altogether, for the colored matter is sparse as if occurring in clumps rather than overlaying the surface. Competent professionals differ in ability to detect color, probably due to varying degrees of sensitivity to color or even color-blindness. Madler, Schmidt and Pickering noticed colors better than the equally assiduous Goodacre. Greens and brown predominate, but blue, violet, red and purple have also been reported. All seem variable, if not actually transient.

The greenish tint is most common on the great plains or seas, or within such puzzling craters as Grimaldi and Ptolemy. The Sea of Conflicts shows most green when illuminated by a low-angle sun, and the color may therefore be a characteristic rock tint, or a chemical reaction set up by the diurnal cycle. The floor of Grimaldi, on the other hand, in a comparable location, is a maverick, *and may be greenest at most any time of day,* thus manifesting the characteristic vagaries of life.

All things considered, the case for life on the moon, on the evidence of something which *may* be vegetation is indicative rather than definitive, but it is . . . indicative.

Aristarchus, clearly depicted by Wilkins, is the brightest crater on the moon, dazzling through large telescopes. Its steep central hill is most prominent. It is twenty-nine miles in diameter and contains peculiar dusky steaks on the inner slope which are thought to be vegetation.

Wilkins' remarkable drawing of Aristarchus and its artificial appearing area recalls the vast, strange geometric designs on the sands of the Nasca desert in Peru, which were obviously inscribed to be read from the air or from space. The great crack known as Schroeter's valley, whose line has peculiar geometrical angularities, is another example.

Wilkins has recently discovered a very fine crack extending from the angular bend of Schroeter's valley at the lower right in the drawing, to the "Cobra Head" just above the center. He believes this crack is new because he discovered it with an instrument of average size; yet this area has been drawn by dozens of observers in the past. An apparent extension of this crack from the Cobra Head to the base of the outer wall of Aristarchus also seems to be new.

Neison has seen the high mountain a little north of Webb's object #149 near Aristarchus as blurred and violet-tinted when surrounding objects were sharp and white.

Aristarchus is so bright as to be visible to the naked eye on the bright side of the moon, and an average size telescope can pick it up on the dark side. Webb says: "There are, however, as already mentioned, *variations in its light,* noted by Schroeter. Smythe, who has seen it every size, from a 6th magnitude to a 10th magnitude star, says it is difficult to account for the fluctuations." Schmidt and others have seen a darker "nimbus" of violet hue around the wall and also in the interior. Webb, himself, saw a bluish glare in Aristarchus in 1867.

The area around the crater Gassendi is even more startling.

It has a marked geometric and hieroglyphic appearance. Part of its wall, next to the sea, has been destroyed by a flow of molten lava, but within the walls are specimens of practically every type of lunar topography. In the center is a group of large hills, one with a pit on its summit. Many cracks intersect or run parallel, some only a few hundred feet wide and visible only because of their length. These cracks give the crater floor its peculiar geometrical appearance. One of its little hills shines brilliantly at full moon. Schroeter noticed many changes here, and there is a strange diversity of drawings by various observers.

◆ Plato ◆

The problem of the lunar crater, Plato, is the essence of the problem of life, intelligence and UFO on the moon.

The interior of the crater Plato, as charted by selenographers, has almost the appearance of a city map; or rather, perhaps, of one of the modern urban sub-divisions which avoid strictly rectilinear streets.

The bright spots and streaks on the floor of Plato are certainly interrelated. They fluctuate in brightness and visibility, and sometimes in a complementary manner. As one fades, the adjacent one may brighten. The bright spots appear almost invariably on streaks which are less bright, and mainly where streaks intersect. The number of spots is variable, and this variability is not always due to the sun's altitude or the angle of its light.

Webb devoted considerable space to Plato, mentioning, among other items, changes in the shading of the four main streaks on the crater floor, prior to 1855. Careful work by Pratt, Gledhill, Elger and others, coordinated, analyzed and checked by Birt, show transitions of a local nature. The number of specks and streaks varies from observer to observer, from night to night, and from hour to hour. Plato's interior darkens progressively with the rising sun which is contrary to lunar features in gen-

PLATO, HOME OF LUNAR UFO: *Puzzling interior of crater Plato, where objects appear to come and go, or move about. Large "object" at right of crater has never been satisfactorily explained.* (From *Our Moon*)

eral. If this is not a chemical reaction, it is almost certainly due to life of some kind.

Mr. R. A. Proctor, a skeptic regarding changes of the moon, unbent with regard to Plato:

There is one spot on the floor of the crater Plato . . . which has been scrutinized with exceptional care, and some observers are satisfied that as day progresses on this crater floor, the surface darkens as though some form of vegetation spreads over it. . . .

The *Journal of the British Association for the Advancement of Science* (volume 14) contains an almost book-length report on Plato. It was prepared by Birt, foremost selenolgist of his day, acting as clearing agent for reports from all observers and he recommended concerted efforts to solve its puzzles. It would have been a better report had it been less inhibited, for Birt apparently strove to avoid offending the more conservative astronomers.

Birt himself shared the professional resistance to acknowledging anything which might be considered as indicating "organic" change on the moon. Yet, only such hypotheses would seem to rationalize otherwise anomalous observations. These observations demand a new concept of what goes on in lunar craters.

In his book *The Moon*, Goodacre, too, tended to deprecate any idea of changes on the lunar surface. However, he conceded that observers have seen many different white spots in Plato, in various locations, and that it is hard to believe that they do not come, go, and move about. From the evidence in intensive studies made by cooperating teams of observers operating at intervals of several years, he was forced to conclude that the bright spots and streaks vary in visibility, independently of solar altitude.

Goodacre further conceded that the surface of Plato is occasionally obscured by mists or clouds, citing observations of fogs forming on the east side of the crater, where there is a peculiar conformation. Neison had seen the whole surface obscured by a fog at (lunar) sunrise which dispersed later.

Waugh has seen the whole surface of the floor of Plato covered with minute specks of light as if reflected from flocculent clouds near the surface. This is the same mottled illumination reported on several occasions in Mare Serenetatis and other places.

On October 2, 1904, from 1300 until 1600 hours no detail could be seen on the floor by Hodges or by Goodacre, independently. Something very remarkable was observed in 1882 at the time of the greatest and most mysterious of comets. The observer was A. S. Williams, who, on March 27, at 8:10 P.M., while the whole floor of the crater was in shadow due to the sun being low in the lunar sky, saw the interior aglow with a milky light which covered about three-quarters of the crater floor. The remainder was completely black in the normal manner. The glow disappeared after an hour. This would indicate some kind of self-luminous material, able to maintain itself in a vacuum over defined areas.

For the serious reader, the *English Mechanic* (volume 27) contains a serialized article on Plato which has much valuable information.

In the *Astronomical Register* (volume XIX, page 180) is a monthly report on the moon. Birt reports that Williams had seen a new spot in Plato, and that over thirty such spots had been listed. Some were double; some very small, round and white; and they were not always seen with equal facility. Elger reported that spot number five *changed its position* in 1870. Williams reported a new streak which he thought might be lava, flowing from spot three. Spot nineteen appeared to be especially variable, sometimes being seen clearly and at other times not at all. Williams called attention to "a remarkable obscuration of the northwest part of Plato on May 10, and 11, 1881"—which was contemporary with another great and mystifying comet.

Everybody who owns a telescope looks at Plato. Its walls are rugged, but the level floor looks smooth except for a few tiny craters and the capricious streaks and spots. At lunar sunrise the towering peaks of its circular ramparts begin to catch the light, and shine like stars in the still unlighted area on the dark side of the terminator. As the light increases, the entire ring is seen, while the interior remains in blackest shadow. As the interior shadow retreats, the spire-like shadows of the eastern peaks are outlined, with a few scattered craterlets between them, each throwing its own tiny shadow. The white spots and streaks show up only when the sun approaches the moon's meridian.°

Some observers doubt that the floor of Plato darkens at high noon, but none deny that strange things happen there, for sometimes nothing at all can be seen on the floor.

° Meridian: the north-south line across the sky, passing through the zenith, which the sun crosses at noon. From this noon-passage we get the terms A.M. and P.M., meaning ante-meridian and post-meridian.

On April 3, 1952, Moore and Wilkins made independent drawings of the crater, using Europe's largest telescope. They agree perfectly. Neither shows the peculiar pit or craterlet at the foot of the eastern wall. This object has frequently been drawn, but on this date not a trace was seen, although customary detail was present over a large portion of the crater bottom. Four hours later a skilled observer, using a large instrument, saw *nothing at all* within Plato. Craters do not come and go capriciously; yet this occurred again on October, 1952, and April, 1953. It seems impossible to avoid the assumption of a moving and transient obscuring medium which unfolded across Plato in one evening—in less than four hours, in fact.

If this was a cloud of gas, what force kept it within the crater Plato? What directed its determinate course over the crater floor?

Why doesn't some group of observers maintain a sentry-watch to catch this cloud in action?

Wilkins states that he, Moore, Haas and Goodacre have all seen these obscurations. So have dozens of other observers. They have been seen in crater Schickard also, but no systematic, uninterrupted scrutiny has been maintained.

Plato is about sixty miles across and Wilkins says that it has often been suspected of being *invaded* by mists or clouds. He have been seen in crater Schickard also, but no systematic, through apertures on the floor or walls. He thinks dust is a better explanation than mist.

On August 12, 1944, in very clear weather, Wilkins viewed Plato with an 8½-inch telescope. It was then near the terminator, and about a quarter of the floor was already streaked with shadows. The remainder was of a dark grey tint, with nothing distinct showing except a *very bright round spot* near the center. Wilkins assumed this to be the largest of the craterlets on the floor of Plato, but says:

Why an object which usually requires some looking for should have suddenly become a large bright spot is a mystery. It looked as though a little craterlet was filled with something which strongly reflected sunlight. Whatever it was, it completely altered the usual appearance, turning a well-defined craterlet into a bright spot.

Wilkins seems to have failed to note the parallelism here to Linné and other "bowler hat" phenomena which he himself has mentioned. The sunlight reaching the interior of Plato was very oblique, and not likely to evoke bright reflections from anything, particularly the interior of a small crater. These white spots behave in a peculiarly volitional manner, and this one seems to be a quick-acting Linné.

Robert Barker has many times reported areas of changing color on the moon, but none more important than the interior of Plato where a reddish-brown tint has been seen on the western wall and adjoining areas of the floor. Barker is convinced these tints represent life, probably vegetation. Where there is one kind of life, there can also be another.

Plato, Shickard and other craters are badly in need of sustained, continuous, intensive and systemic study. Solve the puzzling problems of Platonian metastasis and vagaries and you will be well on the way toward a new and awesome reappraisal of space life in the earth's environs.

◆ Cleomedes ◆

The crater Cleomedes has not had great prominence in astronomical literature, although Birt (*Astronomical Register*, volume XIX) put the puzzle of its variability second only to that of Plato. He mentioned "shades" seen within Cleomedes and averred that they were not shadows, such as are cast by crater walls and mountains. Birt also mentioned an obscuring medium reported by Schroeter within Cleomedes.

There is a most interesting little story about Schroeter (who reported the first recorded obscuration of Linné) and Cleomedes. When he first looked at Cleomedes, he saw nothing inside but a mountain in the lower (northern) part. Shortly afterwards he saw something "eddying" there and suddenly a well-formed crater made its appearance. We are indebted to

Wilkins for bringing this to our attention. Wilkins says: "Schroeter thought he had witnessed a real volcanic outburst, and that *the crater was formed under his eyes,* but we now know that this was very unlikely and the *reason he did not see it at first was that the lighting was not just right.*" (My italics)

In spite of our approval of Wilkins' generally open-minded attitude, it is difficult to excuse this example of negative snap judgment. Bear in mind that in Schroeter's day it was almost universally thought that all lunar craters were of volcanic origin; meteorites had not yet been accepted as objects arriving from space much less UFO. Schroeter could be pardoned for not assuming that he had seen a meteor strike the moon. Yet, the "eddying" must have been the dust created, agitated and blown aloft by the metoric impact, *or by the sudden movement, or taking off, of a UFO.*

There is no reason except bigotry to deny Schroeter's report, or question its accuracy. The denial of this critical observation is on a par with scientific denials today of the sightings of UFO and science's past denial of meteors. We still have scientists denying in the press that the great Arizona meteor crater was formed by a meteor, in spite of tons of meteoric material picked up on the site. Exploding gas is offered as a substitute, *believe it or not!* Here, in Cleomedes, a crater was *seen* in the act of forming or being vacated, and Schroeter's valid sighting is eloquent refutation of those die-hards who object to lunar changes "because no one has ever seen a change taking place."

Cleomedes may be the king-pin on which turns the whole concept of a progressively changing lunar surface.

◆ Fracastorius and Schickard ◆

In the *Astronomical Register* (volume XXI, page 200) selenographer Elger publishes an extensive report on the crater Fracastorius. Forty or more light spots were known, he says, but few were accurately mapped or located. He says of spot (a):

This puzzling object is situated near the center and on the culminating point of the irregularly convex floor. Under high illumination it is generally recorded as a single round spot without definite outline, but with a central bright point. However, it is described sometimes as double, consisting of two large hazy spots with a *minute bright point on each. Occasionally it is seen three-fold or even four-fold.* On January 6, 1881, a small craterlet was seen on a *short tongue of light* proceeding from a large ill-defined spot to the west of it. . . .

(b) A *heart-shaped mountain* sometimes seen as a crater, which Schmidt, in his large map represented as *four ridges surrounding a square space.*

Those white spots with brighter points on the top are indicative of UFO. The bright point may well *be* the UFO.

Elger also described a spot (c) in Fracastorius, which, under a high sun, appears as a large, round, nebulous spot (like Linné). However, in oblique light, it resembled a low, circular hill or "round-topped tableland," which cast a shadow. Then it was one of the "domes," or Wilkins' "bowler hats." In spite of many observations, Elger never saw it as a crater until the 24th of January, 1883, when it *had a remarkable appearance:*

It seemed to be surrounded by a peculiar glow quite different from the lights of the other spots on the floor of Fracastorius, and in the center of the glow I could just distinguish a delicate crater of the most minute type, which would certainly not have been visible had not the definition been exceptionally good.

Only four or five of the more than fifty objects listed within Fracastorius have had their positions accurately determined, and these have produced very puzzling data, hinting changes.

There is also the huge plain of Schickard, not far from Gassendi. It is 134 miles in diameter, and walled in by mountains. Its surface varies from dark to light tints of grey. Wilkins states unreservedly that there can be little doubt of its extraordinary variations. The interior may be beautifully clear one night, so that craterlets and cracks stand out distinctly, but on the next night everything in the interior may be veiled. In this respect it parallels Plato.

Elger commented on the Schickard tints that the phenomenon

has not received sufficient attention. "In no other lunar object are there peculiarities of tint more prominently displayed, or better calculated to induce an attempt to discover some feasible hypothesis to account for them."

Barker is convinced that the changes of tint are produced by vegetation which completes a growth cycle within the fourteen earth days of sunlight comprising the moon-day.

Elger also said:

> In connection with many observations, it is strange that Schroeter should describe as distinct objects two craterlets in the interior of the crater Schickard which are now the faintest craters in its interior, and fail to see many others which are now certainly easily detected.

Reports of lunar activity which lay buried in the archives of nineteenth century astronomical literature are now vibrating with new meaning, and thanks to Patrick Moore and H. P. Wilkins, English selenographical traditions are being carried forward. The new contributions may well be the most sensational made in astronomy.

I believe the discovery of life and intelligence in the environment of the earth-moon binary system is of as great ultimate importance to man as the photographing of new galaxies, millions of light years away. I believe that this discovery, and our consequent awareness of this space intelligence, is of vastly greater and more immediate importance to us. It has the effect of putting us into a new world. Once this new world is established, contemporary science will doubtless forget its opposition and claim credit for a new intellectual outlook.

◆ Alhazen ◆

In the *Astronomical Register* (volume V, page 170) Birt gives an intimate account of the lunar crater Alhazen:

> This crater has been very puzzling to observers because of the protean shapes it has assumed. Sometimes it has presented the appear-

ance of a depressed grey surface within a ring; at others, that of a longish flat ridge. Perhaps the most curious . . . is that of its general *indistinctness* [italics Birt's], while neighboring objects have been well defined—a phenomenon which I have often noticed in other cases; and this is strongly in contrast with its having been seen with extraordinary distinctness even when near the limb. These phenomena were recorded by Schroeter at the end of the last century. In 1825, it could not be found by Kunowsky; but in 1827, Pastoroff and Harding could always see it. Kohler, in 1828, recognized it as corresponding to Beer and Madler's Alhazen, but observed that it was *very variable in aspect*. During the progress of Beer and Madler's survey, it appears to have been missing, as they could discover no ring mountain in its place. In 1862, I found it to consist of two ranges of mountains that under some circumstances assumed the appearance of a crater; but I was then quite unable to detect with an aperture of 2¾ inches, the slightest vestige of a real crater. On July 5, 1867, I saw it under very favorable circumstances with the Royal Society's achromatic of 4½ inches aperture, power 230, Schroeter's pair of craters *lambda* and *delta* in its neighborhood being very distinct. I then ascertained that Schroeter's Alhazen is really a crater situated on the surface between the two ranges of mountains and but slightly depressed below it. Although not greatly depressed, it is sufficiently so to present under this illumination and visual angle the true crater form. It would seem that its apparition as a crater is rare, probably from a number of causes.

Here is another clear-cut case of periodic variation in lunar activity. Again and again, on reviewing recorded observations of specific lunar areas, we find that what Schroeter saw in the latter part of the eighteenth century was not seen by observers in the first thirty years of the nineteenth century. Often these things were again seen in the second thirty years, missed again in the third thirty, and seen again in our own times. This "thirty-year" cycle is only a rough assumption. I am willing to consider any cyclic interval from eighteen to fifty years for these lunar vagaries; but cycle there does seem to be.

◆ Messier and Messier-A ◆

From 1829 to 1837, the selenographical team of Beer and Madler made over 300 observations of the pair of craters which they called Messier and Messier-A (now called Pickering).

Beer and Madler described them as being exactly alike . . . startlingly so. Several observers have since measured them and described them in detail. Pickering is now described as triangular and Messier as elliptical, whereas, earlier, they were identically circular. Pickering usually *but not always* appears larger. Moore thinks these changes are illusory, but does not deny them entirely.

Moore says that Klein twice found mists in the crater Messier, and Moore himself has several times found both Messier and Pickering to be blurred. Again this suggests a strip-mining operation to us.

Moore states unequivocally that on August 20, 1951, there was a brilliant white patch inside the crater Pickering, so brilliant it could not possibly be missed. Such a sighting is pertinent to the problem of UFO. There are far too many such observations for all of them to be accidental, and note the similarity of these transitory white patches to space clouds which have been seen.

Fauth's map of Messier and Pickering shows the two as of very different size and shape. Goodacre thought that Messier and Pickering do not actually change and the apparent changes are due to differences in illumination at different phases of the moon. This obliges him to discredit earlier observers such as Schroeter and Gruithuisen, which he does, saying that their drawings were full of mistakes.

Wilkins says of Messier (1954): "This is the more westerly of the pair, the other being Pickering. They were described by Madler as being exactly alike, but now are not only different shapes but exhibit variations." Thus, the very latest authority establishes that the lunar craters are undergoing variation and change, which suggests that powerful, *intelligently* directed forces are at work there.

Strip (or surface) mining, which can take in large areas, can explain much.

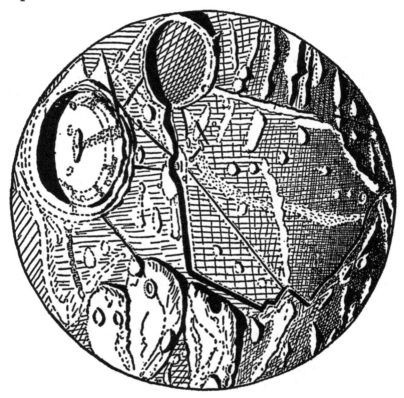

ARISTARCHUS, HERODOTUS AND SCHROETER'S VALLEY:
Showing artificial appearance of certain lunar regions.
(From *Our Moon*)

◆ Selectivity and Structural Similarity ◆

Any description of the lunar surface should contain a comparison with the terrestrial landscape. Scientists of the past have concentrated on emphasizing the spectacular differences and contrasts. Yet there are some similarities as well and, strangely enough, it turns out that the similarities are more sensational than the contrasts.

It has been reiterated that the earth has nothing comparable to the great ring plains and craters of the moon, such as Ptolemy, Plato, Cleomedes, etc. Yet there is accumulating evidence that analogous features do exist. Long Bay, on the east coast of South Carolina, is the western rim of a vast submerged crater. Belcher Islands, in Hudson's Bay, appear to be outcrops of the central peak of a crater whose eastern rim makes a semi-circular notch in the coast. Ungava Bay seems to be a great crater hole, and the proven meteoric crater "Chubb" two miles in diameter, lies between the two. The entire Gulf of Mexico resembles the lunar seas.

Dr. V. B. Meen, of the Canadian National Museum, has demonstrable evidence, on Canadian geological maps, of a walled plain or crater thirty miles in diameter, which has escaped detection from the ground.

But the most striking resemblances are in Mexico, on whose high volcanic plateau there are also clusters of explosion and impact craters not yet studied by formal science. Their extraterrestrial origin is categorically denied by geologists, simply because the craters occur in volcanic regions. These craters range up to at least a mile and a half in diameter. It is among these that we may observe astonishing similarities to certain features of lunar topography.

In the *Astronomical Register* (volume II, page 183), Birt called attention to a phenomenon which he described as "half-craters," which have been brushed aside as mere curiosities.

It seems that many meteoric impacts should be slanting and should produce distorted craters. But almost all lunar craters are circular, girdled with mountainous walls. The absence of distorted craters has been a frequent argument against the impact theory of crater formation. At first thought, these half-craters would seem to fill the gap. Yet they are too scarce to substantiate the meteor-impact theory. Their scarcity and abnormal profile make them objects of suspicion. What caused them? Perhaps the similar topography of the Mexican plateau may provide some clues, particularly the cluster of impact and explosion craters. Some are perfectly symmetrical, circular, walled pits like the minute lunar craters. They are potential laboratory specimens, which, up to now, we have refused to study because they are in a volcanic region. They are proven in many ways to be of extra-terrestrial origin. One lies on a mountain slope and has a secondary crater inside—like many lunar craters. The largest is a mile and a half in diameter.

But they are of two types: symmetrical, circular rings; and elliptical "half-craters," on one side of which no sign of debris but on the other, debris piled up to mountain heights propor-tional to the size of the pits. The underlying lava layers are distorted and bulge upward. Where there is no debris the rims are clean-cut, sharp. The rims on the hilly side are shattered and rugged. An *uncontrolled* explosion or volcanic eruption dis-placing the surface on one side only is difficult to conceive.

About half the group are normal and the rest half-craters. The axes of the half-craters are parallel to each other and the piled debris is at the northwest end of the ovals. The lunar half-craters also have their debris to the north.

Questions: What caused these craters? Why are half of them elongated and non-symmetrical? Why are they in a cluster? Why is there debris on one side only—*the same side in each?* Why are they located in areas almost identical in appearance and condition with lunar areas containing similar small pits? Why are these crater-pits so identical in size and appearance to the small lunar craters which appear and disappear occasionally? Has this small area served as a landing and take-off field? Could some-thing blasting off from the Mexican plateau leave debris on one side only of a huge crater? Is there selection and control in the alignment of the asymmetrical craters? What is the connection between the circular and the non-circular craters in the same group?

The largest of these puzzling craters is a mile and a half in diameter, and the hill of debis on its northwest edge is about three hundred feet high. A local resident who made soundings in a small boat could not reach bottom and declared it to be *"muy profundo."* (The central pit on the top of Linné is also assumed to be "very deep.") Debris is heaped in a gradually ascending ridge around 190° of the rim of this big crater. The remaining 170° is level with the plain. The half-craters on the moon are similar.

Webb observed that incomplete surface rings are more common in the lunar north. Ours are in the northern hemisphere. The heaping of the debris is usually on the northern rim; so, too, in Mexico. There are far more double-craters on the moon than the law of averages can explain. There are at least two double-craters in Mexico and several multiple craters indicative of superimposed impacts or departures. Both in Mexico and on the moon, multiple craters tend to line up along a North-South axis. Both in Mexico and on the moon the craters appear in clusters, and along straight lines.

Webb said that we have nothing on earth similar to the double, multiple and half-craters of the moon; but that was a hundred years ago. We do have them.

In the "incredible decade" a Mexican astronomer saw more than a thousand objects cross in front of the sun, *flying in pairs.* His photo of one, a cigar-shaped affair, was published in the French journal, *L'Astronomie.* This may have been the first genuine photograph of a space ship, but in those days they didn't dream of UFO. What were those thousand objects, in pairs, seen at Zacatacas?

Fauth supports Webb and others regarding the formation of double and multiple craters. In his book on the moon he presented many fine examples. Their arrangement and frequency preclude explanation by statistical laws. Even the arch-conservative Goodacre stressed double objects and multiple craters and illustrated them in his book *The Moon.* There *must* be *some* significance in the analogous structure and distribution of the double craters in Mexico, and on the moon.

East of Mexico City, there is a splendid double or twin crater of a size that would be barely discerned from the moon in an average telescope. It is not a volcano and is not recognized by science.

H. T. Wilkins (not to be confused with astronomer Wilkins) says in a letter to me that he has valid reports that in similar rugged country in neighboring Guatemala, a huge UFO is using a charred and blackened crater in Northern Guatemala for an operating headquarters.

◆ Unfocusable Nebulosities ◆

The editor of the *Reports of the British Association for the Advancement of Science* once said:

> Bright spots on the moon are of two kinds: (1) those clearly and unmistakably slopes of mountains or the interior of craters; and (2) those which appear as round, nebulous spots. The spots of the second class are *apparently horizontal* [his italics] but it is not yet obtained by direct observation whether they are *in contact with the ground* [italics mine]. The three most observed individual spots of this nature are Linné, Posidonius gamma and Alpetragius-d, and these present some quite remarkable differences.

Almost all through the lunar day, Linné appears as a white spot *varying in brightness and size.* It is usually about the same size and brightness as Posidonius gamma, which is the highest part of a ridge on the Mare Serenitas, with a small pit in its summit. Early in the lunar day, Linné exchanges the characteristics of the first class for those of the second, being reduced, toward the end of the day, to a nebulous white spot. Posidonius gamma retains the appearance of a mountain much longer. Alpetragius-d, which seems to be a crater opened in the bottom of a depression, retains its form much longer than the other two.

While the three objects, under high sun, present an identical appearance, the lunar surface surrounding each differs materially. Linné has the appearance of a small isolated cone with an opening on a comparatively level surface; Posidonius gamma is the minutely perforated summit of a mountain range; Alpetragius-d is a somewhat large opening, with a small central cone, in a depression on a mountain range.

To all appearances, under the scrutiny of the most careful observers, these spots appear to be *on the surface*. [Italics ours; note that this was the nineteenth century.] In the case of Linné, the spot spreads around the cone or crater; in the case of Posidonius gamma it extends around the summit of the mountain; in the third case it covers the depression and the included crater. Their variable appearance is doubtless associated somewhat with the altitude of the sun, but there is more to it than this. Any apparent connection with the altitude of the sun is obviously of a more complex nature than simply the changing of shadows. The objects differ greatly but have in common the minute central pit, seen at low angles of illumination; and the white spot at high angles, nearer lunar noon.

W. H. Pickering was among the many selenographers who noted that not only Linné but other small craters have *from time to time been replaced by patches of light, of poor definition and difficult to focus.* The transition is similar in all cases. A few have been known since the earliest days of telescopic lunar study; the others have appeared within the period of modern telescopic observation.

Many white spots were described in the *Selenographical Journal.* McCance reported the crater Messier appearing as a bright spot as big as crater Pickering. And a bright spot was noticed near the busy crater Plato; verification was requested by the astonished observer.

The white spot longest and most consistently observed is probably the "bright spot west of Picard." Herbert Ingall once wrote that recently the bright misty appearance surrounding the spot had been growing fainter.

He notes:

April 10, four hours before full moon, not a trace of the spot west of Picard, but in its place a most minute point of light glittering like a star with about 10° of brilliancy. In size, the point of light could not have been more than one second (or one mile). On May 12, after a full moon this place was close to the terminator and I then perceived a small hollow or pit, the sides having about 5° of brightness and the pit was about two seconds (or miles) diameter. On April 10 and 11, the surrounding Mare was intersected with *bright veins mixed with bright spots.*

Note that there is no way of judging the size of a point source of light at such a distance. That it is seen at all gives it some apparent size. Ingall's statement that the light could not exceed one second of arc is meaningless, since he saw a star-like point of light, not a circle or lighted area. Also keep in mind the rare but puzzling appearance of the *Mare.*

We feel that the *behavior* of this area is of great interest. Consider the absence since October, 1864, when Ingall observed it, of the white cloud-like appearance that exceeded Picard in size. On July 10, 1865, the spot was only slightly brighter than the *Mare* and very small (about one to two miles on the moon). Consider, too, the reduction of the pit-like marking, its wildly variable reflecting power (4° to 10°), and a crater or craters having been seen on the site since October, 1864, widely differing from Birt's observations in 1859. If these observations are considered insufficient to establish physical change as a fact, they at least indicate alterations in reflective power and a change in size of *something* sometimes larger than Picard, *which is thirteen miles in diameter,* to a point one second (mile) across.

How solve the enigma of small clouds associated with minute craters on the surface of an orb with practically no atmosphere? Something must be generating and dispersing these clouds that appear and disappear in a manner not consistent with a highly rarefied atmosphere.

Birt, one of the most persistent observers of the white spot near Picard, writes (*Astronomical Register,* volume II, 1864, page 295):

In the course of my observations, as I observed the locality under oblique illumination, the white cloud-like spot either became invisible or did not exist; which, I cannot say. But its want of definiteness and its similarity in appearance to a cloud led me to hesitate before expressing an opinion as to what it really appeared to be. Further observation brought to light a small pit-like depression in its neighborhood with which the larger cloud-like marking appeared to be connected.

The pit-like depression is of a beautiful whiteness and shows up when the cloud is not visible.

This looks very much like the lair of some sort of UFO.

Captain Noble, another persistent lunar observer, stated that the white spot west of Picard sometimes resembled the puzzling Linné. He reports that from 8:00 to 8:20 P.M., June 15, 1877, it had almost the identical appearance of Linné on January 19, 1869. It is important to note that the change was so rapid that it held this appearance for only twenty minutes.

I cite these older observations because the lunar observers of those days made more systematic studies of evanescent features on the face of the moon, and gave more detailed reports; and also because such unpredictable activity is by no means a thing of the past. Modern observers of the highest calibre also see these puzzling *erratics*, and interest in them is reviving rapidly.

In Moore's recent book, there is a description of the famous "white spot" north of Picard. Moore confirms its continued activity. While he considers many white spots to be small craters, this one, he says, has more the appearance of a surface deposit, sometimes showing haziness, sometimes abnormal brilliance, which leads him to assume that it is a vapor, though he makes no attempt to explain how it maintains cloud-like condensation in the atmospheric vacuum of the moon.

H. P. Wilkins, in *Our Moon*, one of the most modern of lunar treatises, and most generous to lunar activity, says (pages 133-34):

It is curious, to say the least, that the earlier observers, many of them possessed of good telescopes, should have recorded few of the domes or "bowler hats." Nasmyth [a foremost selenographer] says that no such things existed apart from the *one* to the north of crater Birt, near the Straight Wall. Yet, today, they are known in considerable quantities. The author [Wilkins] and Patrick Moore have found nearly a hundred, and most of them have a pit at the summit. To the west of the crater Picard, in the Sea of Conflicts, is a white patch on which various people have noted a minute pit. Epsin, quoted by Webb, declared that the white patch marked a depression. F. H. Thornton found on September 26, 1953, that the patch is a low dome with a summit pit. On that date the terminator crossed the "sea" and had actually passed the site of this patch. Had it been a depression, or even if it was level as most observers thought, it would have been invisible, concealed by the shadows.

But Thornton saw it as a sort of island of light amid the blackness, clearly proving that it was raised, in fact a dome. It is curious that this is the first time that such a thing has been seen. Is it possible that it has only become a dome recently? . . . is this a new blister on the moon?

Now, mark you: this is not ancient history. This is mid-twentieth century.

H. P. Wilkins clearly states (1954) that domes or "bowler hats" are increasing in number—rapidly, and he is confirmed by other observers of today, using the best telescopes. In spite of his own extensive study and review of all other reports, he cannot explain the domes.

"The spot west of Picard," however, is certainly not the only one where there has been confusion as to shape, size, appearance, pits, sharpness of focus, and domes versus depression. The classic is the evasive crater Linné.

The author knows of no report of a similar nature before Schroeter. Most important was Schroeter's notations about Linné in 1788, the *first report of this series of UFO operations*—the disappearing craters, superimposed nebulosities, and the rest. *Their number doubles just about every twenty years!*

Twenty years—a cyclic period that forces itself on our attention. Some authorities put the present number of domes or "bowler hats" at more than two hundred.

Two hundred years ago there were none.

Something is colonizing the moon. And *something* is permeating our own atmosphere in increasing numbers. Is it the clouds we see, clouds that refuse sharp focus in our telescopes (such as were seen *here* by Harrison, Swift, Barnard, Schmidt and Brooks)?

Or are these clouds merely an accompaniment, or a by-product, of something more tangible and, perhaps, more *sinister?*

Elger describes (*Astronomical Register,* volume XXIV, 1886, pages 45 and 207) one of the elliptical white spots as a convex surface on the moon, *although no shadow was formed.* (Italics mine.) Even though this object was not the "spot west of Picard," the description tallies, showing that dome-like structure has been long under debate.

Some of these very low but very broad convex surfaces would cast shadows (if at all) only at the moment of sunrise or sunset. Elger also noted a white spot of 6° of brightness near the crater De Lisle, previously unreported, indicating recent activity. We are coming to recognize that signs of action go together with the peculiar white spots.

Elger adds largely to our understanding of activity that seems related to the peculiar white spots and "bowler hats" on the moon. (*Astronomical Register*, volume XXII, 1885, page 172). He says that east of Crater Alpetragius there lies a large, bright, anomalous spot, designated as "d", shown in reproductions of drawings by Madler, Lohrmann, and Schmidt. In Beer and Madler's map, it is a well marked crater, five miles or more in diameter, with a small crater to the south. In a letter to Birt dated June 5, 1868, Julius Schmidt of Athens says:

This crater "d" is now no longer existing, but in its place is a round spot of light more than ten miles in diameter, extremely brilliant, which has quite the character of the bright spot on Linné, and of the *few others of this kind which are also found on the moon*. The small neighboring crater south of "d" is still distinctly visible.

Nobody but Elger took much notice of this at the time.

These white spots definitely show that something is happening on the moon. As long ago as the mid-nineteenth century reports indicated that such spots were increasing in number. We have every reason to believe they are still increasing. Whereas a dozen or so were known in the period 1860-1870, more than two hundred are now reported by Tulane University.

By mathematically extrapolating the indicated rate of increase backward for the past one hundred sixty years, it can be calculated that the first of these white spots appeared around the year 1800. The first recorded obscuration of Linné was seen by Schroeter in 1788, from which it may be assumed that the "march of the white spots" began about that time. Was Linné the first "colony"? There must be some significance in these unfocusable spots and nebulosities on the moon. What prevents a telescope from receiving a sharp image when the surroundings are perfectly clear?

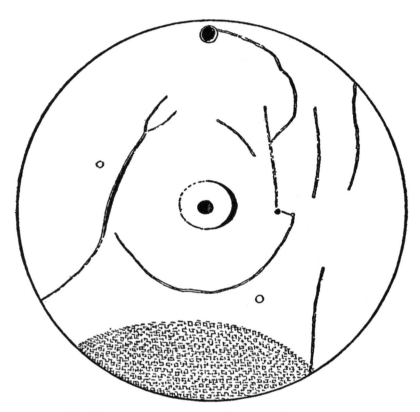

LINNÉ AS IT IS TODAY: *Small-scale sketch by Patrick Moore of Linné as seen through Europe's largest refractor.* (From *Our Moon*)

◆ Disappearances and Linné ◆

In a region west of the crater Parry, objects seem to come and go. While new craters could be explained by meteoric impact, explosions, UFO excavations, collapse of the lunar crust, or other causes, a *disappearing* crater is harder to explain. In the area near Parry, Schmidt reported the disappearance of two "remarkably deep" craters. (Linné was once a deep crater, too!) At least one seemed to become a dome (as did Linné, at times).

Madler mapped a number of small craters just west of Parry, the inside diameter of one of which measured two and one-half miles, the outer five miles; this was described as very deep. Such an object is visible even in modest telescopes; but this and a nearby crater were said by Schmidt to have disappeared before November 1878, the beginning of the "incredible decade." Lohrmann saw no craters at this point, but at the sites designated "B" and "C" by Madler, he saw bright round hills about the size of small craters, which come and go; and, incidentally, about the size of the extra-terrestrial craters clustered on the Mexican plateau.

A changeable widget within the crater Archimedes looks variously like a craterlet, a rock mass, a small hillock and a projection of the crater wall. Birt mapped bright streaks nearby.

Schroeter, circa 1780-95, (was there another "incredible period" at that time?) showed, at one point of the lunar landscape, four deep pits, two about the size of the considerable crater Ptolemaeus-A. About three-quarters of a century later, Webb (a careful observer) definitely located on this site only *two minute craterlets*. Neison, outstanding map-maker, later confirmed Webb. Yet, somewhat later, one of the missing members was reported visible—*but with four bright spots on it!* Some commentators pointed out that the behavior of one of these changeable objects was much like that of Hyginus-N.

Note the association of these disappearing craters with bright spots, domes, lights and clouds. What are they?

And, what is more, note the frequency with which spots, lights and clouds appear in groups of one to eight or nine—on the moon, in space, in the heads of comets *and* in the terrestrial sky.

No story of strange disappearances on the moon would be complete without Madler's "square." On the edge of the Mare Frigorias, not far from the ever-variable crater Plato, there is a large "bay," which Madler described as an almost perfect square, within which was an almost perfect cross formed by white ridges. H. P. Wilkins, using the greatest telescopes in Europe, reports confidently that one side of the square no longer exists and the cross is gone. The area was searched with a telescope ten times the diameter of the one used by Madler. *Something,* then, moved away a huge wall and a great cross.

Many disappearances are only temporary, and some do not seem to be cyclic or repetitive. The Spanish comet hunter Sola once saw only a white patch where there should have been the small, but sharply defined, crater Reiner.

Let me quote here from *Our Moon,* by H. P. Wilkins:

. . . All this is mysterious enough, almost enough for us to sympathize to some extent with the idea often expressed by Schroeter, that some of these appearances are caused by the "industrial activities of the Selenites." We cannot subscribe to this idea because without air to breathe it is exceedingly difficult to contemplate the existence of Selenites let alone to speculate as to their possible activities, industrial or otherwise. *It is equally difficult to explain these things on natural grounds.* [Italics mine]

There is an active mind striving against the fetters of dogmatized science. This is as far as we may ask an astronomer to go in advocating intelligence on the moon, or anywhere else in space. More would cut him off from his profession. Let this man of authority state the observational facts. I, already an outcast, will cheerfully take the rap by stating bluntly what the facts imply—UFO activity!

I am, at this time, offering *an* explanation, not necessarily *the* explanation. If I succeed only in stimulating thought, and encouraging somebody to achieve one more tiny step toward truth, the effort will be worth while.

The classic and possibly the prototype of lunar disappearances is the crater Linné. Nothing else, aside from Hyginus-N, has caused so much comment.

Linné changes with puzzling rapidity, as illustrated by a report from Webb. On November 13, 1866, Webb, Talmadge and Birt observed Linné. Webb saw "an ill-defined whiteness," Talmadge "a circular dark cloud," and Birt—nothing.

Denning remarked about Linné that to an observer of his acquaintance it had appeared on January 8 as a small hill rising up as a very brilliant point from the ravine which was still in darkness. Later considerations led him to conclude that the "hill," if hill it was, was to the west of the center of the white cloud which had replaced crater Linné. Combine this observation with the persistent sightings of a small orifice in the top of this cloud. What is the nature of this object and what accounts for the instability or activity of whatever existed on top of it?

In the *Astronomical Register* (volume VIII, 1870, page 190) Birmingham reports that on June 6 he saw "a very marked central depression on the white spot of Linné—very shallow and rather east of the center of the white spot." More movement.

The following pages recount in chronological order the fantastic history of this outstanding lunar puzzle.

Before 1866, all acceptable maps of the moon indicated a small but prominent crater located at lunar longitude 11° 32' 28" W; and latitude 27° 47' 13" N, on the extensive lunar plain named Mare Serenitatis. But the existence of this crater, with a diameter of approximately six miles, has not been serene. Situated on a low, broad ridge, it was prominently isolated. The maps showed no crater, large or small, nearby, although diligently prepared by famous lunar map-makers, such as Beer and Madler, Lohrmann, Schroeter and Neison.

Although definitely seen, measured and mapped by observers

for two centuries, Linné had not been entirely without its darker history. According to the *Intellectual Observer* (volume X, page 444) Schroeter had turned his telescope on Linné on the evening of November 5, 1788, and had seen not a crater but a darker spot, diffused and without sharp border. Its brightness was rated at ½ on a scale wherein dense shadows are rated zero, and the brilliant, possibly irridescent, interior of the crater Aristarchus is rated 10. This observation did not get too much attention from the astronomical fraternity until late in 1866, when . . . *Linné disappeared.*

Nobody seems ever to have attached much importance to the fact that in the autumn of 1788, for at least one evening, a deep, dark, definite crater almost six miles across was obscured by a dark "something" which, so far as we can ascertain, cast no shadow.

Schmidt, who had known Linné since 1841, saw, on October, 1866, nothing where Linné should have been except a glimmer, a small whitish cloud. This persisted through November.

So Schmidt announced the first authenticated *disappearance* of a lunar crater.

Contemporary selenographers rushed to their observatories to verify it. Birt considered this sudden disappearance "concealment" by a "cloud," though neither he nor anybody else accounted for the fact that this cloud did not cast a shadow. Almost uniformly, the literature of 1866 to 1870 refers to the "obscuration" of Linné as being a "white spot," which, on December 15, 1866, had no defined edges, was almost eleven miles in diameter, and cast no shadow. If Linné was still there underneath, it was a changed Linné.

Similar cloudy spots had been observed from time to time. Between 1858 and 1863, Birt had made several sightings of a white cloudy patch west of the crater Picard. A very bright, cloud-like patch nearby, seen by Ingall in 1864, had practically faded out by the end of the year. These patches were associated later with minute craters or orifices. Something of the sort eventually developed at the site of Linné as well. It has never been determined at what point these little black points made their appearance. The interest in Linné was heightened by the fact that this was at least its second obscuration in eighty years.

Something was going on at Linné. Birt has tabulated the brightness of the location (or object) over a period of years:

Observer	Date	Degree of Brightness
Schroeter	1788, November 5	0.05
Lohrmann	1823, May 28	7.0 plus
Breed and Madler	1831, December 12-13	6.0
De la Rue	1858, February 22	5.0
De la Rue	1865, October 4	5.0
Rutherford	1865, October 4	6.0
Buckingham	1866, November 18	2.0

The location of Linné is shown on the photograph on page 65.

Schmidt's announcement appeared in a number of publications. In part, he says (*Intellectual Observer*):

I have known this crater since 1841, and even at full moon it has not been difficult to see. In October and November, 1866, at the phase of the moon when previously it has had maximum visibility, this deep crater, with a diameter of 5.6 English miles, had completely disappeared and in its place there was only a little, whitish, luminous cloud.

There is significance in this cloud's being *luminous*.

Webb was among the earlier observers in England to confirm the defection of Linné. In the *Intellectual Observer*, (pages 11-58) he lists some observations:

1866, December 13: I was much struck by finding that the site of Linné was occupied by a whitish cloud.

December 14: The whitish spot in the place of Linné is barely as large as *Sulp. Gallus;* it is the most conspicuous object in the E. half of *M. Seren.*

December 25: Fine definition. Linné a very conspicuous white, nebulous patch, containing some very indistinct and almost doubtful markings within it.

1867, January 12:   On the site of Linné nothing but a small ill-defined whitish cloud, not quite so large as *Sulp. Gallus.* There seems to be some slight marking as from a small shadow, towards its center, but far too indistinct to say whether caused by hill or hollow. The white cloud was by no means bright or conspicuous, although perfectly distinct.

Repeatedly the earlier literature had described Linné as being deep and dark. Beer and Madler, a sort of Damon and Pythias of astronomy, referred to "the deep crater Linné." Nobody made such a reference after October, 1886.

This reported change on the lunar surface attracted much attention in its day, but contemporary astronomers are indifferent. Their concern today is outer space, the problems of cosmogony, the constitution of stars and nebulae. But it may be that we have overlooked something important close by.

It is interesting to note that the diehards consider that the intense observation *after* the disappearance of Linné in 1866 served only to establish its *true state,* and not to verify its change!

At about this time Temple expressed great interest in the *increasing number of white spots on the moon's surface,* attributing them to what he called *chemically warm activity,* as opposed to any brightness depending upon oxidation or other atmospheric effect. His comments appeared in the *Astronomische Nachrichten* (Number 1655) and were translated by Lynn (*Astronomical Register,* pages 58-219). He believes that *two* obscurations of Linné indicate that these nebulosities are something more than ground markings.

Birt's resumé in the *Reports* for 1867, referred to above, quotes Schroeter as follows (*Selenotopographische Fragmente,* 1-181; November 5, 1788):

The sixth ridge [in *Mare Serenitatis*] comes from a depression close upon the south boundary of the mountains, passes northward towards *v* where it has within it a somewhat uncertain depression about the same size, but quite flat and resembling a white very small spot.

Schmidt says that "*v* corresponds . . . to the place of Linné," and thus identifies Schroeter's description of the first obscuration of Linné.

But note the entirely different description, reported by Lohrmann as of May 28, 1823 (*Topographie der Sichtbaren Mondoberflache*, page 92):

". . . (Linné) is the second crater on this plain . . . near a ridge beginning at *Sulpicus Gallus;* it has a diameter of somewhat more than a mile [German mile, about 4½ English miles], is *very deep*, and *can be seen under every illumination.* [Italics mine]

Of observations made by Beer and Madler of the region adjacent to Linné on December 12-13, 1831, Madler wrote in 1867:

The crater Linné, situated in 27° 47' 13" N. Lat. and 11° 32' 28" W. Long., has a diameter of 1.4 geographical miles (6.4 Eng. M.). In full moon the edge of it is not very sharply limited, but in oblique illumination it is very distinct, and I have measured it seven times with great facility. The light of the edge is permanently 6° and the small inner space retains its brightness until shadows begin.

In February, 1867, Schmidt assigned to the original crater a diameter of just over seven miles and a depth of just over 1,000 feet. His earlier observations included about 1,300 drawings of the lunar surface, some pertaining to Linné and its environs. The latter included the following:

1840: On a general chart of the moon, diameter 12", constructed from my own observations about the end of 1840, Linné is marked as a crater.

1841: April 27. In a sketch, (#4) Linné is wanting, but two small craters are strongly marked in the NW.

1841: May 28. In No. 11 Linné is not marked.

1841: September 6. In No. 36 Linné is not marked.

1841: December 2. In No. 52 Linné is marked as a crater.

December 2. In No. 53 Linné is given proportionately *very large as a crater.*

December 3. In No. 54 Linné is represented *distinctly as a crater.*

1842: January 3. In No. 63 Linné is not marked, although close to terminator.

February 16-17. Linné which was near to the light boundary (terminator) was not seen.

July 14. Observed Linné at Hamburg with a good telescope by Banks; with power 88 it was represented as a *very small crater.*

1843: May 9. The air being particularly favorable, I counted with the last mentioned telescope 22 craters in the Mare Serenitatis, and amongst them is certainly included Linné.

August 17. With the great telescope of the Hamburg observatory, the two mountain veins running northerly from *Sulpicus Gallas* were well visible on the evening terminator, but of Linné no trace.

Now, while these many observations leave no room for doubt about the previous existence of Linné as a crater, or crater-like object; and while a careful study of the exact times of observation shows that its appearance and details depend somewhat upon the degree and angle of solar illumination, we must ask whether there were no indications of alternate appearances and disappearances during the century of 1788 to 1866. Although Schmidt and Birt provide no suggestions, we cannot escape the suspicion that something out of the ordinary was going on around Linné during those years.

Astronomers soon noted that the spot obliterating or replacing Linné fluctuated in size. Birt assembled the measurements:

Authority	Date 18__	Sec. of Arc	Eng. Feet
Schmidt	66.794	6.90	48,688
Birt	66.953	11.61	81,932
Birt	66.961	7.07	48,871
Birt	66.964	7.32	51,652
Birt	66.969	6.75	47,644
Schmidt	66.986	1.81	12,789
Birt	67.036	7.95	56,105
Buckingham	67.197	6.00	42,340

Authority	Date 18__	Sec. of Arc	Eng. Feet
Wolf	67.443	4.50	31,755
Birt	67.518	7.85	55,423
Huggins	67.518	7.85	55,423
Huggins (2nd)	67.518	6.14	43,314
Birt	67.518	7.00	49,426
Birt	67.520	5.36	37,848
Birt	67.528	6.31	44,528

So the "thing" covering Linné was fluctuating in size as well as brightness.

Now if this "cloud" occupied a crater or depression, how could it fluctuate in size to such a degree without disclosing the outer walls? If it was elevated above the plain how could it avoid casting a shadow, or showing a lighter hue on the side towards the sun? If below the surface, why did the walls cast no internal shadows? What was the central hill and/or crater seen *on* this white spot by observers with superior instruments? If this was a real cloud, what prevented it from dissipating into the vacuous atmosphere of the moon? If it was too tenuous to cast a shadow, why was it opaque enough to obscure the surface below it? If it was lava, why did it change size, and why did the old walls sometimes show through, as seen by Noble and others? If the spot was made up of the debris of the destroyed "old Linné," where did all the material come from to fill the "deep" crater?

Schmidt and others made nine measures of the brightness of Linné relative to the bright spot called Posidonius Gamma:

		Compared with Posidonius		
Observer	Date	Fainter	Equal	Brighter
Schmidt	Nov. 17 (1866)	X		
Schmidt	19	X		
Schmidt	22	X		
Schmidt	23-24	X		
Schmidt	Dec. 14			X
Schmidt	16		X	
Birt	19	X		
Schmidt	Jan. 13	X		

Observer	Date	Compared with Posidonius		
		Fainter	Equal	Brighter
Schmidt	14	X		
Birt	14	X		
Birt	15	X		
Birt	Feb. 11	X		
Birt	Mar. 14			X
Buckingham	14		X	
Birt	May 11	X		
Birt	15	X		
Birt	17		X	
Birt	July 13		X	
Birt	Aug. 10		X	
Birt	12	X		

This shows considerable fluctuation in the brightness of the cloud over Linné, as determined by simultaneous comparisons with Posidonius gamma, even after eliminating the effects of variable sunlight.

Whereas the original Linné was a deep crater with heavy internal shadows, the new object appeared level with the plain, and shadowless. Early observations placed Linné on a long, low ridge, but after the change, the ridge appeared discontinuous, as though partially blotted out. Gradually, seen under high-altitude sunlight, Linné began to resemble Posidonius gamma which was definitely seen as a mountain about 1,000 feet high at low illuminations. Both light spots had minute dark spots near their centers, at high altitude illuminations which often appeared to be minute craters or crater openings, reminding one of the opening and closing of manhole covers.

Some observers described the minute black spot as being *on* Linné rather than in it. Occasionally an observer described the bright spot as convex. Some observers saw a "ghost" of the old, original crater outlined in the brilliant white spot. This would indicate fluctuation in the thickness or density of the cloud, as well as in its size and brightness.

The small, black "crater" on Linné was first seen February 11, 1867, whereafter it appeared frequently. Strangely enough the similar one on Posidonius gamma appeared about the same time.

At sunrise, when shadows should be longest, Posidonius gamma cast very distinct shadows, as the original Linné had done, but the new Linné was *entirely invisible,* not even appearing as a bright spot until the sun rose considerably higher in the lunar sky.

Repeat: *At sunrise Linné was invisible and neighboring Posidonius gamma was distinct with shadows.* At high illuminations both became bright spots, with tiny black points centrally located, sometimes described as crater holes.

At times, when nearby craters were plainly seen, the new Linné was invisible or a mere white spot.

The consensus of Schmidt and most of the other observers was: (1) in the first half of the nineteenth century, Linné was a crater somewhat deeper than average; (2) *sometimes* between 1842 and 1866 it disappeared; (3) after 1866, at sunrise, when shadows are longest and nearby craters are most prominent, Linné was invisible; (4) at high-angle sunlight, Linné became a bright spot of variable size and brightness, sometimes well defined, sometimes nebulous, sometimes convex, sometimes with a minute crater in the center of the cloud, sometimes with a small hill which cast a shadow; (5) Schroeter, in 1788, saw Linné in about the same condition as after 1866; (6) there are other bright spots on the moon which have similar characteristics, sometimes including the same minute black crater. The observations of Lohrmann and others, between 1788 and 1841, which were not given sufficient consideration, also show unexplained variations.

It is especially notable that, while the new Linné was constantly altering its appearance, at no time did it revert to its original deep cup shape.

At one time, Goodacre described Linné as a cone on the edge of a shallow depression.

In 1954, Wilkins said:

Today Linné is a pit on the summit of a low dome, and situated in the center of a white area. If Lohrmann, Madler, *or* Goodacre correctly described it as it really was in their time . . . then a change of some sort has certainly occurred *for today Linné is the reverse of a crater, being in fact* a hill or dome with a minute pit on its summit.

INTERIOR OF CRATER GASSENDI *as seen by H. P. Wilkins with Europe's largest refracting telescope. Note the geometric layout.* (From *Our Moon*)

V

ETHNOLOGY SPEAKS

◆ Little People, Green and Otherwise ◆

The rash of news reports anent "little people" and "little green men," throughout 1954 and 1955, emphasized the persistence of this theme in the field of UFO. After the climax of Miss Dorothy Kilgallen's sensational report in May 1955, a hunch made me stop in the Miami Public Library to read up on Pygmies "just in case." It proved a minor revelation.

Of course I had read Scully's yarn. Of course I had noted the erratic reports from France in late 1954. Of course I knew about Miner Black and the dwarf who appeared, seeking a pail of water, not too far from mysterious Chico, California. I was casually familiar with the literature about little people and UFO, but had sensed an element of unreality there.

My first rundown in the encyclopedias stopped me cold. Here, before my eyes, was evidence of an entire race of "little people," who might have, probably could have, and maybe *did* invent space flight eons ago.

On my arrival in New York in June for an extended sojurn, I walled myself into the New York Public Library with stacks of books on Pygmies. In a short time I had come to the following conclusions:

1. We have had persistent reports of "little people" observed in, or in connection with, UFO.

2. These "little people" are obviously of high intelligence, and are sometimes dark in color—or even green.

3. We have undeniable evidence that space craft (UFO) have existed for a very long time, thousands of years in fact.

4. There is no evidence that our "second wave" of civilization has ever developed the ability to create space craft, although there is some slight evidence that lifting machines were used in the *very early* stages of this wave.

5. As pointed out in *The Case for the UFO*, remnants of artifacts, made by intelligent "hands," have been recovered from coal beds and stone quarries originating at least as remotely as Tertiary times.

6. The current period of civilization to which we refer as "historical times" is only two to eight thousand years old, depending on the area under discussion. Culture areas whose records are less graphically preserved do not extend backward more than 25,000 to 50,000 years.
   Thus our vaunted civilization is still a "beginner." About 98 per cent of its total development occurred within the past 5,000 to 10,000 years; and almost the entirety of its scientific development within the past 300 to 400 years. This disregards possible remnants of the archaic science of the "first wave," such as the Great Pyramid of Gizeh.

7. Pygmy man is known to have existed since Miocene times, a period of approximately 33,000,000 years. He is not a missing link, but a fully developed human race—although *not related to other races* through any known genetic connection.

8. Thus our scintillating intellectual progress has run its gamut in 1/10th of 1% of the total time during which fully developed *homo sapiens* is known to have existed; and its scientific upsuge has taken place within 1/1000th per cent, or within 1/100,-000th of the known life span of the Pygmy race.

9. It seems within the bounds of reason, then, that a comparable intellectual surge could have occurred during the vast span of Pygmy history. If wiped out, or nearly wiped out by cataclysm, it could easily have been lost in the subsequent shuffle.

10. Since we know that space flight has existed for at least 3,500 years, and, according to the research of Leslie, H. T. Wilkins, Churchward and others, we have reason to believe that space flight may have been in existence for 70,000 to 100,000 years, there is reason to believe that space flight derives from a time in the pre-cataclysmic era which developed a first wave of civilization. In this case, it is an improbability of lesser order to assume that space flight originated on this planet in an earlier wave of intellectual development, than to assume that the UFO phenomena, more recently observed, are coming from another planet.

11. If we do, indeed, have "little people" within the UFO, as reported by observers of varying responsibility, then we may assume that the Pygmies, at some remote epoch, developed a civilization which discovered the principle of gravitation and put it to work.

These general conclusions are supported, sometimes positively, sometimes by default, sometimes vaguely, by the findings of history, archaeology, ethnology, mythology, paleontology, philology, theology, genealogy and geography.

Edward Potter and William T. Walsh have posed a very tantalizing question. They suggested that there may have been a sudden change in the earth's gravitational attraction in a remote period. Giant animals and plants, so large that we consider them freaks and monsters, once throve on earth—huge dinosaurs like *Brontosaurus* and the even larger *Diplodocus*, and the gigantic tree ferns. Did these living forms reach such dimensions because gravitational pull was smaller? Did they then *weigh* less than they would if living now? I might add a related question: Was this a temporary period of partial release from gravitation, lasting perhaps only a few million years?

It is suggested that there may have been similarly phenomenal growth of indigenous residents (or colonists) on the moon. Ancient literature, myth, and tradition swarm with giants. There are persistent stories of a race of giants appearing in Peru (with no hint of where they came from) who were so large that they killed the native women with whom they attempted intercourse. Were they colonists returning from the moon? Were the enormous megaglyphs at Nasca, Peru, made by those giants as a *means of signaling to observers with fine telescopes in space or on the moon?*

In such speculations we are dealing in millions of years, not mere centuries. Startling things could have happened; still I see no certain connection between these huge animals and the moon or space travel.

One other thought: If evolutionary growth could increase the size of beings on the moon, the reverse would be true of colonists *from* the moon. We have had Pygmies here for 30,000,-000 years who, as far as we can trace them into the past, were small but fully developed humans. Is the Pygmy an equally monstrous under-growth produced by evolutionary processes acting on terrestrial colonists? Is the Pygmy related to the giants of the past as the present-day horned toad is related to the dinosaur?

The UFO problem *is* complex.

Only a few years ago, a Swedish expedition was reported (in the *Svenske Dagblat*) to have found very small Pygmies in the Cameroons of Africa, the adults only about three feet tall. This, if substantiated, would make them the smallest known living Pygmy tribe. The ethnologist Walter Kaudern, specializing in Pygmy races, thought the earliest were possibly smaller than those of today, and there has been a tendency for increase in stature. This is pertinent in view of what we shall learn of the mysterious Zimbabwe ruins of southeast Africa.

A recent report comes from France, checked by M. Marc Thirouin who edits a UFO journal called *Ouranos*. A Mme. Leboeuf was picking blackberries, when her dog started barking. Raising her head, she spied a queer "thing" standing motionless and staring at her "with intelligent-looking eyes." It was about three and a half feet tall and seemed to be without arms. A shroud like a deep-sea diving costume, made of plastic or cellophane, covered its entire body. As it started moving toward her in jumps, Mme. Leboeuf fled. The shock made her take to her bed for some days, during which time the dog whimpered continuously. On the same day a UFO was seen high in the nearby sky.

H. T. Wilkins states as a certainty that Pygmies existed in ancient South America. He records that two gold-prospectors are said to have found a fourteen-inch Pygmy mummy, with a lively and intelligent facial expression, encased in granite in a cavern which had been blasted open with dynamite. If this case is verifiable, the body had been within solid, igneous rock for millions of years, from pleiocene times, in fact. This episode is of the "erratic" class. It is difficult to conceive of any process of preservation which would permit the body to escape being consumed by molten rock. We must consider this with reservations.

At a very remote time there were Pygmy tribes in North America. In 1885 their bodies or bones, it is reported, were found in various burial grounds. Their faces differed from typical Indian features, and the remains indicated elements of civilization. They were found in prehistoric stone graves in the Cumberland Valley, not far from the Ohio Mound Builder area. The corpses were buried with small, finely worked implements of quartz and chalcedony.

The Maya of Yucatan and Central America have legends of dwarfs who may have been the first people there. They were said to have done their work in darkness. The dwarfish Picts of Britain are also said to have worked only at night.

A curious fragment of tradition comes from the few surviving works of the Maya and Quiche Indians. A great cataclysm or flood is said to have been caused by cosmic forces, associated with Venus, concurrent with a major distortion of the earth's orbit. The Maya had a respectable knowledge of astronomy, and there may well be some truth in this. The Roman historian Varro suggested the same thing. This was said to have ended the first period or cycle of the little people.

There are vague memories among Polynesians of a race of "small people" possessed of great strength in spite of their small stature. Numbers of colossal stone structures are said to be their work. Lewis Spence and Robert Graves have mentioned similar attributes among Celts and Picts—brute strength and the building of megalithic stone structures, such as Stone-henge. This points both to the immense antiquity of "little people" and to the ancient world-wide distribution of a Pygmy culture of a high order.

There are rumors, also, of Pygmy survivors of the "great sea that swallowed the land" in the Pacific, and of the salvaged weapons with which they fought giants. This may relate to the submergence of the continent of Mu. There are megalithic stone structures in the South Sea Islands comparable to those of Peru and Africa.

Most megalithic structures are found in the tropics, and they *do* encircle the earth. It is significant that many were obviously built for the use of "little people," especially Sacsahuaman, Zimbabwe, and the Great Pyramid.

There seems little room for doubt that the ancient Pygmies had some science, though it differed from the science of today. It appears to have been based on non-metallic substances, primarily stone, handled and worked by means unknown to us. It was probably not electric or electronic.

Some science cultists hesitate to admit any other types of science than our physical science of the past few generations. However, the handling and working of great stone masses must have been accomplished by a form of power not yet discovered by us. These accomplishments may have been rather in the nature of accidental discoveries than of the systematic developments we term "physical science," or invention.

We hear that there were little people in forgotten cities buried in the jungles of Amazonia. This finds support in what we will have to say later about the tunnels of Cusco, Peru. There is a hint of the lost science in a report of a "cold light" eternally burning in one of the lost jungle cities. What is that light? And, come to think of it, what was the light used by the ancient Egyptians, when carving the vast interior tombs in the Pyramids and the Valley of the Kings—a light that left no smoke traces?

There are caves in Europe which have been shaped inside by masonry methods. They are 10,000 to 20,000 years old. Their rooms and passages are too small for normal-sized adults of today, and children use them as playhouses.

Similar caverns exist in the remote mountains of Spain, near the age-long home of the Basques, whose language roots, as in the case of the Pygmies, have never been traced.

The Pygmies of neolithic days left behind them delicate stone implements in India, Africa, and France. The tiny "Hayden" flints, which have left a trail from Eastern Asia to California via the Bering Strait, are equally puzzling. They have been used by archaeologists as evidence that the American Indian tribes emigrated from the Orient. But it is just as likely that the migrations began here and moved westward. More likely still, these mysterious items were made by Pygmies in an age long forgotten before the Indians settled in western North America.

Jesuit records indicate that there were Pygmies living in small numbers in the Swiss mountains as recently as the sixteenth and seventeenth centuries. Human remains of small stature have been found there which seem to be about 9,000 years old.

The Greek historians Herodotus and Hecateaus mention the African Pygmies, showing that Mediterranean travelers penetrated into Africa as early as 450 B.C. Herodotus said that the Pygmies of the Congo were *sorcerers,* evidence of a lost science, perhaps gone "black" and occult. At this point we wonder when *and how* communication was maintained with Zimbabwe or Central Africa?

In the early part of the nineteenth century, Dr. Grayson investigated some ancient tombs in the Mississippi Valley, said to be the graves of Pygmies. The bodies are all buried with their heads toward the east. Why?

Both H. T. Wilkins and Dr. Flower, an English ethnologist of the late nineteenth century, reported Pygmies in ancient Japan, and the small stature of the modern Japanese would confirm this. Note, also, that Japanese of relatively short stature often are very strong and show the tremendous shoulder span of the Picts. It is believed the Pygmies were in Japan "ages" before the yellow-negrito savages from the old land of Pan invaded and conquered the stone-age Ainu aborigines. The latter have reported that the "little people" were about four and one half feet tall and had tails. Their artifacts are said to have been found.

Then there is Zimbabwe, in Rhodesia, one of the world's most puzzling ruins. It is said to have been discovered by an American named Renders in 1868; yet there is a remarkable map, in Dutch, published in Amsterdam in 1763, which locates and describes the site with astounding geographical detail, including the locations of Pygmy tribes in the hinterlands—of which more later. For the moment: What brought that knowledge of Zimbabwe to Holland *before 1763?*

"Why," you ask, "Zimbabwe? What's that to do with UFO or even 'little people'?"

That's easily answered. These slumbering remains of an ancient mining project have been a frustrating enigma to archaeologists. Zimbabwe, like other recalcitrant erratics, becomes eloquent when underwritten by *space flight and "little people"*!

Did you ever meet a stranger on the street and wonder if you had met him somewhere? After pondering vague resemblances for a while, did you finally conclude that this unknown person had a "family likeness" to some person or *group of persons* you had known? Zimbabwe has a vague and haunting "family likeness" to Sacsahuaman, Easter Island and Phoenicia . . . perhaps Egypt . . . perhaps the Orient. And, in all, sharing an aura of the world's least explained archaeological puzzles.

"Well," you ask, "for instance?"

Well, for instance: the *little steps* leading up the 350-foot ascent of its "Acropolis" . . . steps so small they are a positive hardship to climb . . . which recall the little steps leading to the "Inca's Throne" at Sacsahuaman, and the basaltic stone staircase *in the mountain.* The passages in the Zimbabwe ruins are too small for the normal adult of today, as are the little tunnels of Cusco, near Sacsahuaman.

Entrance doors in Zimbabwe are under five feet high! Ancient gold mines in the Zimbabwe area have entries and passageways too small for an adult white man!

Students of archaeology, who have commented on Zimbabwe, have each, in turn, attempted to establish Zimbabwe as an outpost of some other *one country.* Always they have failed, largely because of their own artificially created barriers—usually *time barriers*—and their restricted concept of tansportation. They have failed to recognize the true antiquity of a world-wide civilization. Seen as a link in a world-wide network, the jigsaw pieces of Zimbabwe begin to assume their place in a pattern.

In common with Peru, Easter Island, Baalbek, and other megalith sites, Zimbabwe shows every sign of having been precipitously vacated. Why? What happened all over the world to drive strong people from prepared strongholds? So quickly that they left tools and treasures behind? It is estimated that at least 100,000 people lived for centuries in Zimbabwe but left no burying ground, no mummies, no bones. Why? What was the mode of exodus? Where did they take their dead . . . and how?

The Zimbabweans were phallic worshippers, so were the Easter Islanders, and the Phoenicians. There are no writings or inscriptions at Zimbabwe—and none on Easter Island except a few remnants on wooden slabs. The Zimbabweans carved large birds in wood; so did the Phoenicians.

Those people who mined $300,000,000 worth of gold and cast it into ingots for export must surely have known how to write. To whom did they export? How was the gold carried away? No native tribe within hundreds of miles of Zimbabwe has attached any value to gold within historical times. Who wanted it badly enough to live in jungles to mine it, yet would not bury his dead in Zimbabwe? What mode of transportation was so convenient that dead bodies could be carried "home"?

And the stonework! A million or so neatly cut *granite* blocks of approximately uniform size: about six by twelve inches; over 100,000 tons, shaped and fitted with the same skill as at Sacsahuaman, Easter Island, Angkor Vat, and the great Pyramid, yet without a trace of *local* quarrying. Where did that stone come from? How transported, if not by levitation or flight? The same problem faces us in Peru, Easter Island, Baalbek, Egypt: *ease in handling heavy stone* . . . and anomalous crudity in almost every other field.

But, withal, a race desiring gold so badly that they established an isolated colony of 100,000 souls to mine it! (The Incas and pre-Incas loved gold. So did Solomon . . . and the Queen of Sheba.) The logistics of such an enterprise would stagger a modern army.

No roads, no tractors. And these were little people, Pygmies. So were the pre-Incas. So, probably, were the pyramid builders. And their transportation problems were similar, and solved in ways mysteriously similar. How? Was there a world-wide civilization which "discovered" aerial or space transportation, without the aid of what we call science? What was their secret?

Nobody has ever determined the age of Zimbabwe—nor of Easter Island, nor Sacsahuaman, nor Baalbek. Nor—I may be in a minority here—of the Pyramid. Miss G. Caton-Thompson explored Zimbabwe and decided the ruins could have been built only after 900 A.D. She also visited Easter Island. Did she ever publish a comparison of Easter-Sacsahuaman versus Zimbabwe? R. N. Hall after several years at Zimbabwe, decided that the period of building covered at least three hundred years and was done by "some civilized race from the Near East." Mauch dated Zimbabwe from the time of the Queen of Sheba. Randall-McIver could find no trace of either European or Oriental motif, and significantly declared the structure to be typically African. Estimated dates run from 400 to 4,000 years ago. So do the estimates of Sacsahuaman, Easter, and the other enigmatic areas.

Consider the isolation of Zimbabwe. It totally lacks connection with its surroundings. Why? Neville Jones, antiquarian of the Southern Rhodesian Government, says:

> Here, away in what was until recently the unknown interior of Africa, we are confronted with the evidences of a race of people who, whether they were immigrants or indigenous natives, have disappeared as a cultural unit. They have left for our inspection hundreds of ruins, of which Zimbabwe is the noblest, which display great imagination and immense energy, and have bequeathed to us no clue as to who they were or whither they went.

In view of all these dead ends, may I suggest that this colony came, with their material and equipment, by aerial transport and took away their dead in the same manner? May I be pardoned if I underwrite this aerial transport with a form of true space flight carried on by "little people." If you reject this, can *you* explain how else?

It is certain that this gigantic ruin was not erected by the local natives who had no money and no use for gold. And how did the Dutch map-maker of before 1763 know of it? What closed group obtained and used knowledge of inner Africa a hundred years before Livingston?

Why was this area *unknown, yet mapped?* And how was it mapped? How are we to explain that the map of 1763 located the Pygmies of West Africa, and yet these Pygmies are said to have been discovered less than one hundred years ago! If Livingston did, in truth, discover the Victoria Falls, why are these falls noted on a Dutch map of 1763. Was Churchward right in saying a secret group of esoterics have had knowledge not available to you and me? A very early use of aerial transport would explain many things.

It is about 250 *roadless* miles from Zimbabwe to the coast. But the gold must have been *exported,* for it was cast into ingots on the site. How was the gold brought to the coast or to its destination? How were workers, building stone and supplies brought in if not by air?

What caused the sudden departure from Zimbabwe? From Baalbek? From Easter Island? Only two explanations are possible: World-wide cataclysm, or destruction of the common home-base of all those colonies. A minor catacylsm could account for the latter, such as took place in the Caribbean-Central America area with the impact of great meteors or comets. But, *if that home-base were not on this planet?*

If the base for these many colonies of "little people" was in space, then each had its own lines of communication. A world-wide catastrophe would have precipitated evacution from all points. Otherwise, where did all of these isolated colonies go to so suddenly that they dropped their tools and personal effects in their very tracks?

How many times am I to be reminded of some verses in the Gospel of Saint Mark:

14. But when ye shall see the abomination of desolation . . . standing where it ought not . . . then let them that be in Judea flee to the mountains.

15. And let him that is on the housetop not go down into the house, neither enter therein, to take anything out of the house.

16. And let him that is in the field not turn back again for to take up his garment.

26. And then shall they see the Son of Man coming in the clouds with great power and glory.

27. And then shall he send his angels, and shall gather together his elect from the four winds, from the uttermost parts of the earth, to the uttermost part of Heaven.

Does the fact of Zimbabwe being on a Dutch map of 1763 imply that the ruins were then being worked? Maybe, but we doubt it. The literature of that time could not have omitted discussion of one of the world's greatest sources of gold, if it had been worked then.

The stonework of Zimbabwe is skillfully executed. The blocks are well cut and joined without mortar. The walls vary in height from twelve to thirty-five feet. They are fifteen feet thick at the base, nine feet at the top. There were originally large stone monoliths on top. The towers are of phallic significance. The surrounding outcrops of rock show no sign of quarrying. The whole complex was built on a hill about 350 feet high, just as at Sacsahuaman.

In the many mine workings in the neighborhood, almost invariably the passages are too small for men other than Pygmies. They were made by and for little people . . . and the mines, like the ruins, were abandoned in a hurry. Artifacts remain, but no human remains. How did those people get out without leaving their dead?

Phoenician coins and artifacts show conical towers, phallic designs, etc., resembling those of Zimbabwe. These have been interpreted to link Phoenicia to Zimbabwe. We grant the possibility; but similar coins have been dug up in North America. Some of the Zimbabwe phallic models bear the lotus design, a prime Oriental motif. Moreover, according to Churchward, the lotus was a major symbol of the ancient races which preceded the Asiatic races (except the Pygmies, which he did not mention). The lotus is certainly not a pattern native to Africa.

But antiquity of puzzling vastness constantly haunts us. Consider the gold thread found in solid rock in England, and the beautifully worked metallic vessel blasted from rock in New

England. And the coins dug from mound-builder tombs in Ohio, and those dug from deep underground in Illinois and Virginia. Well, there was workmanship at Zimbabwe, too. A coil of gold wire, thin and well-made, was found there. Gold may be preserved for thousands of years where iron would disintegrate. The Bantu make *coils*, but nobody has ever been known in all Africa who could make *wire*.

Zimababwe? It has almost all of the elements of mystery common to the many sites around the world which were abandoned precipitously and which do not appear to have undergone long-term evolutionary development. If you can explain it on any other basis than little people and space flight, I will listen to your hypothesis long and attentively.

◆ The Voice of Little People ◆

As every UFO fan knows, there has been a brown-out of UFO or flying saucer news for several years. Only a few publications have kept faith with those who *know* that UFO are a reality. Some general magazines have printed sporadic articles on flying saucers, but in recent months these have been largely a re-hash of widely known incidents; opinionated and unverifiable expositions based on erroneous scientific concepts; or, worse, damaging hoaxes.

Miss Dorothy Kilgallen's International News Service report from London in May, 1955, was the first UFO report given complete national distribution in several years, though there has been no dearth of UFO activity. Miss Kilgallen's report was featured in many important papers. After hearing it via radio, this author saw it first in the Miami *Herald*. Subsequently clippings were received from all over the country. We quote the story as run in the Miami *Herald*, May 23, 1955:

I can report on a story which is positively spooky. British scientists and airmen, after examining the wreckage of a mysterious flying ship, are convinced that these strange aerial objects are not optical illusions or Soviet inventions but originate on another planet. *The source of my information is a British official of cabinet rank who prefers to remain unidentified.* "We believe, on the basis of our inquiries thus far, that the saucers were staffed by small men—probably under four feet tall," my informant told me. "It's frightening, but there is no denying the flying saucers come from another planet." *This official quoted scientists as saying that a flying ship of this type could not possibly have been constructed on earth.* The British government, I learned, is withholding an official report on the flying saucer examination at this time, possibly because it does not wish to frighten the public. In the United States, all kinds of explanations have been advanced for often-sighted flying saucers. But no responsible official in the United States Air Force has yet maintained the mysterious flying ships had actually vaulted from outer space.

We take one minor exception to the statements as reported: It is jumping to conclusions to say the strange ship came from another *planet.* To make another planet the only alternative to terrestrial origin is so oversimplify, and to disregard masses of evidence. Such assumptions indicate that our conceptions are too narrow as regards life and intelligence. The existence of life in surrounding space is more acceptable to reason than assumptions that the great number of observed UFO must, of necessity, come from another *planet.*

As for the "little men," at least *they* are not new to earth. We have had "little people" for millennia—for eons, and nobody has set forth any logical earth origin, though it *may be possible,* eventually, to find a niche for them in the accepted chain of evolution.

There are "little people" in African and New Guinea jungles today. They have been written about, photographed, measured and studied. But *nobody* knows their origin or ancestry. They are, perhaps, one of the "erratics" of ethnology. Were these people, these isolated tribes, "planted" in the tropical African jungle from UFO thousands of years ago? Did UFO land, or crash, and establish racial germs or colonies? At Zimbabwe? For there are evidences of Pygmy races in many other parts of the world.

"Common denominators" help us to organize knowledge which is in chaos. In the present chaos of UFO lore, can the concept of "little people" serve as a common denominator? Let's glance at the encyclopedias.

In the *International Encyclopedia* (1930 Edition, volume XIX, page 396), Kollman says that the *primitive ancestors of mankind were Pygmies*. He cites three principal geographical areas where Pygmies still live.

A. The wavy-haired, Asiatic Pygmies, the Saki or Senoi, live in the southern part of the Malay Peninsula; the Toala in the Celebes; and the Vedda and some jungle tribes in the Deccan (India). They are considered survivals of a pre-Davridian race.

B. The woolly-haired Asiatics, Negritos, include the Andaman Islanders; the Semang in central Malay Peninsula; the Aeta, in the Philippines and others in New Guinea, etc.

C. The woolly-haired African Pygmies scattered through Equatorial Africa.

Extensive references on Pygmies can be found in:

Pygmy Races of Men, by W. H. Flower, in the Journal of the Anthropological Institute of London, volume XVIII; *Pygmies,* by Frederick Star; *Man: Past and Present,* by A. H. Keane; *The Pygmies,* by Quatrefages (translation from the French).

One of the best *brief* discussions is in the 11th edition of the *Encyclopedia Britannica*. It cites a description in the *Iliad* of a Pygmy race in the far south (Africa). Pliny mentioned Pygmies in Asia and Africa, the Catize dwarfs in Thrace, and a similar race in Caria. Ctesias wrote of Pygmies in the heart of India . . . "black, ugly, hairy."

Relics of Pygmy races exist in Sicily and Sardinia, *along the highroads between pleistocene Africa and Europe.* Dr. Kollman found neolithic skeletal remains of European Pygmies near Schaffhausen.

Some anthropologists believe that a dwarf race, inhabiting ancient Europe, gave rise to the legends of elves, goblins, gnomes, etc. Were the fabulous Picts in this group?

Some scientists hold that a now-submerged Indo-African continent was the original home of primitive man. (Churchward's lost continent of Mu.) The *Britannica* also postulates that the Miocene ancestors of the Pygmies may have reached Java from this sinking continent. This fits into our own postulates of the vast antiquity, possibly reaching back millions of years, of intelligent mankind on earth.

Do you recall the accounts of low types of animal life falling from the sky? And our speculations that UFO crews may grow larval, insect, or reptilian life in their craft for food? Well, it is established that the Pygmies often eat larvae, ants, grubs, etc.

Among many points of distinction, The Andaman Island Pygmies believe in a god, Puluga, *who lives in a stone house in the sky;* and Malay Pygmies have a language which has no root similarity to any known tongue.

Then, there is the little hand-worked meteorite from the tertiary coalbeds, and the small worked stone from Tarbes, France, reported so graphically by Charles Fort. Such wrought objects extracted from coalbeds or rock quarries or dropped from space are small and delicate, *as though made by little people.*

We have inferred an ancient race on earth, with enough intelligence to have developed true, wingless flight; and that they either moved into space or were deposited on earth by UFO from space; and that they may have been "little people."

Pygmies.

Dorothy Kilgallen's news feature from England was but the climax of a long series of reports.

Have we, then, a common denominator: *Pygmies?*

Maybe yes, maybe no . . . but, harking back to the accounts of things which fall from the sky, we see significance in an incident communicated to the *UFO Reporter* recently by Miss Mildred E. Danforth. She suggests checking it in New York since she cannot vouch for it personally. During construction work on the Cathedral of Saint John the Divine, workmen left a high scaffolding in place over a weekend. When they returned, they found lying on the scaffolding the body of a little man with one eye in the middle of his forehead. A New York *Times* reporter is said to have written it up, but his story was "killed" to avoid the charge of sensationalism. Army authorities were said to have removed the body. Do little people then fall from the sky occasionally, as well as frogs, snakes, periwinkles, fish, etc.?

The following generalizations about the little people have been formed by scientists:

1. The Pygmies cannot be considered a degenerate form of any known race of mankind.

2. They are of a very ancient human stock.

3. It is not yet *fully* established that the Pygmies are the oldest type, or prototype, of the human race.

4. There appear to be several variant races of Pygmies, but it is not clear if all came from the same terrestrial stock.

5. The question of relationship, or affinity, between the Asiatic Pygmies is especially puzzling.

6. The Andaman Islanders are considered an entirely unmixed breed, but all tribes have very ancient racial components carried through many thousands of years of development.

7. Apart from some few pronounced racial traits such as frizzy hair and color of skin and, of course, stature, there are vague anthropological affinities between the Melanesian Pygmies and others. But the question remains unsettled.

◆ The Voice of Geography ◆

Such students as Kaudern and Nippold, making exhaustive studies of world-wide Pygmy distribution, have conceded that this is one of the greatest of all ethnological puzzles.

There are conflicting schools of thought on the matter of the geographical distribution and origins of the Negro and Pygmy races. One, for which Logan is spokesman, holds that they originated in Africa and slowly penetrated into southeast Asia and Oceania by way of the sea. Another school from whom Dr. Flower is spokesman holds that the Pygmies spread eastwards and westwards from southern India. Equally puzzling is how they could have been distributed into so many isolated communities, scattered over a wide band, *encircling the earth.* Where and how did they originate?

Professor Seely supposes that the African Pygmy races reached Malaya via a sunken continent (Lemuria) which scientists believe connected northeast Africa with India. This supposition is not in conflict with Churchward's statement that there are submerged cities of incalculable antiquity in the shallow waters just west of the Indian mainland. If such a continent existed, as seems probable, the migration could as easily have been from east to west, as Dr. Allen posits, and would fit Quatrefages' deduction that central Asia was their origin.

In his book, *The Pygmies*, Quatrefages says that we cannot separate the history of the black races, including the Pygmies, from that of the yellow and white races. He says man originated in tertiary times in northern Asia and migrated southward, eastward, and westward, and developed basic racial variations. The central highlands of Asia, he points out, still have three of the basic races. The Pygmies were the first to arrive in the Eastern Archipelago and in the Bay of Bengal. New data, however, make parts of his theory questionable.

Note that throughout all the published discussions on the Pygmy races, certain peculiar conditions are reiterated and emphasized. One is the large number of *isolated* Pygmy tribes. We have Pygmy tribes in New Guinea, far to the east in the South Pacific; a distinctive Pygmy race in the Andaman Islands far to the west in the Bay of Bengal; and equally distinctive Pygmy tribes scattered through the Philippine archipelago. There are also variant branches of Pygmy races in southwest Asia. Note also that none of these scattered groups are large. Seldom did any one group obtain more than a few thousand individuals, even before contact with civilization reduced their numbers.

Also note that the same conditions obtain in Africa; namely, that they occur in *isolated* tribes, though they have certain basic characteristics in common, but exhibiting intra-tribal individuality from long isolation.

Flower set the southern limit of the Oriental Pygmy races at the Sunda Strait and the northern limit at Taiwan (Formosa) with traces in Japan. The eastward limit is New Guinea; the westward, the Andaman Islands and probably India.

Some experts believe that the Pygmies once inhabited a vast area of Southeast Asia, and that all these groups are interrelated. Today only scattered remnants survive. This also seems to apply to the African tribes.

Attempts have been made to show that the Pygmies in the

Philippine Islands, the Andaman Islands and New Guinea, all reached these places by sea. This has been seriously challenged by Kaudern, who doubts that the Pygmies ever had boats. According to other hypotheses, the Pygmies reached these islands from the Asian mainland by way of land bridges. This would give them great geological antiquity. There is a difference of opinion among scientists about the submergence of such land bridges, whether they occurred before or after the advent of man.

Most challenging, perhaps, of the puzzles relating to this incomprehensible human group is the origin of the Philippine Pygmies. Geologists do not postulate land bridges from the Asian continent within any time during which mankind could conceivably have existed. And, if the Philippine Pygmies arrived via bridge from Sumatra and Borneo, why are there no traces of Pygmies in these two great islands?

Walter Kaudern considers the riddle of the origin of the Philippine Pygmies insoluble. By this extreme statement we suppose he means insoluble by conventional science. He is convinced that, throughout all their millions of years of history, the Pygmies lacked the intelligence to create any kind of seagoing craft, and that land bridges must have existed for the convenience of the little men. Yet he concedes that no great tectonic or volcanic activity took place there, in or since quaternary times.

The only other condition which could have produced land bridges was glaciation prolonged enough to lower the sea level throughout the world by transferring much of its water to extensive ice caps.

About three hundred feet of fall in sea-level would have provided a land bridge from the Malay mainland to the Andaman Islands, which have Pygmy inhabitants. This assumes that the contours of the ocean have not changed appreciably during these millions of years—a risky assumption.

But it would have required a drop from three to nine thousand meters in the water level to expose a land bridge from the Asiatic mainland to the Philippine Islands. No change of such a nature is conceivable. It would presuppose an almost incalculable accumulation of ice at the poles. According to Kaudern, the greatest conjectured lowering of sea-level through glaciation is approximately nine hundred feet, which is not enough to link the Philippines with the Malay peninsula.

Consequently, if the Pygmies did migrate by land from the Asiatic mainland to the Philippines they must have done so in slow stages, during quaternary times, and via very circuitous routes, first from the mainland westward to mountainous country the peaks of which, as the slopes were submerged by melting polar ice, became the Andamans. From there the little folk would have had to move tortuously southward, then southeast for hundreds of miles, to reach Sumatra. Thence, to reach New Guinea they would have gone eastward, over mountainous terrain for 3,000 miles. They might have branched off from Sumatra to Bornea and thence to the Philippines, via, perhaps, the Celebes, a distance of 2,000 miles or so. Sumatra and Borneo are at the center of this area. Why are there no Pygmies or Pygmy remains there?

A trek to south Africa would have been more than twice as far. Again we are faced with choice between high improbabilities, and if more logical means of global migration can be found, they deserve consideration.

Kaudern finally concluded that there must have been such variations in sea-level, since no other means of exposing land bridges can be admitted in the light of present geological knowledge. But it is not a satisfactory explanation.

The weakness in Kaudern's reasoning lies in his assumption that the Pygmies never reached cultural levels high enough to devise water transportation. In our own thinking the Pygmies may have developed a high civilization in ancient times, and attained an intellectual level almost infinitely beyond anything contemplated by Kaudern or other ethnologists.

It will be helpful to the reader to consult a large-scale map of the Indian ocean, and the Indonesian area southeast of Asia. It will at once be apparent that any land migration of Pygmies from the Andaman Islands to the Philippines must have proceeded over the huge islands of Sumatra and Borneo, or by even longer routes.

It will be seen from the map that these isolated Pygmy settlements are on the edges of the Malaya-Indonesia complex. Since we do not find Pygmies in the center of the area, hypotheses of means of distribution based on submerged land bridges are questionable. Even Kaudern and Haddon have admitted the tenuous nature of their own speculations. But if Pygmies did not migrate via land bridges or by sea, then *how?*

Must we not seek another method of distribution?

In *The Case for the UFO*, when no "natural" explanations could be found for proven phenomena, and where will or intelligence seemed evident, we did the logical thing and looked for them in *other* than "natural" manifestations. Perhaps this is our "way out" too from the maze of Pygmy scattering and origin. Maybe there *is* another explanation?

We have long postulated a race of superior mental development in very ancient pre-flood times. We found much to indicate that possibility. With only a slight mental adjustment, we can picture Pygmies as that prehistoric race which developed space flight in those eons between the Tertiary age and the flood. If they were operating space craft around the earth; or if they came to earth from space, it would follow that these isolated tribes might be survivors or colonists from space craft which either crashed or landed. Prolonged isolation may have produced their well-known racial fear of "strangers."

Also if space navigation was devised by early Pygmy cultures *many* thousands of years ago, some of these space craft may have been operating away from the earth when the flood wiped out most of their kin. Thus, while these "sons of mankind" were "away on a far journey" mankind may have escaped "by the skin of his teeth."

◆ The Voices of Chronology and Antiquity ◆

The dilemma of official science on this subject is evidence of what is stressed in this volume: that the present framework of science is inadequate to encompass the reality of the world in which we live.

It is doubtless praiseworthy of science that it eternally

strives to secure each foothold before proceeding to the next. But thereby it tends to limit itself to the quantitative at the expense of the qualitative. Science is continually being frustrated through its failure to recognize an adequate time-scale for human intellectuality and to acknowledge the scope of archaic mental activity.

Let us review some chronological considerations as given in geology, bearing on the Pygmy question, and the relationships of the Pygmies to "little people" and the UFO.

AGE OF SOME OF THE MORE RECENT GEOLOGICAL PERIODS

Geological Eras		Millions of Years	
		Duration of Era	Time Since Beginning of Era
Quaternary {	Recent	—	—
	Pleistocene	1.7	1.7
Tertiary {	Pleiocene	13	15
	Miocene	18	33
	Oligoscene	9	42
	Eocene-Paleocene	11	53

One of the big questions about Pygmies, ranking with the problems of their distribution and origin, is: "How long have Pygmies been here on earth?"

According to ethnologists the Pygmy man of the Miocene times, more than thirty million years ago, was a full-fledged human being—not a missing link. Thirty million years ago is 15,000 *times* as long as the Christian era, and 5,000 times as long as our recorded history.

Did the Pygmies (or any other race) in that vast stretch of time develop a high order of civilization? Certainly they were firmly established as a race for as long as any other, and perhaps a good deal longer. If our civilization has developed to its present towering peak in a few thousand years, others could have done so (and disappeared) many times over. We need only reflect upon these "races" and "civilizations" that have come and gone *within* recorded history.

Fossil remains are important in the establishment of chronological and other scientific data. But *fossil remains of Pygmies are surprisingly scarce.* Therefore, paleontology, archaeology and anthropology have failed to throw much light on the age or origin of the Pygmy people, or on any archaic Pygmy civilization above Stone Age level. Yet there are positive hints from combined archaeological-geological sources. With Kaudern, we can turn for a moment to zoogeography (the world distribution and movement of animal life) for clues to the antiquity and antecedents of Pygmy stock.

Certain cultures are often said to have appeared as going concerns complete with writing, mathematics and various amenities as far back as we trace them. They do not show the developmental stages normally leading out of Stone Age existence. Some archaeologists dispute this, but there remian the puzzles of Egypt, the Orient, and South America.

However, few scientists have been so brash as to postulate that an entire race appeared suddenly and without normal evolutionary development. We will not be that brash, either. We simply say that no matter how far back one goes—perhaps thirty million years to the Miocene—there were Pygmies. Not midgets, but *fully developed human beings, whom science has not been able to connect with other races.*

It might be observed in passing that that perennial best-seller, the Bible, mentions an abrupt creation (or *arrival*) of fully developed man.

In its fauna, Indonesia is, strangely enough, more closely related to Africa than to India. Some zoologists refer the Pygmy to the Pleiocene, postulating their spread from the Orient to Africa, along with Oriental fauna. This assumes some kind of land connection either very deviously by way of India, Asia Minor and Arabia; or by way of a now sunken land mass which may have stretched from Northeast Africa to Oceania. This closely approaches Churchward's concept of a now submerged continent of Mu, though differing somewhat in location, and is plausible in the light of geological, botanical and zoological data.

The Australian Bushmen have been rated the most primitive

people on earth, and they share certain characteristics with the Pygmies, although they are not quite so small in stature.

Flower considers the Bushmen of South Africa the earliest race of which it is possible for us to have knowledge. This could mean that these ethnological kinfolk of the Pygmies comprise the oldest living race in direct lineal descent from primitive man. But from new studies made since Flower's time, I consider the pre-Dravidian Pygmies the oldest—older even than the Australian Bushmen, which makes me wonder why the most primitive races in existence today seem also to be the oldest pure strains? Why is orthodox science unable to establish their origin?

I believe, with Kaudern, that the Pygmies were in existence many thousands of years before the periods of glaciation. Conditions must have favored the rise of archaic civilizations during the interglacial eras and in the previous millions of years during which there were certainly Pygmies . . . who may well have been the dominant species on earth.

This is more or less in line with Churchward's thesis that ancient civilizations spread westward from a now submerged continent which he called Mu. If we accept his hypothesis, and also admit that such a civilization was made up, at least in part, of Pygmies who are known to have been an established race at that time, we may consider that world-wide cataclysms, one of which was the "Flood," may well have destroyed all of civilization except a few remnants scattered here and there over far-flung, and somewhat inaccesible, areas.

This might indicate that we have been mistaking as origins what were actually surviving vestiges of a pre-Flood civilization of vast extent. In other words, the first development from Stone Age conditions took place prior to that destruction, and what we are seeing is the re-emergence of a previously developed race.

It seems evident that these isolated Pygmy tribes occupy sites which were once the mountain tops or plateaus of now submerged areas. The survivals may then be from the backward, perhaps even degenerate, portions of the early races making up the "first wave of civilization." The archaic "hill-billies" far from the sea-board centers of trade and culture would hardly have been the most advanced elements of the race.

Bible students may recall that Christ left instructions for mankind to make a dash for the mountains at the first shock of disaster. Does this mean that a future cataclysm will repeat the one which almost annihilated the world's earlier civilizations?

Some of our dilemmas might be resolved merely by accepting a new timetable for civilization, allowing for advanced intellectual achievements before the Flood. After all, Noah must have inherited some technical knowledge to have built an ark (large as a modern tanker) capable of riding out the deluge. Even Churchward may not have been sufficiently liberal in his chronological scale. Perhaps he should have placed the mother civilization of Mu in the Pleiocene or Miocene; possibly even antedating the tertiary coalbeds in which was found the hand-worked bit of meteoric steel.

There seems little doubt that the Pygmy people were a part of the terrestrial scene in the Pleiocene. If they were also active in the Miocene, this race is more than 30,000,000 years old and was fully developed as human beings at that time. Who, then, are *we* to deny that they could have developed even one civilization in all that time—one capable of flight of a type simpler than our heavier-than-air flight? Of space flight?

◆ The Voice of Psychology ◆

There is one peculiarity of Pygmy tribes which is of considerable significance to our UFO problem. Not only do Pygmy groups always appear isolated, but all have an antipathy to intercourse with other races.

The mind of the Pygmy seems to be almost pathologically conditioned to isolation. He is universally resentful of foreign intrusion. Some kind of *racial* lesson seems to have been so etched into his brain as to make it a racially inherent characteristic. The mind of the Pygmy is the mind of a prisoner kept too long in solitary confinement.

Now, *where* was the Pygmy held captive, or where did he develop this xenophobia, or fear of outsiders—this introversion?

Would it be—could it be—that centuries of confined living in the cells of space ships (or on the moon, in air-tight structures) would produce these characteristics? Leave him with the instinctive feeling that he is a stranger on earth?

◆ The Voice of Genealogy ◆

Chronology and origins are related to the evolutionary continuity of Pygmies with other mammalia; and to whether the Pygmy race appeared abruptly, as a going concern, no matter how far backward we may look. Scientists have told us that the Pygmy of the Miocene was already a distinct human type.

I have been referring to "little people" and "Pygmies" rather indiscriminately. These terms have been used deliberately. A Pygmy is a person well-proportioned and normal in every respect except his small stature. A dwarf or midget, on the other hand, is a stunted and often deformed individual.

From time to time, throughout the reporting of little people either in UFO sightings or in ancient history, we encounter the statement that a specimen or race had normal features and bodily proportions. Science establishes that Miocene Pygmies were fully developed, normal human beings of small stature. Thus we are identifying a race, and not freaks.

There seems to be a discontinuity in the evolutionary stream of the Pygmies' beginnings; at the junction or point of contact with origins of other human strains. Areas of discontinuity suggest intelligence and choice. We seem to be drawing ever nearer to recognizing the distinction between the statistical realm of Godhead and Divine Law, and those environmental elements controllable by the intelligence of man, man-like beings, or even uncarnate intelligences operating below the omnipotent level of Godhead.

In his work *The Pygmies,* Quatrefages states: "*Modern science is sometimes misled by its own rigidity*"—an understatement worthy of John Bull himself. That was said in the nineteenth century, but the rigidity has not relaxed very much, so that one fears this may be one of those rare cases in which *rigor mortis* sets in before the death spasms. It has caused misreadings of traditions and legends, in which nuggets of truth are encrusted. Unbigoted researchers often pry out these nuggets and add them to the treasure trove of human knowledge, and they are nowhere more valuable than in the study of racial origins.

All variants of the Pygmy races seem to have some basic genetic inter-relationship, but no specific, direct or tangible *physical* connections have been established by the most painstaking students. *It almost seems that there has been a relationship in time, but not in geographical space* nor physical contact. Not only does each community of Pygmies differ greatly from neighboring non-Pygmy races, but authors disagree as to which other races are *least distinctly* related to the Pygmies—not caring to concede that other races may be *closely* related. If geographical distribution is the greatest puzzle of Pygmydom, then certainly the Pygmy genetic relationships and antecedents are a puzzle second only to the problems of their distribution.

Flower believed at one time that the Andaman Island Pygmies might be the parent Pygmy race. At another time he ascribed the descent of the entire Oriental group of Pygmy tribes to an early pre-Dravidian (Indian) race. The two ideas are not entirely incompatible, and fit in with Quatrefages' postulate that all human races sprang from a common source somewhere in mid-Asia.

The word "Dravidian" is generally applied to the races of the subcontinent of India. They are universally conceded to be of great antiquity, and Churchward supposed that they had arrived from a motherland to the east, now submerged, which he called Mu, some hundreds of thousands of years ago. Therefore, if the Pygmies are pre-Dravidian, they are of greater antiquity than any other known strain of Homo sapiens. Quatrefages, one of the best authorities, indicated that the Pygmies are definitely not a "missing link," but have been fully established human entities in their own right since the earliest times to which they can be traced. He believed that fully developed Tertiary man had all the essential human characteristics and . . . again . . . we search for "beginnings." As we have seen this may go back as far as the Miocene or as much as 30,000,000 years, enough for the establishment of any number of civilizations before ours, in which space-flying may have been discovered.

Obvious similarities between the Asian and African Pygmies, but none with *any* other race! Each Pygmy group differs from surrounding non-Pygmy groups, is an ethnological island—and, considering their nomadic habits, a floating island!

If the Pygmies and other races do come from common stock, their divergence occurred in the inscrutable past; or the site of this common stock was one from which all Pygmy "colonies could have been established independently of terrestrial surface movement."

Have you ever looked at a gorilla, a chimpanzee and an orangoutang side by side? Under their fur, the skin colors are *yellow, black, and white.* Correlate this with the geographical areas in which they are found, and you begin a most intriguing train of speculation.

According to Flower and other authorities, the Negrillos of Africa predate the Negroes of the same area, just as the Negritos of the Orient predate the other Asiatic and Melanesian types. For *millions of years,* it seems, the Pygmies have been *separate* from all other humanoid types. Their precedence seems to be established in spite of the lack of any genetic or evolutionary links with other races. Yet anthropological dogmatists insist that no race could maintain its original state over so long a period.

Was there, then, *no other race* with which the Pygmies could blend during those millions of years? But what if their parent strain lives in space? Would this dissolve some paradoxes?

We recognize racial similarities between the Pygmies of Africa and the Orient, but we find no direct links between these two major streams, nor can we envision any zoogeographical mechanics by which one could have arisen from the other. Both P. W. Schmidt and Walter Kaudern have shown that, while a common origin of the African and Asian branches cannot be established, the features they share in common, including small stature, short head, and frizzy hair, cannot be denied. Therefore, if they are related, their common ancestors belong to almost unacceptably remote geologic times—*unless some new and unprecedented method of distribution is envisioned.*

Since genetic links between the Pygmies and their adjacent neighbors are absent, just where *do* we stand with regard to the relationship of the Pygmies with the remainder of mankind? Or with the entire environment of the earth?

To date, science has been forced to admit its failure to establish: (1) the genetic origin of the Pygmy race; (2) the geographical origin; (3) the route and mechanism of their distribution through Asia, Melanesia and Africa, and (4) a reason for the lack of affinity between the Pygmy and other races by whom, for thousands of years, they have been surrounded.

Again there is a haunting sense that these relationships have, somehow, jumped geographical, geological and genetic gaps. There is no trace of intermediate evolutional stages. It is exactly as though there were a "time-fault" or discontinuity in the human-terrestrial adventure. But space travel, or permanent habitation in space, could rationalize all this. A common origin in *space* could explain the unconnected diversity of the Pygmies, the geographical isolation of their little groups, and other puzzles.

In all: a prize quandary for ethnology.

◆ The Voice of the Sphinx and the Pyramids ◆

The team of astronomy-archaeology has something to add to the subject of Pygmies-science-antiquity-gravitation. For one thing, the passages in the Great Pyramid are adapted *only* to the "little people."

The passage to the so-called Queen's chamber is approximately 46½ inches high. The height of the passage to the "King's chamber," at the top of the Grand Gallery, is approximately 43 inches. The vertical height of the main passage is about four feet four inches, while the height perpendicular to the floor is about 47 inches—just under four feet.

It is not for me to say that this vast pyramid was built by a Pygmy race. Nonetheless, it is almost unthinkable that a race, intelligent enough to construct such an edifice, manifesting astronomical data of the most profound and complex nature, would make the passages too low for convenient use.

In *The Great Pyramid*, D. Davidson, a British engineer, outstanding analyst of pyramid data, maintains that a highly developed civilization existed in times which are generally and vaguely referred to as "pre-historic." He indicated that among other reasonable inferences is the probability that this former civilization came to a catastrophic end and very little of its culture survived except in the form of tradition. This parallels my own conclusions, but omits consideration of many great works of stone which have survived the cataclysm, but which may not have been familiar to Davidson.

The men who founded the modern "wave" of civilization built on and from the lore carried over from a former culture. Huge, archaic structures, particularly in Egypt, Peru, Yucatan and Tibet, indicate a high development at the earliest known stages of their construction, albeit imperfectly understood by us. As many writers have pointed out, these isolated, yet similar, reviving remnants of past civilization appeared almost ready-made, which is evidence of highly cultured predecessors.

Tradition, from all sources, declares the former civilization was destroyed by cataclysm. In Egypt it was called "the destruction of mankind": in ancient Mexico, Peru and other places, "the destruction of the world," and in the ancient Near East, China, Egypt and elsewhere, the "deluge" or the "Flood." Many appear to be versions of the deluge narrative in the Bible.

I concur in Davidson's belief that the Pyramid was built for the perpetuation of scientific knowledge transmitted from the ancients. But I dissent from his interpretation of mathematics and metrology of the Pyramid in Christian apocalyptic terms, electing Britain as the "chosen" nation.

The Pyramid is a solid, concise, geometrical expression of natural laws known to a former civilization. Unquestionably it refers to both linear measurements and the motions of the solar system. Motion implies or infers time—and gravitation. It will suffice here to say that the geometry of the great Pyramid depicts, among other things, the dimensions of the earth's orbit, its eccentricity, period of rotation, procession of the equinoxes and other astronomical concepts involving space, time and gravitation.

In the diagram, the circumference ABCDA, stated in pyramid or "primitive inches" is 36,524.2465 and the length of the solar year is 365.2425 days. The circumference $Ae_1e_2Bf_1f_2Cg_1g_2DH_1h_2A$ is 36,525.64715 P'', and the length of the sidereal year is 365.25647 days. The circumference A m B n C o D p A is 36,525.9973 P'' and the length of the anomalistic year is 365.2596 days.

The sidereal year is the time required by the earth to make one complete revolution of 360° around the sun, as measured from the absolute positions of the stars. The solar year is the time

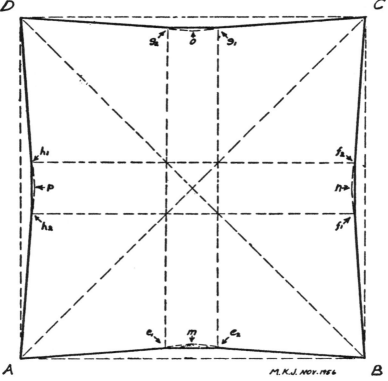

ACTUAL BASE-LINE OF GREAT PYRAMID *(solid line) shows true outline of base with hollowing-in effect, which depicts the three periods of revolution of the earth in its orbit. Not drawn to scale.*

required for the earth to make a revolution around the sun from vernal equinox to vernal equinox. The earth's orbit is also revolving slowly and the anomalistic year is the time required for the earth to go from perihelion, the point in its orbit where it is closest to the sun, back to perihelion.

The sum of the diagonals AC and AB in P″ is 25,826.5 and the period of the procession of the equinoxes is 25,826+ years. It is this period of approximately 26,000 years which I believe constitutes the error in Davidson's calculations. I believe the Pyramid was built 26,000 or 52,000 years earlier than has previously been admitted. It may have been 78,000 or 104,000 years ago or longer.

Many other astronomical quantities are built to scale in the Pyramid, with the primitive inch as unit measure (1/500,000,000th of the arc from equator to pole). One of these is the eccentricity of orbit (deviation from a true circle) also defined by the same circumferential base lines used for laying out the length of the various years. Some of these quantities take thousands of years of close instrumental observation for accurate determination.

The Pygmies may not have had such a highly developed science. However, *somebody did*, but hardly the Egyptians of 3,000 B.C.

Davidson thought that the state of scientific astronomy reached by the antecedent culture was equal to, or superior to ours. The data built into the Pyramid indicate an advanced knowledge of *gravitation* and the mathematics of planetary orbits. Obviously some underlying natural law of beautiful simplicity, *encompassing gravitation,* is represented in the pyramidal form. Only Einstein in our civilization has approached it and even he did not entirely achieve it. Clearly the Great Pyramid was constructed to perpetuate that astronomical and mathematical knowledge.

Davidson concluded that the builders were survivors of the cataclysm. They must still have possessed the libraries or other stored data. Such a structure as the Pyramid could not have been built from orally transmitted knowledge. There is no indication that the Egyptians after 5,000 B.C. had the knowledge or the ability. The faulty nature of some of their chronology is evidence that in the centuries immediately preceding the Christian era they lacked the knowledge to build or even understand the Great Pyramid.

Davidson considered it proven that the former civilization was "more highly skilled in the sciences of gravitational astronomy, and therefore in the mathematical basis of gravitation, than modern civilization." It has taken man thousands of years to rediscover what he had more precisely known by a surer and simpler method than ours in an earlier phase.

This is in keeping with my repeated proposals that the first wave of civilization had stumbled onto or discovered some physical laws more basic than any which we know today, particularly in relation to gravitation; which brings up again the question of whether this knowledge originated here or in space.

Using complex astronomical theory, Davidson calculated that the entrance passageway was oriented for observation of the star Alpha Draconis when it was the pole star in either the year 2144 B.C., or the year 3434 B.C., deducing from this that the Pyramid was built at one or the other of those two epochs. It is remotely possible that he is correct, but then it is hard to explain why the Pyramid seems to have been a traditional landmark in Egypt in earlier periods. By Davidson's own admission, the knowledge necessary for such a construction must have come from a previous civilization wiped out thousands of years before. Such knowledge could not possibly have been transmitted by tradition over such a period.

The same reasoning as that used by Davidson would permit the Pyramid passageways to have served the same purpose approximately 26,000 years (or any multiple of this period) earlier than his given two dates. This is indirectly conceded by Davidson when he observed that "no other date for 30,000 years in the past, or 30,000 years in the future, would fit all the observed facts."

My contention is that the construction of the Pyramid took place 30,000 or 60,000 years ago. I feel that Davidson misinterpreted certain elements of a chronological scale in deference to the dogmatic insistence of science and theology that no major civilization existed before 7,000 or 8,000 years ago.

The levitation of heavy stone megaliths for structures such as Sacsahuaman, Easter Island, Baalbek, Tiahuanaco, etc. has been discussed elsewhere. Here we need only reaffirm that it is explained by the mechanical and gravitational genius associated with the ancient civilization we now credit with the acumen to have incorporated an entire astronomical-gravitational science into the Great Pyramid of Gizeh.

Furthermore the oldest known authentic record of the visitation of a fleet of UFO was in Egypt. (Reproduced on page 180 of *The Case for the UFO*).

Certain astronomical data were held by the ancient Chaldeans and the Chinese, in common with the Egyptians, and we must at least consider the possibility that it was inherited from a common source. Churchward believed that such astronomical knowledge came to India with the Nagas, from Mu, a submerged continent to the east. From India, he believes, it spread to China, the Middle East and Egypt. We must also realize that the Maya Indians of Central America had a calendar system superior even to that of the Egyptians and the Chinese, and an intimate knowledge of planetary movements. Churchward believed the Maya to be an eastern colony of Mu.

◆ The Voice of Philology ◆

According to Flower, the isolated African groups of Pygmies are experiencing gradual extinction through inbreeding, the hardships of their nomad life, and the intrusions of other races. Modern observation confirms this.

Flower described the Andaman Pygmies as moral, even by our own codes, in spite of a nasty, pugnacious nature. No taint of cannibalism existed among them. Though some of the literature presents them as amoral, their sexual relations, intra-family and intra-tribal obligations, and other ethical restraints have analogues in our own codes.

Dr. Flower described many tribes as having taken refuge in the mountains and some as living in natural caves. Other writers speak of the aversion of some Pygmy tribes to living in confined places as a sort of claustrophobia, and observe that they will not live anywhere except in the forests. This is not true of the semi-Pygmy bushmen of South Africa, who live in natural caves; and of some Oriental Pygmies. Is there a racial memory which inhibits some races from living in caves? I think of the smashed tunnels of the Andes.

The French authority on the Pygmies, Quatrefages, believed that they were basically intelligent but that their minds are asleep. Up to the ages of twelve to fourteen, Pygmy children have I.Q.'s approximately equal to those of our children. And other ethnologists have recorded that the few Pygmies trained in white schools have shown considerable ability and capacity to learn.

The language spoken by the Andaman Island Pygmies probably preceded all those spoken in neighboring Malaya, Thailand and perhaps even India. This is in line with ethnological speculations that the South Asian Pygmies occupied India and Southeast Asia before the "pre-Dravidian" races.

The Andaman Pygmy has only two cardinal numbers: one and two. From these he counts up to ten, but no further, by touching his nose with each of his fingers successively, and adding the words "this one also."

Every folk has its own version of the Flood, indicating that this catastrophe was world-wide and so calamitous that it was indelibly impressed upon the racial memory.

Legend among some of the Pygmy groups has it that descendants of the first pair of humans became too numerous for their original locality and scattered widely, which agrees with the theories of Quatrefages.

After creating the first human couple, Tomo and Elewadi, the God Puluga taught them a language, which the Andaman Pygmies believe was the one still spoken in a district in Middle Andaman Island. Philological study supplies no reasons for doubting them.

The tradition runs that the second generation after Tomo became so morally lax that Puluga sent a chastising flood which covered the whole earth and destroyed almost all living things. However, two men and two women in a canoe (the ark story in miniature) escaped to become ancestors of the present islanders.

(How closely this parallels the belief that all present races are but reviving embers of a glorious past!) Puluga threatened a repetition of the penalty if they did not behave, and they live in constant dread. They are on their good behavior according to a moral code that may be the oldest in existence.

Some Malay Pygmies have a language which is totally unrelated to any other known terrestrial tongue; yet, they seem to have a racial memory of the use of writing.

What created and maintained the isolation necessary to develop and perpetuate such linguistic purity? Theories of migration by sea or by land bridges break down before linguistic homogeneity of such rigor. These tribes had to originate from some place almost literally "out of this world." For they could hardly have done much migrating without picking up a few "foreign words."

Moreover, it would seem that they might have arrived from that source at a comparatively recent time, to account for such a conspicuous lack of inter-cultural influence.

From where and by what means could this have been accomplished, other than from the profound depths of the earth-moon binary space? Or from another planet? And via UFO?

◆ The Voices of Theology and Mythology ◆

The Malay Pygmies, according to explorers who have lived among them, believe that God exists *above* them, and created them. The universality of such beliefs about "heaven" is one of the phenomena of world-wide religion, and cannot be explained away as mere coincidence. There must be some common cause for this world-wide belief, and the most acceptable one is the postulate of a physical, existent "Heaven" surrounding the earth, *and* known to the original parent community.

It is of especial pertinence to our current theme that *the African Pygmies believe their gods to live overhead, beyond the blue sky.* It is one of *our* most basic religious concepts that *our* God and his agent, Christ, together with their angels, *dwell above us, beyond the sky.* Of all fundamental religious tenents, this, which points toward life and intelligence in the space around us, seems to be the most universal. We can almost say that this is *common knowledge* rather than merely *common belief.*

The book *Among Forest Dwarfs of Malaya,* by Paul Schebesta, has some particularly significant reports to make about the Kenta. According to their tradition, the world in the beginning was all water. The great god Kaei *dwelt above in the firmament* and *beside him was the sun.* Compare that with the thesis developed in *The Case for the UFO* that the mother bases, or craft, from which come our smaller UFO, are located in space, almost directly in line with the sun.

The ethnologist Mann thus summarized the religion of the Mincopies, who are considered a Pygmy race:

Puluga, their God: (1) resembles fire, but is invisible; (2) was never born but is immortal (see Hebrews 7:3, anent Melchisadek); (3) created the world and all good things, both animate and inanimate. He is believed to *dwell in a great stone mansion in the sky.* He eats and drinks. When it rains, he descends to earth to gather food. During the dry season, he sleeps most of the time. Puluga prefers certain roots, fruits and seeds for food. Whatever man has, he got from Puluga. When angered Puluga comes forth from his house, blows, thunders, and hurls blazing fagots. So the Mincopies explain their most dreadful tempests. (Remember controlled organic clouds.)

The Hottentots also have personified the clouds which bear thunder and lightning as a divine family. Throughout Pygmy religious beliefs, one finds storms and clouds serving as weapons for wrathful gods. Puluga uses the storm cloud as his vehicle.

The Mincopies' belief that Puluga descends to the earth to gather food when it rains may take on significance for us when we recall descriptions of apparently purposeful storms. The irate Puluga, coming forth from his house, blowing, thundering and hurling blazing fagots, is in line with those clouds that develop in a calm sky, proceed with intelligent deliberation, spit stones and debris and pass away.

How significant are the characteristics of Puluga? To resemble fire, yet be invisible, fits many descriptions of UFO. The stone mansion in the sky is important in view of our growing conviction that the very ancient "first wave of civilization" worked with stone to the almost complete exclusion of metal. It is not impossible that the UFO in space are made of stone, or stone-like material. They may even be intelligently manipulated asteroids.

In *The Pygmies*, Quatrefages makes an allusion of remarkable significance in connection with reports of little people inhabiting UFO. The Mincopies' god Puluga is not alone in his stone celestial mansion: *"He lives with a woman of green color*, whom he created for himself. They have a son and many daughters, *black angels who amuse themselves by throwing fish and crustaceans into bodies of fresh or salt water to be used for human food."*

Puluga's *green consort*, living with him in a stone mansion in the sky, accords with reports of green "little people" associated with crashed or landed UFO.

The heavenly concept of the Pygmies is not radically at variance with the descriptions of "heaven" in our own Bible; of "our father's mansions"; and the general synonymity between "Heaven" and a religion of intelligent activity surrounding the Earth.

Recall the dumpings of fish, periwinkles, crustaceans and lower forms of life in general, and you will note some significance in the black angels' tossing of fish and crustaceans to earth. Numberless instances have been reported, occurring in all lands, and obviously observed by the Pygmies. There is reality in these reports—and there must be a reason.

Churchward is among the few writers seriously to propose that our modern civilizations and races are but the slowly and painfully recovering remnants of the civilizations and peoples overwhelmed by the "Flood." This cataclysm served as a *sieve in time* through which rivulets of the human race were permitted to filter. Survivors were in inaccessible areas to which the full tide could not penetrate.

There is some evidence of lost arts among the Pygmies, who appear to have weak racial memories. This is of some significance to the thesis that in a very remote past, there may have been advanced Pygmy cultures. It is quite as if a racial intellect had been numbed by some terrific catastrophe.

The Mincopies worship a block of stone, thirty feet in diameter, which shows irregular markings. Although they have no writing or other means of recording anything, the Mincopies claim that this block narrates the history of creation—a remarkable notion in a race without any form of writing. It suggests racial memory of writing and its purpose—another minute but significant item of evidence of filtration through the time-curtain drawn by the universal cataclysm.

Quatrefages thought that the Pygmies, for the most part, were not pugnacious, as reported by some explorers; and that, in many ways, they are superior to the surrounding races. This is an indication of a latent ability which might have manifested itself directly in a now-extinct civilization.

All in all, the religious beliefs and traditions and myths of the Mincopies and other branches of Pygmydom can serve as a common denominator for our developing concepts of the space life of the UFO. The Pygmy "heaven" has remarkable similarities to ours, as it has to the heavens of many scattered and obscure races. It seems improbable that all could have developed the same ideas of "heaven overhead" or "beyond the sky" without some physical basis.

All point to *intelligence in space.*

◆ The Voice of Witchcraft ◆

With respect to "little people," there is every reason to believe that they have been here since the earliest advent of man; further, there is no provable evidence of their connection with a scientifically acceptable evolutionary tree. It is my contention that a pre-cataclysmic civilization of world-wide scope existed, and that the Pygmies constitute the race most likely to have produced it. This race had the power of levitation and worked in stone instead of metals. It did not develop electronic physics, but it understood basic gravitation better than we do. It used mental powers temporarily lost to us, but may have survived somewhat among direct descendents of early Pygmies.

Where traces of this "mental science" have been observed, they have been called, or attributed to, "magic." Where the magic seemed to have application and reality it has been derisively called "black magic" in contrast to the equally ritualistic but less substantial mysticism of the orthodox churches.

Witchcraft is indigenous among Pygmy peoples everywhere. Whatever may be the state of its validity today, or of its practical application, witchcraft indicates a residue of the science of a past civilization. Witchcraft, then, becomes an integral part of the background which we have to study in rationalizing two of the world's great interlocking mysteries: UFO and religion.

We have taken a close look at Pygmies in many areas, most of them in the tropical regions. We have found common characteristics, the universality of which could not be explained by known terrestrial mechanisms of migration or communication. Thus far we haven't discussed their traces in areas outside the tropics. Clues to them may be found in the records of witchcraft in the isles of Britain. These show that the Pygmies of ancient Europe and the northlands shared the powers, the racial characteristics and the scientific attainments of their brothers in milder climes. The Pygmy empire was world-wide.

Of the several works on witchcraft now in print, none serves our purpose so well as *Witchcraft Today*, by G. B. Gardner (Citadel Press). This book describes how the "little people"— the picts, gnomes, etc.—fell before the Celts and Saxons and other invaders. While the "little people" gained stature through intermarriage, they lost much of their racial heritage of mental or physic power. It is from this pictish strain that the early Britons drew their mystic and occult ability. There is evidence of a collateral nature that the Druids and the builders of such structures as Stonehenge were directly connected to the precursors of ancient Egyptian and Middle Eastern civilizations of thousands of years ago.

When Christian fanatics drove the rites of the little people underground, witchcraft became clandestine. Although weakened, it changed more in quantity than in kind; and it survives today. The appellation "Witchcraft" is a johnny-come-lately, being only a thousand or so years old and the associated stigma is a product of bigoted ignorance of Christian Crusaders.

But we are more concerned with showing the links between world-wide Pygmydom and the science of a remote past, a science which understood levitation and, most likely, developed space ships or inherited them from a parent race from the spatial reaches of the earth-moon binary system.

Scots, English and especially Irish folklore is full of tales concerning "little people." The significant similarities between some of the Irish folk tales and those of older and more remote areas of the world constitute a subject worthy of separate study. The fantastic parallels are more than merely coincidental.

◆ The Voice of the Andes ◆

There exists in Peru remnants of stone work which were the product of little people. In the highlands of Cuzco, and adjacent to the famous ruined "fortresses" of Sacsahuaman, there are tunnels, stairways, passages and remains of rooms, etc., ripped right out of the mountain's solid rock by glacial action, and/or some tectonic force even more powerful and destructive. The ramparts of Sacsahuaman appear to be post-glacial; but these other works carved in the living rock of the high Andes, were there before a glacier sheared off the mountain tops. This writer has seen and touched a cross-section of these tunnels.

There can be no doubt about the glacial action because the tracks of the glacier are all around, in the form of grooves in the stone which are typical of glacial action. In some, these grooves are so smooth today that you can coast down them as you would on a playground slide.

The accompanying drawing shows the proportions, shape and size of this cross-section of a passageway. What the writer saw was the result of a force which rent the solid rock asunder and carried some of the pieces away.

Ask yourself what people could use a tunnel of this description—obviously only Pygmies. Even the larger races of Pygmies would experience difficulty traversing such a tunnel. It is only about three and a half feet high at the center and roughly three feet at the sides.

But this is not all. On the plateau north of Sacsahuaman, at a distance of a few hundred yards, there is a huge, ovate boulder as big as a large house. It is marked and pitted with remnants of chambers, passages and a stairway. It had been torn out of the living rock by a force which would seem to have been tectonic rather than glacial. Of the stairway only a fragment of about six steps remains intact, the ends jagged at the points where the rock was torn asunder. The proportions fit these already described. The width of the stairway is not over eighteen inches, and the threads and risers are about six inches.

In recent years this fragment of stairway (itself a sizable boulder) has broken off from the rest, but its original connection

CROSS SECTION OF TUNNEL

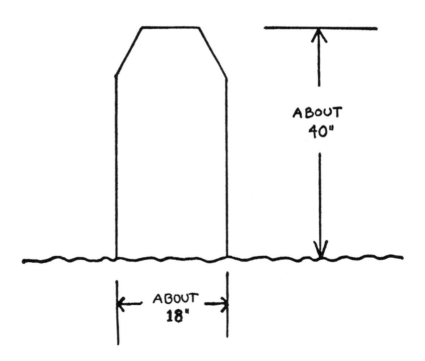

ABOUT
40"

ABOUT
18"

therewith is obvious. As one sees them on the ground the steps are upside down. The original risers are horizontal; the original treads vertical. The treads can be identified by the hollows worn into them by long usage. Such small steps would prove inconvenient to people of our stature; but the stairway passage not wider than the tunnel previously described, would be almost impossible.

Large areas of the surface around these archaeological remnants are covered with rectilinear-shaped depressions. These have been assumed by many archaeologists to be the result of quarrying. It is quite obvious, on mature consideration, that these chambers were exposed by glacial or tectonic action, and are associated with a one-time vast interior complex inside the mountains. It is as though you had cut through swiss cheese, disclosing parts of the bubble cavities within.

The big rock with the fragment of stairway is at a considerable distance from its origin and a force of tremendous power must have put it there.

Nearby is a scrambled pile of stones, a three-dimensional jigsaw jumble. Some are ten to twenty feet long and heaped in such a way that a man can crawl under or between them. These stones also have been ripped out of the solid mountain. One face of each stone is smooth, dressed with considerable accuracy, showing the signs of a cornice at the top, perhaps a tunnel section or possibly part of a chamber wall. The other sides are irregular as though blasted from a solid mass. The inescapable conclusion is that these stones were once the sides of passages or rooms.

The workmanship which went into this internal stone structure differs from that which created the so-called fortress of Sacsahuaman, which is obviously of later origin. The stones of Sacsahuaman, although very large, appear to have been ground into place *in situ*. Archaeologists report indications of tunnels underneath the main structure of Sacsahuaman, thought to have been used by the defenders in the time of the Spanish invasion. This is unproven, for the tunnels and chambers which we are discussing are obviously pre-glacial whereas Sacsahuaman is post-glacial. The glacier's course was such that it would have engulfed and destroyed the rampart structures.

The race which made this internal citadel must have had

a well developed culture to be capable of such construction. They must have had both good reasons for tunneling into the mountain and efficient techniques, considering their small stature.

About two years ago, a body was disinterred high in the Andes. It was perfectly preserved and had many ornaments. Its size was so small that, quite automatically, it was described as the body of a child. I wonder?

Of the world's examples of megalithic stonework, Sacsahuaman is outstanding, though not the largest. There are comparatively few examples of extensive citadels cut into solid stone—but there are some in Egypt, some in Asia Minor; and some reported in Ceylon are so ancient that no one has so far been able to date them.

A geological cataclysm, violent enough to expose and destroy these intra-mountain workings, is so obvious and its magnitude so great, that we are constrained to wonder whether it was the actual formation of the mountains, rather than the glacial action, which destroyed the original citadel. Glacial action is unmistakable but not all the destruction may be attributable to the glacier. Possibly glacial action occurred before this particular mountain peak was raised, the glacial markings being on the summit and not in the valley.

Furthermore, as pointed out by several writers, cities then existed in this part of the Andes, and their vestiges show signs of having been submerged under the sea, although they are now from 10,000 to 13,000 feet above sea level, as indicated by recent discoveries around the shores of Lake Titicaca and Tiahuanaco to the south. This is clearly evidence of at least two waves of civilization. The Incas, overrun by Pizzaro, were late-comers. Sacsahuaman and Tiahuanaco were of pre-Inca origin.

There are many reasons for believing that the Incas were not indigenous to the Andes region, as even archaeologists concede. Churchward, in his *The Children of Mu*, maintains that there was a Mu colony on or near this site before the Andes were pushed up, and when the Amazon basin was an inland sea. Churchward considered this area a way-station between Atlantis and Mu.

The original Inca group was definitely post-glacial and contemporary with other elements of our second wave of civilized development. The builders of Sacsahuaman probably preceded the Incas by hundreds, possibly thousands of years.

Not so the builders of the internal citadel. These may have been the people mentioned by Churchward as having occupied the postulated submerged continent in the Pacific. This archaic race was in the first upsurge of civilization. Or, if we hesitate to say "first" unequivocally, at least in a wave previous to our own.

Here, then, in the high Andes, lie the indisputable remains of a pre-Flood or pre-cataclysm Pygmy civilization, the antiquity of which almost defies speculation. They could not have developed the capacity to produce such works in some of the hardest rock strata in the world, in a few decades or generations. Moreover they were evidently "little people," and of an extremely ancient race. That they were intelligent and skilled is beyond question. Whether or not they were Pygmies in the accepted sense may be debatable.

Conceivably, the cataclysm may have been the same one that raised, or partially raised, the Andes mountains, though probably not the same as wreaked havoc in the Atlantic Ocean and destroyed Atlantis.

Churchward, for reasons not entirely clear, assumes the destruction of Mu occurred about 270,000 years ago, whereas the destruction of Atlantis is said to have occurred much later, possibly 9,000 to 13,000 years ago. Such a hypothetical chronology is suggested by the archaeological remains in the Cuzco area, where we have evidence of *at least one* and possibly two cataclysms superimposed one upon the other.

The internally constructed chambers and passageways of the high Andes appear to be of an age comparable to that attributed to Mu by Churchward. It is conceivable that the first terrific destruction occurred hundreds of thousands of years ago, while the glacial action occurred in comparatively recent times. There is much evidence to suggest that this area was one of the geographical points where the filtration took place from the first wave of civilization to the second. Tiahuanaco has been shown by astronomical-archaeological data to have existed some 26,000 years ago. This means that the mathematical and astronomical knowledge exhibited by the ruins existed at least 26,000 years ago, and takes much time and skill to accumulate.

We have pointed out that the races which built megalithic stone structures all over the world thousands of years ago, in all probability had a means of lifting or levitating stone masses about which we have no knowledge. The Cuzco-Tiahuanaco area is certainly one of the areas where this knowledge existed. I have previously postulated that this power originated with, or in, space craft. I have no reason to change my hypothesis.

Not far away, perhaps two or three hundred miles, on the desert coast of Peru, is one of the most puzzling and least understood of all the world's archaeological remains: tremendous geometrical markings, some several miles in length, visible in their interrelations only from high up in the air. They include parallel lines, angles, triangles, spirals, and in a few cases, caricatured animal and human forms. It seems an inescapable inference that these figures were designed to be read from the air. If so, from what, unless it be some flying machine?

These megaglyphs are unquestionably ancient but probably did not precede the formation of the Andes. They probably belong to the second wave of civilization. Again, then, we have evidence of an area where a filtration from the first civilization took place and enabled the second wave to begin its revival.

Swedish newspapers of February 21 and 22, 1953, reported the discovery of fossil remains in India of a race of very small stature, and a dwarf cow said to be only forty-five centimeters or about eighteen inches high! Even assuming a mistake in transmission, and that forty-five inches, not centimeters, was intended, we would still have a conspicuously small cow, since forty-five inches is under four feet.

For us, however, what is remarkable here is that the discoveries were made in a long *pre-historic staircase*. Nothing was said about its size or dimensions but it would be worth investigating further in the light of the passageways and staircases of "little people" in Peru.

◆ The Voice of the Observer ◆

The intriguing theme of "little people" was tossed into the UFO field fairly early in the hullabaloo ensuing from Kenneth Arnold's celebrated observation of 1947. Since then there has been a thread of continuity relating to "little people" in the many sightings of UFO.

In 1950 there were numbers of reports of landed "saucers" piloted by "little people." One declared that the wreckage of a space ship had been picked up near Mexico City. It was said to measure forty-six feet across, and its dead pilot was twenty-three inches high. The man reporting this, said to be a sales manager of high standing, had not personally seen the UFO, or flying saucer, the term then used. He said American military men had viewed it, and for military reasons hushed the matter up.

A lecturer is said to have stated that three or four saucers had been discovered or captured after landing or crashing and had been inspected by scientists. A total of thirty-four corpses, measuring between thirty-six and forty inches in height, were found, it was said, in three of the UFO. Sixteen men, apparently in their late thirties, were taken from the first. Their bodies had been charred a dark-brown color. No explanation of the charring has been given except an inrush of air when their UFO crashed—which is patently absurd.

Sixteen dead "little people" were said to have been found in the second craft, but uncharred. Except for their small stature, these men were not different from us. They appeared to be normal, proportionately developed *Homo sapiens.* The third ship had only two men in it, who were said to have died while trying to climb out. All appeared to be well formed, which is pertinent to their being associated with the Pygmy race and not with dwarves or midgets.

A fourth, but empty, saucer was reported to have been found near a government proving ground. It was stated that some field scientists who inspected it left it to secure photographic equipment, and on their return they saw several "little men" hop into the saucer which immediately disappeared.

I strive to avoid bigotry in any matter of observational data. But in justice to my readers, I confess that I have, until recently, indulged a healthy scientific skepticism toward those 1950 reports. But in the light of events in 1954 and 1955 a new assay of the evidence may be necessary. A nationally known magazine which has published much pro and con relative to flying saucers, devoted considerable space to debunking these reports. I prefer to reserve judgment until the facts are all in and verifiable.

A more authentic-sounding report of "little people" is the "Steep Rock Episode." The account was published in the *Steep Rock Echo* (a house organ) in September-October of 1950.

Briefly, at about dusk on July 2, 1950, a man and his wife saw a flying saucer land on a river in Ontario, Canada. Although the landing itself has not been verified by other evidence, UFO were seen in the neighborhood at about the same time by other observers.

Ten occupants of this UFO emerged and walked on top of it. They were about three feet, six inches tall. They were described as moving like automata rather than living beings. They had a peculiar gait, seeming to be able to reverse their direction without turning around.

The man of the couple who made the first sighting returned on a subsequent day with a friend who confirmed that the UFO was manned by "little people."

Then there is the case of John Black and John Van Allen, workers in a titanium mine near Marble Creek, California. On May 20, and again on June 20, 1953, they reported sighting a strange silver object composed of two large discs of metal twelve feet wide and about seven feet thick, which landed on a sand bar. They were only about a hundred feet away and could see clearly. A being, like a broad-shouldered man, about four feet tall, descended by a rope ladder. The "being" filled what looked like a bucket with water and handed it to "something" inside the UFO.

Mr. Black says he found two campfires near the sand bar

around which were five-inch footprints. Much has been done to discredit this report. Particular emphasis has been placed on Black's presumably unreasonable report that this saucer had been seen several times, always on the 20th of the month.

Nevertheless, Norman Bean, an electronics engineer in Miami, thinks there are very good reasons to accept the report.

In *Flying Saucers on the Attack,* H. T. Wilkins mentions an Oklahoma woman who tells the story of an old time "prairie roamer" (This was in the 1880's) who claimed to have seen a "round thing" settle down from the sky on the bald top of a mountain. From this "thing," the roamer said, two very small and very "pretty" men had emerged.

In 1954 and 1955 there was a spate of UFO to-do in Europe, particularly in France. Quite a number of average citizens saw UFO, and several reported seeing "little people" in them.

Excitement ran so high that *Life* Magazine took notice and published reports and photos putatively taken by witnesses. Among those who reported seeing "little people" were Pierre Lucas and Serge Pochet. Lucas said that after he saw an orange ball fall from the sky he was startled by a small bearded figure about four feet tall tapping him on the shoulder. Pochet said two small figures, about three feet tall, approached him. Jean Narcy described a helmet-shaped UFO from which a little whiskered man in a fur coat emerged.

Life also reported an encounter by an Italian woman with two merry little men about three feet high who descended from a "spool"-shaped object. The lady, Signora Dainelli, said they stole some flowers and a stocking.

Early in October, 1954, there was quite a wave of UFO news from across the Atlantic. Reports came from Germany, Belgium, Egypt, the Lebanon, French Cameroons, etc. In Muenster, Germany, a forty-two-year-old movie projector operator reported that he saw a cigar-shaped object hovering about six feet above the ground. Four creatures, three and a half feet tall, emerged. They had thick-set bodies, oversized heads and delicate legs, and wore rubber-like clothing.

The English newspaper, *Evening News,* carried a report by a thirty-four-year-old French steel worker, Marius Dewilde of Grenoble, France, who saw from his kitchen window a flying saucer and two "little men" about three feet tall who wore enormous helmets and "overalls." His dog was barking madly at the creatures. When Dewilde tried to get near, a green light shot out of the object which rose into the air expelling black smoke.

Another account of "little men" came from Coldwater, Kansas. The Pratt *Daily Tribune* carried the story on September 14, 1954. It received better nation-wide publicity than most UFO stories in the past few years. *Fate* Magazine was kind enough to lend me one of their news clippings.

LAD SPOTS WEIRD LITTLE MEN WHO TAKE OFF IN A "CUCUMBER SHIP"

Coldwater—John Jacob Swaim, 12-year-old Comanche County farm boy, has created quite a stir in the southeast part of this county with a story of having seen a gnome-like man and a weird flying machine in a field on his father's farm.

The story of the incident, which occurred several days ago, has just come to light.

The boy, son of Mr. and Mrs. John Swaim, sticks by his story which created as much excitement here as the flying saucer episodes of a few years ago.

The boy was in a terraced field on his father's farm about dusk one evening, so the story goes, when he noticed something peeking over one of the ridges at him. As he approached it, John said, the object or individual moved behind another ridge.

He said his first thought was that one of his brothers was trying to play a joke on him. Finally he got a good look, saw a man about three feet tall, dressed in shining garments with two cylinders strapped to his back.

The wide-eyed boy said the little creature went to an object about three feet long and about the same height, which was hovering just above the ground. John says it resembled a cucumber. The little fellow milled around the contraption, finally climbed aboard.

The machine disappeared in the twinkling of an eye, according to the boy's story. There were several lights on the "cucumber ship."

The boy, wide-eyed from excitement, was so positive in his account of what he saw that his parents called Sheriff Floyd Hadley.

The sheriff found queer-looking footprints around a circle, just as the boy had said. Hadley took impressions of the tracks but wouldn't venture an observation as to how they were caused. He sent some of the prints to the FBI, but at Topeka Director Lou P. Richter's office plans no check of the story.

The boy described the feet of the strange visitor as resembling paddles deep sea divers sometimes attach to their feet. Hadley said the prints appeared to be about 4½ inches long and 2½ inches wide across the toe.

Coming from a twelve-year-old boy, with such a vivid description, this story has a ring of sincerity.

Gray Barker's *Saucerian*, published in Clarksburg, West Virginia (P.O. Box 2228), is one of the best of the saucer magazines. Barker adds a spice of humor to his UFO-ing, and his sixty-four page book is most readable. We thought Gray was a tobacco-chewer until we learned that the bulge in his cheek was due to his tongue. The *Saucerian* recently reviewed some reports on "little people." We are going to quote some of them. With scientific objectivity, Gray gives them their face value, leaving speculations to us. Here is something from France:

MISTAKEN FOR MARTIANS

With *The War of the Worlds*, featuring the modern version of H. G. Wells' story of an invasion from Mars, playing currently in French theatres, and the widespread tales of four-foot midgets wielding paralyzing ray guns, it was natural that Gallic wit often turned to jumpy nerves.

M. Pierre Langlois was a genial farmer who laughed a lot until he ran smack into a man from Mars right in the middle of National Road 76, in the Cher Balley district. There, bending over some diabolical, other-worldly engine, was a strangely luminous figure, appearing to be half floating around it. The figure was attaching something, a ray gun the farmer surmised, with a protruding metal claw. Grabbing a shotgun from his house, he gave the man from Mars both barrels.

Next day, in court, M. Langlois had a lot of explaining to do. For the "Martian" was M. Andre Lacoste, a traveling salesman from Bordeaux who, wearing a white raincoat, had been fixing the carburetor of his auto with a monkey wrench. His figure had been illuminated by the headlights of the car.

The panic spread. In the village of Troussey, sugar beet gatherer Alexandre Ronnejki, who needed a haircut, was attacked by a crowd who thought he was a hairy saucerian.

At Taint-l'Hermitage, Central France, a vineyard worker declared that a neighbor, M. Neyret, looked "extraordinary" in the dusk and beat him severely. Only after he had torn off one of M. Neyret's ears did the worker discover the man was not a Martian.

In the Lorraine village of Walschied women fled to a church in hopes of obtaining divine sanctuary, as their men attacked some big chrysanthemums they had seen glowing weirdly. The flowers, which some one had covered with a brilliant cloth to protect them from frost, were the men from Mars that terrorized residents said had landed there in the garden. And there they were, Pygmy size, with heads glowing, and just standing there motionless.

Most indicative of the attitude of earthlings toward saucer-men may be an account from a village near Milan. A man was returning from the movies on a bicycle when he noticed a very bright light in a sports field. Two small shadows were moving about in the light, emitting strange guttural sounds.

Greatly frightened, he pedalled back to town to inform the populace. A group of people returned with him and, sure enough, there was the weird light, but now they could see several small figures, dressed in white pants, grey jackets and helmets, moving around the disc. In the brilliant light they were able to see faces of dark color with large noses, which someone said looked like elephant trunks. [Possibly a breathing apparatus?]

With the intention of attacking the saucermen, the mob tried to force open a gate, but when they failed they began to throw stones and fruit. The little figures fled towards the saucer. One man tried to sic his boxer dog onto the retreating saucerians, but the dog added to the confusion by turning around and biting his master. . . .

Although they were greatly outnumbered by the men, saucer-women were also reported:

A vacationing schoolmaster, M. Martin, said he met two beautiful ladies, presumably from Mars, on the island of Oloron, off the French Atlantic coast. One report had them about four feet tall, another five feet seven inches, but all dispatches agreed they wore leather helmets, gloves and boots. They borrowed M. Martin's fountain pen and scribbled some mysterious signs for him on a piece of paper, which he had kept as evidence of the interplanetary encounter.

As the reports pyramided it seemed that saucers and little men had virtually invaded France. Thousands of Frenchmen, including meteorological experts, doctors, seamen and just plain everyday people, were seeing saucers, and of these many claimed to have seen them close up, along with Pygmy pilots.

Two inhabitants of Lexignan saw a thirty-foot disc land in a field between the villages of Lagrasse and Aude. When they approached it, the machine flashed a blinding light on them, and made the usual getaway. Two human forms, which looked like children, were observed by a farmer named Henri Lehrisse to land in his courtyard in a saucer only one yard in diameter. The machine remained in the yard only a few seconds before flashing off again.

Our next is from Hopkinsville, Kentucky. It was taken seriously enough to make the wire services at a time of general UFO blackout.

LITTLE MEN WITH INDIRECT LIGHTING
GLOW GREEN ALL OVER KENTUCKY FARM

Hopkinsville, Ky., August 22 (UP)—Hundreds of curiosity seekers tramped across Cecil Sutton's farm today after the Suttons said "little green men" from space paid them a visit last night.

Sutton, his family and several relatives said they were up all night fending off the little men who, they said, glowed with an inner illumination.

Kentucky state police and sheriff's officers investigated the weird reports, but were unable to find any trace of the "space visitors."

"That is because they used lights all over the place," Sutton said. "You can't see them except in the dark."

When asked if they expected the space men to return tonight Sutton said: "You can't tell, they might be back."

Mrs. Sutton said she was "Skittedy about it."

The Suttons told this tale: About 7:30 Sunday evening, Bill Taylor, a visiting relative, went to a well near the home and came back to the house excitedly talking of a "space ship" in a nearby field. A few minutes later a "little green man" approached the house, they said.

"He was about three feet tall, with eyes like saucers and set about six inches apart, with hands like claws and glowing all over," Sutton said.

About five feet from the door of the house he stopped and retreated when the Suttons fired a shotgun off into the air. But soon he returned, and the Suttons fired at him. The creature fell down from the blast, then ran off into the fields, according to the Suttons.

Later more of the men returned and climbed about the trees and on the roof of the house, Sutton said. After three hours, the Suttons ran for their car and went into Hopkinsville to call the sheriff.

The police officers said there definitely was no one drinking at the Sutton home last night.

The following from the Clarksburg *Saucerian* takes us to Venezuela. Like Barker, I pass it along to you. There are, without doubt, some grains of truth in all of this hubbub, despite the confusion introduced by hoaxers.

FRACAS WITH SAUCERMEN

The "little men" tale to end all little men tales of 1954, came out of Venezuela, reported in the November, 1954, *APRO Bulletin.*

Gustavo Gonzales has a grocery delivery service in Caracas, and on November 28, he and his helper, Jose Ponce, were going to the suburbs to load up. They braked their panel truck to a screaming halt upon reaching a street leading to a sausage factory, for their way was blocked by a luminous sphere, eight to ten feet in diameter, hovering six feet from the middle of the street.

As they jumped out of the truck they discovered a man the size of a dwarf coming right at them. Gonzales, the braver of the two, grabbed the little man, intending to put him into the truck, but with one push the creature knocked him for fifteen feet!

When he had lifted the little man, Gonzales noted the unusual lightness of the creature. He said the feel of the body was like stiff hair, and very hard.

Ponce was distracted from watching the struggle by two other little men who came out of some bushes with what looked like hunks of earth in their hands. With this new development and the way the little man was defeating his boss, Ponce thought it was time to make a disorderly retreat for the Traffic Inspector's office just around the corner.

As the other little men jumped into the sphere through an opening in the side, the men Gonzales had grappled with then leaped into the air six feet and came at him, his eyes glowing. Gonzales pulled his scout knife on the creature and as it approached him with claws extended he made a stab at its shoulder. But to his surprise the blade slid off as if he was striking metal.

By that time one of the little men who had fled to the saucer emerged, apparently to break up the fracas, carrying a tube-like affair which he pointed at Gonzales. The weapon shot a blinding light at Gonzales, incapacitating him momentarily, but he did see both creatures jump into the sphere which shot up into the air and was soon lost to sight.

Overcome with exhaustion and fright, the two men related their stories to unbelieving policemen, who thought they were drunk. But they examined the two men, found them sober and took them to a doctor who gave them sedatives and kept Gonzales under observation, worried about the strange reddish mark on his side, the only proof of his tussle with a saucerman.

Skeptics were more credulous when they heard a similar story related by another man, a typesetter, who had been afraid to tell it for fear of ridicule. He was in his launch in the Delta district on November 4, when he saw a luminous sphere suspended off the ground a little way from the shore. He approached the spot, tied up the launch, and while some Indians with him fled in terror he hid behind the bushes and rocks to watch.

He saw three or four little men making repeated trips to the sphere with handfuls of dirt.

The APRO organization, usually extremely conservative about spectacular sightings, has stated they feel the story is true, and the original accounts do seem to have a very true ring about them.

And so the accounts went, all over the world. It was evident that many of them were hoaxes, or the garbled narratives of over-excited, over-imaginative people. But as time went by it was difficult to discount all of the stories. There was bound to be fire somewhere!

◆ The Voice of Cincinnati ◆

The first task of an honest and objective scientific investigation is to gather all available facts for classification, analysis and interpretation. Scientists of the eighteenth and nineteenth centuries followed this course rigorously. They recorded much information which they were then unable to classify, much less understand. This left us a vast treasury of information for studying UFO. Today, unfortunately, science rejects data which are not in conformity with its artificial restrictions. "Erratics" like UFO data require a great deal more imagination to cope with than "acceptable data." In science, today, there is an even more intensive concern with the quantitative, rather than the qualitative. For the benefit of future research, I entreat each reader to forward as much information on "erratics" as he can possibly find. This material will be assembled, and eventually offered to the Library of Congress, for its value in the greatest problem of the twentieth century, and probably of human history. The Library Research Group can be reached through the publisher of this book.

As an example of the type of objective reporting which all but died out with the pompous growth of the complacency of modern science, I present the following courageously published by my good friend L. H. Stringfield, who publishes a news sheet called *CRIFO Orbit*, at 7017 Britton Avenue, Cincinnati 27, Ohio. It provides factual coverage of a field which newspaper editors fear. It publishes evidence for *your* appraisal and criticism.

I try to do likewise, and I close the case as presented by ethnology with a comprehensive tally of current events.

Case 101, Northwest Cincinnati, Ohio, August 25, 1955: A huge object described as "bright, round and tannish in color" was witnessed by scores of people near the Fernald atomic plant north of Cincinnati. Two county policemen in separate cruisers, Sgt. Weber and Patrolman Ernest Neher, radioed dispatcher Thomas McGuinn at approximately the same time—10:40 P.M.—that they were watching the object. Sgt. Weber estimated the altitude at 5,000 feet, directly above the plant. Same night, four teenagers, in the vicinity, were terrified by a "little green man."[*]

THE CONTROVERSIAL LITTLE GREEN MEN AND THE TINGLING FACTS

Like their craft, the flying saucer, the little green men recently have come in for a public showdown. However, amid the sneers and chuckles, are a few shocking facts. Studying these, we advise our readers to stop laughing.

First, we have received numerous reports of "saucer" *landings and little men* from points of UFO concentration. Among these and not to be dismissed are the incidents occurring in Venezuela, Brazil, Argentina, and from new evidence, those occurring in France and Italy, in the later part of the summer of 1954. Although the newswires have hushed the stories emanating from the USA, we know of several incidents where the facts corroborate each other. In all known incidents the witnesses, unfortunately, have been dubbed lunatics—a subjective reason why more stories have never been related, especially so, where *prominent people* are involved!

The Cincinnati story is this month's feature not because of dearth of material. Nor is it featured because of the UFO concentrations, which alone is interesting. Our purpose is one of greater importance, for the facts show that the fringe areas of Cincinnati have been a *repeated site for landings and the appearance of little green men.* The officials are aware of this new menace, and we know that more than a handful of Cincinnatians have become more than passively alarmed.

Before the Hopkinsville "little green men" story broke over the nation, CRIFO had silently gathered some unpublished facts concern-

[*] Later learned three policemen, in separate cruisers, witnessed the object.

ing such ogrish encounters near Cincinnati. As it is our policy not to publish names in connection with many of these events we should like to cite a case involving a prominent businessman, living in Loveland. Occurring several weeks ago, this person, who is a non-drinker and a churchgoer (we must add these virtues, it seems, for credibility) saw four "strange little men about three feet tall" under a certain bridge. He reported the bizarre affair to the police and we understand that an armed guard was placed there. A similar event supposedly took place near Batavia east of Cincinnati.

The Hopkinsville incident broke *after these events, and no two parties knew each other.* But, if the Hopkinsville case is not sufficient evidence, of *verdi-sapiens extraterrestrialis* being now amongst us on earth, we have still another case that erases any doubt in our mind. We cannot even hint as to the identity of these people, but we can say that it involved three persons holding *crucial positions* in the city. The incident occurred near Indianapolis, July, 1954. The encounter was enough to terrify these people and break up their planned vacation!

But, we have more recent evidence and each story lends credence to the other for we have checked each person involved and got their personal account. One case occurring near Stockton, Ga., on July 2, 1955, terrified Mrs. Margaret Symmonds who at the time was driving to Florida. The hours was 3:30 A.M., and in the back seat of her car her husband lay asleep. Suddenly Mrs. Symmonds jerked the car away to the side of the road, almost careening. She screamed, awakening her husband and drove away as fast as she could.

To CRIFO, Mrs. Symmonds explains that she saw four little men glowing green. She said their eyes were huge and piercing, their faces dark. They wore some strange-looking garment like a "cape" and were carrying a rod that looked metallic in the reflection of the car's lights. "They did not move at first," she said, "but as the car approached, one moved one step backwards." They looked hideous, said Mrs. Symmonds. Her doubting husband wanted to return to the scene, but Mrs. Symmonds said she was "too petrified."

Mr. Symmonds admits that his wife was terrified by something and was awakened by the car spinning to the side of the road.

The most recent "little men" episode occurred near Greenhills August 25, the same evening when the huge object was seen hovering over Fernald atomic plant. Four teenagers, interviewed by CRIFO, told of their harrowing experience with a little green man, standing by some bushes. All were "certain" as to what they had seen, explaining that the car's lights shone directly on the creature. They all agreed that the little man, about three or four feet tall, had large, bright "yellow" eyes, a dark face behind, and a "sort of shimmering green body." The creature wore an odd garment and they saw a "claw-like" hand. One witness said that the biped took three steps toward the car, but no one waited to see what would happen. The driver of the car, Bill Wallace, 18 years of age, drove away in a state of terror. Without hesitation they informed the police department of their encounter and the area was later investigated, but nothing in the way of evidence was found. Wallace's mother whom we later interviewed, claimed that her son had never been so frightened. He was shaking when he came home and "locked all the doors." One of the girls in the group became hysterical. (Reprinted by permission of *CRIFO Orbit*.)

Ethnology rests its case.

EPILOGUE

The background of the UFO is as broad, as deep and as old as the background of mankind. It may very well be broader and older. It is certain that we find associations, direct and indirect, between all phases of our cultural life and science (with the possible exception of electronics) on the one hand, and the realm of the UFO on the other hand.

The more I study and ponder this unlimited subject of Unidentified Flying Objects, the more I become convinced that the background of the UFO *is* the background of humanity—provided only that we recognize the observable facts for what they really are, and open-mindedly admit them as integral parts of our universal environment.

Made in the USA
Monee, IL
29 October 2020